A THAMES PARISH MAGAZINE

St. Andrew's Church, Sonning

Earley St. Peter's Church

St. John the Evangelist Church, Woodley

All Saints' Church, Dunsden

A Thames Parish Magazine

The History of
The Parish Magazine
serving Sonning and sometime
Woodley, Charvil, Dunsden, Earley

VOLUME ONE

1869 – 1945

GORDON NUTBROWN

First published in Great Britain 2015 by
The Parish Magazine
Serving Charvil, Sonning and Sonning Eye

Text typeface:
Goudy Old Style

ISBN 978-0-9933448-0-0

Printed and bound in Great Britain

Contents

Illustrations

Foreword

I recently attended a forum for parish magazine editors in the Reading and Basingstoke area that reinforced my belief in the value of these unique and sometimes maligned publications. About 60 editors from a variety of magazines published for many different reasons, for example, fundraising, uniting a group of churches, or, as with *The Parish Magazine*, raising the awareness of how the church serves everyone, not just churchgoers, took part in the forum. Despite our differences, we shared two things in common: we were all volunteers and, as well as serving our church, we were creating a valuable social history record of the parish in which we lived.

The value of this record was highlighted for me last year when it seemed that the whole nation turned its thoughts to the events of 100 and 70 years ago. *The Parish Magazine* has been published continuously since January 1869 and from the very beginning one of its aims was to provide future generations with a valuable insight into the life and times of the past. Last year, hardly a week went by when I did not receive a request from an historian, exhibition organiser, or journalist for such information from our archives.

Print technology has changed beyond recognition in the last 147 years and by the time *The Parish Magazine* celebrates 150 years it will have changed even more. The archived copies are becoming frail and constant use by researchers only adds to the wear. I therefore welcome and commend Gordon Nutbrown's excellent summary of, not only the history of *The Parish Magazine*, but of the significant local, national and international historical events recorded on its pages. Not only will it reduce the need for hours of page turning and so extend the life of our archives, the profit from its sale will be used to begin making digital copies of every past issue thus preserving the wealth of information for generations to come. And if you are simply interested in learning more about what makes the Parish of Sonning - which today includes Charvil and previously, Woodley, Earley and Dunsden - such a special place then his book will give you a fresh, informative and interesting way of doing so.

Bob Peters
Editor, *The Parish Magazine*
May 2015

Preface

Publication of the earliest English parish magazines can be traced back to the 1850's. One of the first recorded parish magazines, dating from January 1859, was created by Rev. John Erskine Clarke of St. Michael's Church, Derby; the church was subsequently deconsecrated during the 1970's. There are earlier claims which include the parish magazine of St. John's Church in Frome, Somerset (*Old Church Porch 1854*), however, the publication of this magazine also ceased some years ago.

The Parish Magazine, originally known as *The Sonning Parish Magazine*, is distinguished not only as one of the very earliest parish magazines to be published, in January 1869, but quite possibly one of the longest surviving. It is thought that this magazine has been published every month from its inception until the present day. Unfortunately, it has not been possible to locate issues between the years 1926 until the early 1930's. However, within the Sonning Parochial Church Council minutes of 1927 and 1928 are references to the existence of the magazine, which help to encourage the expectation that issues continued to be published during those "missing years". Further information relating to the period of unconfirmed issues, during parts of the late nineteen twenties and early nineteen thirties can be found printed chronologically within this volume.

For almost a century and a half this magazine has existed, and recorded from a parish perspective many happenings, of great and lesser importance, during the reign of six British monarchs. The magazine was the inspiration of the Rev. Hugh Pearson (1817-1882) who, during his forty years of ministry at St. Andrew's Church, left an indelible image upon the parish. Hugh Pearson had declared in the first issue of the magazine that it should fulfil three objectives:

To supply amusing and instructive reading of a general character, at the lowest cost.
To publish every month, an account of all matters of interest connected with the
Church and Parish.
To contain, from time to time, notices of the past history and antiquities of the Church
and Parish of Sonning.

When the magazine first appeared, during the mid Victorian period, responsibility of the church in Sonning extended widely and included Woodley, Earley and Dunsden. Hence, the publishing of a monthly magazine enabled parishioners from a wide area to be kept informed of matters both of interest and importance to them.

This abridged version of all available past copies of the magazine is published as three volumes: the content of volume one comprises the years from 1869 until 1945, volume two from 1946 to 1985 and volume three from 1986 to 2015. Major changes in the appearance of the magazine, which occurred during the publication of more than one thousand six hundred monthly issues, have been noted and illustrated where appropriate.

To produce this monthly magazine for such a long continual period is undoubtedly a great achievement, and a tribute to those who have given their time and expertise to the continued existence of the publication. Much of the content within this work has been extracted from the original issues of the magazine. These passages, which have on occasions been abbreviated in order to contain space, are enclosed with single quotation marks and are reproduced adopting the original use of upper case and lower case type and punctuation.

I have found it a fascinating and rewarding experience to "wander through" each available monthly issue which has been published during the last one hundred and forty seven years of this magazine's existence. I take this opportunity to thank all who have helped in the research, production and distribution of this work. In particular, I wish to acknowledge: the Rev. Jamie Taylor whose support has been greatly appreciated; Mr. Peter van Went the magazine's honorary archivist, who provided me with detailed information that has been invaluable when researching local history; several members of my family, whom I will not mention by name, but have helped greatly with design, production and proof reading! Last, but by no means least, Mr. Bob Peters who is solely responsible for taking the current magazine to a seriously high level of editorial journalism, and gave me the initial enthusiasm to commit to this rewarding project.

Within these pages are contemporary comments which confirm that the continued publishing of this magazine, during often challenging times, was in part, driven by a desire to ensure detailed local history would be available to future generations. For that noble reason alone, this unique and quite often moving account of bygone days must surely be preserved and protected for those who, in turn, will follow us.

May we express the hope that *The Parish Magazine* will continue to be published into the far and distant future. The further development of communication and recording systems may well cause the printed book to become redundant and consigned into a distant Caxtonian era. However, in whatever future form it is presented . . .
may it survive and flourish!

Gordon M. Nutbrown
Sonning,
May 2015

Cover page: First issue January 1869. (21.5 x 14 cm)

CHAPTER ONE

1869 - 1882

When the first issue of *The Sonning Parish Magazine* was published in January 1869 it was offered for sale at one penny. The editor of the magazine was not named, but it was quite clear that the Rev. Hugh Pearson, who was the driving force behind the publication, played a considerable part in editorial matters.

The January 1869 issue comprised of six pages and was printed in black ink by the letterpress printing process. The printing was undertaken by the firm of E. Blackwell and Son of London Street, Reading. Although early forms of mechanical typesetting were being developed, it was to be many decades before the machines were introduced and revolutionised the composing departments of printers. The lead type used by the printer to compose early issues of the magazine would have been taken by the compositor, letter by letter from a type case, in order to assemble each line and ultimately each page. This was a time consuming task even allowing for the compositor's dexterity, and would be expensive to justify should only a modest number of printed copies be required.

Within the Sonning archives are bound volumes that include examples of magazine insets which would have been purchased for inclusion in *The Sonning Parish Magazine*. The page design of Sonning's parish magazine was very similar in size, layout and type style to the insets, and it was quite likely that many readers could have considered that both parts were inclusive. In addition to founding one of the earliest magazines created for an individual parish, the Rev. Erskine Clarke commenced the publishing of a monthly inset which was named *Parish Magazine*. Another similar publication *Church Progress*, which recorded home mission work, appeared during the late 1860's. Both magazine insets were likely to have comprised sixteen or more pages which would

THE SONNING MAGAZINE, which makes its first appearance in the present number, has in view the following objects:

First, to supply amusing and instructive reading of a general character, at the lowest possible cost.

Secondly, to publish, every month, an account of all matters of interest connected with the Church and Parish; such as,

(1) Announcements of Church Services, Offertories, &c.

(2) A Register of Baptisms, Marriages, and Burials.

(3) Reports of Parochial Institutions and Charities.

(4) A Statement of Parochial Funds managed by the Clergy.

(5) A General Record of Events in the Parish.

Thirdly, to contain from time to time, notices of the past history and antiquities of the Church and Parish of Sonning.

The Magazine will be published on the first of each month at the price of *one penny*. It is believed that a work of this kind will be found extremely valuable as affording full information on the affairs of the Parish, and the work of the Church; and as time goes on, it will become interesting for purposes of reference and comparison.

The numbers should be kept, so that they may be bound up in a volume at the end of the year. Copies of the Magazine will be supplied by the Clergy of the Parish; and they will be glad to receive the names of all who wish to take it in regularly.

Church Services.

—

SONNING PARISH CHURCH.

Sundays, 11 o'clock in the Morning.
3 o'clock in the afternoon.
Half-past 6 o'clock in the Evening.

Saints' Days and Festivals, 11 o'clock in the Morning.

Daily, Half-past 8 o'clock in the Morning.

The Holy Communion is administered on the first Sunday in the month in the usual Morning Service, and on the third Sunday in the month, at half past 8 o'clock in the Morning, and on all the great festivals.

Holy Baptism is administered on the second Sunday in the month in the Afternoon Service. It is particularly requested that children may be brought to be baptized on this Sunday only, unless there is some urgent reason for choosing another time.

The Churching of Women will be immediately before any of the Services.

(For the rest of the Parish News, see last two pages)

Text page: First issue January 1869. (21.5 x 14cm)

have included reproductions of drawings relating to a series of short stories. These publications were designed to be sold as a complete monthly magazine or as a parish magazine inset. In time, further insets were published for inclusion in local magazines. Parish magazines, which often comprised of only one folded quarto size sheet, clearly benefitted from the additional reading matter provided by an inset.

January 1869

During the formative period of *The Sonning Parish Magazine*, very few reports of parish events were included. Far the greater portion of the space available was given over to extensive interest articles which were continued within several future issues.

Subjects included in the first issue, and which became regular features, were details of church services, confirmation, evening school and mothers' meetings. Information concerning a penny bank and two pages devoted to details of offertory accounts were also included. The final page of this six page issue recorded baptisms, weddings, burials and a calendar of church events for the current month. The design of the front page, which was mostly retained for several decades, included a line illustration of St. Andrew's Church, Sonning. (*see: page 12*)

February 1869

Although the format and general content of the magazine continued throughout the year of 1869, the pagination was increased to eight pages from February. Two and a half pages of this issue were devoted to the history and recent restoration of St. Andrew's Church, written by Hugh Pearson; this article was the first in a series that continued in several future issues and provided a detailed view of the building, its monuments and other contents.

[*The series of articles: 'Memorials of St. Andrew's Church' and 'Memorials of the Parish of Sonning' were later published as a book - see reference May 1882.*]

March 1869

The Magazine: It was made clear that the magazine was expected to be self funding, and not subsidised, with the comment that the magazine was: 'published below its cost price, and it is hoped that those who can do so, will make some additional donation.' A further statement followed: 'The magazine will be sent each month to those who wish to take it regularly, if they will leave their names either at Sonning Boys' School or at Woodley School.'

The Sonning Church Choir: The choir performed a concert in February and it was noted that: 'the music was divided into two parts, sacred and secular.' The latter included compositions by Sullivan and Rossini.

Sonning Penny Bank: 'The bank came into operation on 21st May, 1860, and the number of depositors on that day was 9; it has reached, throughout the interval, the number of 344 and 115 is the number on the ledger now. £645 has been received in deposits; £467 is the total amount that has been withdrawn up to 31st December 1868. An amount of £51 16s 9d has been distributed to depositors as a bonus (at the end of each half year), at the rate of 1d. on every 4s. deposited.'

April 1869
Two extensive interest articles, one with the title *Recollections of a Journey on the Continent 1867* by W. R. S. and the other *'Music'* by W. G. were included. These two articles, as with further articles featured within future early issues, included only the initials of an author.

Woodley Clothing Fund: Accounts of the fund were printed together with details of a collection of clothes and toys donated to the London Hospital for Sick Children.

May 1869
The continental journey article continued from the previous month, together with part III of Pearson's history of St. Andrew's Church.

Sonning School Inspections: A report by the Diocesan Inspector of Schools confirmed a good report for the school: 'Writing and arithmetic was admirable all through the School. The reading of the first and second classes is capable of improvement.' The inspector addressing the parents stated: 'I would entreat them to exercise a little self denial, and do their best to enable their children to profit by the excellent education offered them in this favoured parish'.

July 1869

Choral Festival: A three page report gave an account of the seventh annual Choral Festival of the Reading and Henley Choral Association held in St. Andrew's Church. This was clearly a memorable occasion with sixteen choirs performing and consisting of 360 choristers. The visiting clergy who attended included the Lord Bishop of the Diocese, the Dean of Westminster, the Dean of Chichester and the Rural Deans of Henley and Reading.

August 1869

This issue included a three page article on the history of music and the sixth part of Pearson's history of St. Andrew's Church.

School Feast: 'The Feast was held on Tuesday, July 27th, and was as successful as possible. The day was perfect, bright, but not too hot. We had a large assemblage of friends and neighbours, and 190 children from Sonning, All Saints and Woodley Schools were entertained. The games went on till past eight o'clock.'

Parish Magazine: A list of subscribers to the magazine was included, and it was noted that the circulation: 'is about 270 copies a month'.

September 1869

Foreign Travel: An account of a visit to Auvergne in Central France gave an interesting insight into the history of Clermont by W. R. S. The travelogue of the Auvergne visit continued in a further issue a few months later.

Sonning Cricket: It was reported, with accompanying score cards, that two cricket matches had been played and won by Sonning against Swallowfield and Tilehurst.

November 1869

A contribution from an unknown author with the title *Impressions of Sonning* was included in this issue. The article, which was in three monthly parts, included the following passage: 'Sonning seems to me, almost an ideal type of an English village, and there, everything that is picturesque and beautiful, has been carefully cherished.'

St. Bernard's Latin Hymn: A version of Paul Gerhardt's *O Haupt voll Blut und Wunden* which had been translated into English was included.

December 1869
An announcement mentioned that the January 1869 issue was to be reprinted in order that: 'all who now subscribe will be able to complete the volume for the year.' The decision to reprint and produce further copies of the first issue is interesting; unless there had been a conscious decision to retain the typesetting of that issue, with the expectation of printing additional copies at a later date, the cost of re-setting the type in order to print, what was likely to be a *few* further copies, would have been very costly.

January1870
A leading article explained the need for the pagination of the magazine to be reduced to just four pages; this was due to the magazine's receipts falling: 'alarmingly short of expenditure.' However, whilst the page extent of the magazine had been halved, and space for editorial matter severely reduced, the front page was still exclusively committed to a displayed title design.

February 1870
Parish Magazine: Donations amounting to £18 3s 6d towards the cost of the magazine were received during 1869 and listed together with the names of the donors.

Mothers' Meeting: 'The Mothers' meetings at Woodley School will be continued during the month of February. The meeting on Wednesday, February 23rd, will be the last of the season.'

On one and a half pages of this issue appeared Rev. Hugh Pearson's continuing informative article on St. Andrew's Church.

May 1870
School Inspections: The annual inspections of the Sonning and Dunsden schools were recorded. It was noted that the Boys' School comprised of 69 pupils, the Girls' School 33 pupils and Dunsden School 58 pupils. Each school received a good report, particularly the Girls' School where

the comment was made: 'the school is now all that can be desired, and I have nothing to suggest.'

June 1870
It was noted that significant contributions had been made to two funds; £44 19s 4d was raised for the Propagation of the Gospel in Foreign Parts and a further £36 17s 8d was given to the Royal Berkshire Hospital.

Sonning Cricket: The result of a cricket match between the boys of Sonning and Wargrave schools was noted in which Sonning won.

July 1870
Laura Palmer: An announcement was made of the death of Miss Laura Palmer, a generous benefactor, at Holme Park, Sonning on June 22nd. Laura Frances Palmer (1806-1870) was a member of the Palmer family (unrelated to the Palmers of the biscuit manufacturers Huntley & Palmers); they were substantial local land owners and benefactors, who resided for five generations at Holme Park, Sonning.
(*see: Palmer family tree –page 22*)

Sonning and Woodley Parochial Schools: Accounts for the year 1869 in respect of the Sonning parochial schools were published and listed expenses that included half of the master's salary £25, the annual salary of the mistress at the Girls' School £35 and an annual salary of £24 for the mistress at the Woodley School.

September 1870
Franco-Prussian War: The issue was devoted almost exclusively, with the exception of baptism, marriage and death announcements, to a report upon the war that had broken out in July 1870 between France and Prussia. There was clearly concern in England that the Franco-Prussian war could have dramatic repercussions for Europe. The report gave an emotional view of the war from the French perspective, whilst providing an eye-witness account of Prussian celebrations following the news of successes in their campaign: 'The masses rushed to the front of the Royal Palace, cries were raised for the Queen, and as she stepped forward and bowed, it was an indescribably beautiful scene.'

October 1870

Franco-Prussian War: News of the continuing Franco-Prussian war was again dominant. The opening paragraph emphasised the interest and concern of the magazine's readers: 'For the last two months and a half, little has been thought about, or talked about in England, but the calamitous war now raging between France and Germany.' In the same issue it was reported that collections had been made in the Sonning and Dunsden churches in aid of the Franco-Prussian war sick and wounded.

November 1870

An article entitled *Our Village Schools,* which gave an account of the history and development of local education, commenced in this issue and continued into future issues. In 1870 the future of education in England was a topic which no doubt exercised the minds of politicians and those particularly employed in teaching the poor and working classes. Although the children of many poor parents were not given the opportunity of school education, due mainly to the need for their children to be gainfully employed and to bring income into the household, limited compulsory education was but a decade away and no doubt this series of articles was found to be informative.

December 1870

Woodley Coal Club: 'We are happy to announce that the Coal Club has been very successful. The subscribers numbered 91. Their payments amounted to £36 8s 8d. the quantity of coal delivered in November was something under 43 tons.'

January 1871

The page extent of the magazine had increased for the month of January to six pages and continued the article upon local schools.

Franco-Prussian War: A Quaker, who was engaged in humanitarian visits to the war zone, contributed an article entitled *The Suffering of War* which dealt with the severe treatment of French prisoners who had been captured at Metz during the continuing Franco-Prussian conflict. An eye-witness account reported: 'stood for hours at Treves on the platform, and saw them arrive like cattle in trucks, no shelter, most of them had to be lifted out, so ill were they with fever and dysentery, and crying like little children over their suffering; and these were soldiers of the Imperial Guard of France!'

February 1871

Queen Isabella of Valois at Sonning: An article which explained Sonning's connection with royalty appeared in this issue and was continued into the April issue. It gave an account of the incarceration in the Bishop of Salisbury's manor house at Sonning of King Richard the Second's young queen consort, Isabella of Valois, the eldest daughter of King Charles V1 of France. Her confinement began in the autumn of 1399 and continued until the spring of 1400. Following King Richard's death in captivity, Isabella who was then just nine years of age was returned to France.

May 1871

School Finance: A school balance sheet detailing the account of the schools' finances for 1870 was printed. Of the £355 6s 0d income received to meet the expenditure of running the Sonning, Dunsden and Woodley schools, in excess of two hundred pounds was provided by the Palmer family.

June 1871

The Defence of England: The issue carried an article which expressed concern for Germany's territorial ambitions, following their recent victory in the Franco-Prussian war which had ended on May 10th. The article included the following premonition for the future: 'One thought was certainly uppermost in all minds, and that was thankfulness for the "silver streak of sea" which divides us from the rest of Europe, and prevents the possibility of Germany pouring her iron soldiers, by hundreds of thousands, at any moment, on our shores.'
[*The aftermath of the Franco-Prussian war saw the creation of Germany as a nation. Thereafter, a state of tension continued in Europe and was to contribute over forty years later to the outbreak in 1914 of World War 1 - "The Great War".*]

The Army Enlistment Act: Information was provided upon long service and also short service enlistment opportunities, including pay, pension entitlement and conditions.

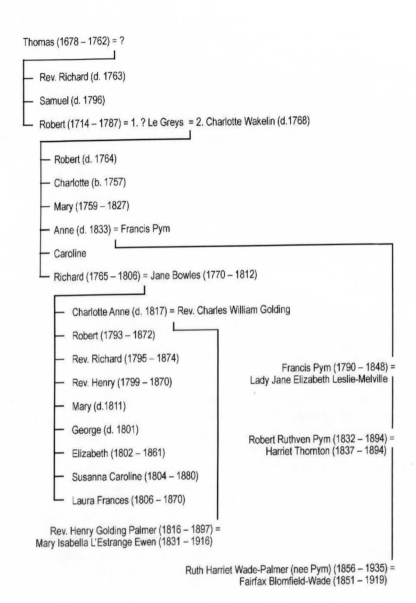

Thomas (1678 – 1762) = ?

Rev. Richard (d. 1763)

Samuel (d. 1796)

Robert (1714 – 1787) = 1. ? Le Greys = 2. Charlotte Wakelin (d.1768)

Robert (d. 1764)

Charlotte (b. 1757)

Mary (1759 – 1827)

Anne (d. 1833) = Francis Pym

Caroline

Richard (1765 – 1806) = Jane Bowles (1770 – 1812)

Charlotte Anne (d. 1817) = Rev. Charles William Golding

Robert (1793 – 1872)

Rev. Richard (1795 – 1874)

Rev. Henry (1799 – 1870)

Mary (d.1811)

George (d. 1801)

Elizabeth (1802 – 1861)

Susanna Caroline (1804 – 1880)

Laura Frances (1806 – 1870)

Rev. Henry Golding Palmer (1816 – 1897) =
Mary Isabella L'Estrange Ewen (1831 – 1916)

Francis Pym (1790 – 1848) =
Lady Jane Elizabeth Leslie-Melville

Robert Ruthven Pym (1832 – 1894) =
Harriet Thornton (1837 – 1894)

Ruth Harriet Wade-Palmer (nee Pym) (1856 – 1935) =
Fairfax Blomfield-Wade (1851 – 1919)

Palmer Family Tree

July 1871

The Length of Life: A thought provoking article by Thomas de Quincey, the author of *Confessions of an English Opium-Eater*, explained how man spends *time* and often wastes it – sleeping, eating, drinking, bathing etc. Within the then accepted human life span of three score years and ten, de Quincey calculated that there are 25,550 days and, in addition, a bonus of seventeen or eighteen days on account of leap years!

August 1871

A Scotch Service: Far the greater part of this issue was given over to an account of religion in Scotland. The opening paragraph commented: 'The Scots are a very remarkable people in religious matters; in one respect, they are a most united people, and, in another, a most divided one.'

September 1871

Indiscriminate Charity: Two articles which appeared were intended as warnings to the readers. Indiscriminate charity concerned bogus charities to which unsuspecting donors might be duped into making a seemingly worthwhile contribution. The other article by the Chief Constable of Berkshire was devoted to vagrancy; advising readers not to entertain giving charity to beggars. This was underscored with the following message: 'Measures were adopted at a large and influential meeting at Reading for securing to the honest wayfarer, proper relief in food and lodging, at the Workhouse. The plea of starvation, therefore, can no longer be used with truth with beggars to extort alms, and the public may safely refuse, as they are earnestly invited to do, to give anything to them.'

Children's Hospital, East London: 'In the month of April we were enabled to send another box to the sick children in East London, containing clothing, toys and six shillings, the result of a penny subscription in Woodley; a box of games from Sonning Boys' School, dolls, bricks, balls, pictures, slippers.'

School Feast: 'On Friday, August 4th, the feast of the Sonning and Woodley schools took place in the Vicarage Garden. Great amusement was got out of various races, there were 187 children present.'

October 1871

The first of a continuing article entitled *On the Ecclesiastical Architecture of England, between the Norman Conquest and the Reformation* appeared in this issue. The article sought to compare ecclesiastical buildings during the eleventh to sixteenth centuries with building standards current in mid nineteenth century England. The quality of Victorian building received the following broadside: 'From sordid motives of economy, or from ignorance of their craft, they have covered the earth with buildings so mean, bald, flimsy and prosaic in appearance, as to make the eyes sore.'

Mothers' Meetings: 'The Meetings will be held during the winter at Woodley school-room, on every Wednesday at two o'clock. Members, who are unable to buy at every meeting, are welcome to attend, bringing their own work.'

November 1871

St. John's Church, Woodley: The extent of this issue had increased to six pages and recorded the ceremony of laying the foundation stone of the Church of St John the Evangelist at Woodley. The ceremony took place on Wednesday October 25th and the stone was laid by Richard Palmer, Rector of Purley, Berkshire on behalf of his elder brother Robert, by whom the church was built and endowed.

Harvest Thanksgiving: 'On Sunday, October 8th, Thanksgiving Services for the Harvest were held in Sonning Church. The Annual Collections were made for the Schools of the Parish, amounting to £24 1s 0d.'

Elementary Examination: 'At the Elementary Examination of Schools in the Rural Deanery of Henley, which was held at Henley on October 25th, the second prize for Boys' Schools was awarded to William Wright of Sonning, and the second prize for Girls' Schools, was awarded to Martha Elphinstone, of Sonning.'

December 1871

Woodley Clothing Fund Sale: 'The proceeds of the sale on 14th November amounted to £11 8s 0d. Many thanks to all who kindly helped the Woodley Clothing Fund by their assistance, and subscription.'

The Passion Play: Four pages of the six page issue were devoted to *The Passion Play* at Ober Ammergau in the Bavarian Tyrol. The article included a fine line illustration depicting the stage of the play.

January 1872

The Old Year: The leading article reflected upon the old year with relief for its passing. A brief account of the suffering and devastation caused by the Franco-Prussian war was followed by a list of other occurrences; famine in Persia, devastating fires in America, which caused great destruction in Chicago, and the illness suffered by the Prince of Wales from which he had recovered. The magazine's editor expressed the hope that such happenings would not reoccur and that the New Year would be a far happier one.

February 1872

All Saints' Church: The issue included a report upon the dedication service conducted by the Lord Bishop of Oxford for the new chancel to All Saints' Church, Dunsden, the church having been built some thirty years earlier.

Chicago Visit: A three and a half page commentary of a visit to Chicago the previous year by K. M. M. provided an interesting view of the city prior to its devastation due to the Great Fire of Chicago, which occurred during October 1871.

April 1872
Sonning Church Ringers: 'A much greater interest has lately been taken in the ringing, and great improvement effected in it. We look forward to a still further perfecting of the art under the present society of ringers.' Details of the *Rules for the Sonning Church Ringers* were included, of which the following is an abbreviated version:

1. Ten Men shall be appointed by the Vicar and Churchwardens to be Ringers.
2. The Ringers shall practice once a week.
3. It shall be the duty of the Captain of the Ringers, on all occasions of ringing to make up the peal at least the day before.
4. A fine of Six pence shall be inflicted for non-attendance on occasions of which a peal has been made up.
5. On Practice Nights a fine of one penny shall be inflicted for being a quarter of an hour late; two pence for half an hour and three pence for non-attendance. The Captain shall receive the odd shillings when guineas are paid, but be fined six pence if he neglects his duties.
6. All monies and fines shall be entered into a book and the whole divided at Midsummer and Christmas.
7. The Bells may be rung on occasion of any marriage in the Church; the Ringers to be paid One Guinea for one peal, but if more required, Two Guineas.
8. No Drinking or Smoking to be allowed in the Tower.
9. The Bells are not to be rung without the consent of the Vicar or Churchwardens.
10. During Ringing or Chiming no other person will be admitted to the Tower without the consent of the Captain and the majority of Ringers.
11. Any dispute or misconduct to be referred to the Vicar.
12. These rules shall be strictly enforced.

May 1872
An article by a contributor using the initials K. A. M. M. with the title *Recollections of Sonning in Foreign Lands*, which was somewhat reminiscent of Robert Browning's poem *Home Thoughts, from Abroad,* recounted the emotional comparison made by two English travellers between Sonning and some notable French and Italian tourist destinations.

Lighting of Sonning Church: 'On Sunday evening, April 24th, a collection was made, amounting to £5 0s 4d towards meeting the heavy expense of lighting the Church for the Evening Services.'

School Accounts 1871:   The accounts of the Sonning, Woodley and Dunsden schools were published. Income was shown as £262 15s 9d, of which half was donated by the Palmer family. After deducting expenses the balance in-hand was 3s.

June 1872

West Country Journey: Continuing with the travel theme, the main contribution within the June issue was an account of a tour from London to Land's End. The author of the article, who had travelled virtually the whole distance by train, commented: 'having brought our reader 326 miles by railway from London, it remains for us to conduct him 10 miles further by road.' It was possible in the 1870's to travel from London to Penzance in some twelve hours via two of Brunel's most famous engineering achievements; Sonning Cutting and the Royal Albert Bridge, the latter crossing the River Tamar between Devon and Cornwall.

Hospital Collections: It was recorded that a donation had been made to the *Royal Berkshire Hospital* of £36 9s 5d together with a box containing clothes. A further donation of toys and ten shillings was sent to the *Great Ormond Street Hospital for Sick Children,* from which a letter of appreciation was printed.

August 1872

A series of articles *Memorials of the Parish of Sonning* written by Rev. Hugh Pearson commenced in this issue. Pearson's earlier series had given a detailed account of St. Andrew's Church, both the structure and contents. In this further series Pearson concentrated upon the village of Sonning and provided an interesting and detailed insight into the history of the parish.

October 1872

A contribution which fully occupied all of the available space in this issue, *One Hundred Years Ago,* sought to compare Sonning in the year of

ROBERT PALMER, of Holme Park, J.P., D.L.,
High Sheriff, 1818; M.P. for Berks, 1825–1849;
Born 13st January 1793; died 24th *November 1872;*
Buried at Sonning, 29th *November 1872 – the "Old Squire".*

Reproduced from August 1910 issue, in a series of portraits
"Benefactors of Sonning".

1872 and its lifestyle, with the year 1772.   The author of the article, having the initials C. P. explained the vast material improvements that had taken place over the last century, noting the modern wonders available in 1872 with the 'Electric Telegraph at their head'.

December 1872
Robert Palmer: The death of Robert Palmer was recorded. He died in his eightieth year on Sunday the November 24th at his Holme Park, Sonning residence which he had inherited from his father, Richard, in 1806. Palmer was undoubtedly a major public figure who had been a substantial benefactor. He contributed to many local projects which included substantial munificence for the construction of local churches; St. John's Woodley, All Saints' Dunsden and St. Peter's Earley. Further Palmer benefaction included the restoration of St. Andrew's Sonning, the provision of land for the enlargement of the Sonning churchyard, the building of the Robert Palmer almshouses in Pearson Road, Sonning and the installation of the village water pump situated in Sonning's High Street.
(see: Palmer family tree – page 22 and portrait – page 28)

February 1873
Unfortunately, the January issue of the magazine, which presumably carried a tribute to Robert Palmer, is missing from the archives. This February issue included the continuation of the tribute to Palmer by Rev. Hugh Pearson

March 1873
A further extensive tribute by Hugh Pearson appeared in this issue. This tribute, which occupied most of the seven available pages of the eight page issue, was to his late brother Henry Hugh Pierson (*sic*), a gifted composer who lived a large part of his life in Prussia (later Germany). When he assumed Prussian residency he had changed his name to Henri Hugo Pierson, the original spelling of the family name.

St. John's Church, Woodley: This issue carried an announcement that the consecration of the Church of St. John the Evangelist, Woodley would take place on March 27th when the service would be taken by the Lord Bishop of the Diocese.

May 1873

The annual meeting of the Easter Vestry was held on Tuesday in Easter Week, April 15th, when the election of four churchwardens was noted: Mr. F. H. Buckeridge (*Sonning Town*), Mr. W. Pottinger (*Eye and Dunsden*), Mr. W. P. Hollis (*Woodley and Sandford*) and Mr. C. Stephens (*Earley*).

Parish Magazine: Readers of the magazine had their attention brought to the matter of overdue subscriptions. Reference was made that payment from a number of subscribers to the magazine was overdue. It was stated: 'we are very anxious to get them in, as we are between two and three pounds deficit.'

June 1873

The School Accounts: During 1872 expenditure of £299 7s 9d had been incurred for running of the Sonning, Dunsden and Woodley schools. The income was derived from trust funds and personal donations of which the Palmer family were far the largest benefactors having given £166 3s 11d.

July 1873

The annual concert of the choir which took place on May 27th in the boy's schoolroom was mentioned, it was noted that some compositions by the late Mr. H. H. Pierson had been played.

Berkshire Friendly Society: Information concerning the society was given. The benefits offered to members by the society, on payment of a small monthly contribution, were explained as:

1. A weekly sum in sickness.

2. A weekly pension in old age.

3. A sum of money payable to the member, or any person nominated by him, at the end of a certain term of years, as an endowment, for the advancement in life of the member or his nominee.

4. A sum of money payable on the death of a member.

A further notice from the Post Office (Government Insurances etc.,) was printed. This notice relating to life insurance and annuities included examples of premiums and the future benefits: 'A man aged

30 may secure an annuity of £10 to begin when he is 60 years old by the payment of £24 3s 4d down or pay £1 8s 4d a year until he is 60.'

August 1873
Bishop of Winchester: A further extensive obituary appeared in this issue. The death was announced of Bishop Wilberforce, the Bishop of Winchester who, as the Bishop of the Diocese, was so intimately connected with the Sonning parish. It was noted that he had preached at the re-opening of St Andrew's in 1853 and was a frequent visitor to Sonning.

October 1873
The first of a continuing commentary entitled *Notes on the Natural History of Sonning* appeared in this issue. This first part concentrated upon bird life and explained the many species which could be seen locally, these included finches, birds of prey, owls and heron. The commentary included historic accounts of Sonning's birds together with their diet and breeding habit.

Harvest Thanksgiving: 'Sunday, September 28th, was observed in the Parish as a Day of Thanksgiving to Almighty God for the blessing of the Harvest. Our three churches were tastefully and richly decorated. Collections were made as usual in aid of the Parochial Schools, and amounted in Sonning to £19 3s 10d, in All Saints' to £ 8 4s 8d and in St. John's, Woodley to £2 12s 5d.'

November 1873
Memorial Window: The issue carried a proposal to place a stained glass window in St. Andrew's Church in memory of the late Bishop of Winchester, inviting the magazine's readers to contribute to the cost of the funding appeal.

December 1873
Both this issue and the month previous included further instalments of *Notes on the Natural History of Sonning* and *Memorials of the Parish of Sonning*. This December issue was fully occupied with these two continuing articles, save for details of church services and the recording of births, deaths and marriages.

March 1874

Sonning Concert: 'A concert was performed on January 28th in the Boys' Schoolroom by the members of the choir. A quartette for pianoforte, harmonium, violin and violoncello played during the evening and was received by the audience with great applause.'

Sale of Children's Clothes at Woodley: 'There will be a sale of children's clothes at the Woodley Schoolroom, on Friday, March 27th from one o'clock to four o'clock. Open to all in the parish. All work to be sent in by March 21st.'

April 1874

Parish Magazine: The continuing loss sustained by the magazine, which had become increasingly reliant upon subsidy by donations, was raised with the following comment: 'We venture to remind our readers that the expense of the magazine is very great. We lose upon every number in consequence for selling it for a penny only.' It was further noted: 'For last year there is a deficiency of no less that £7.'

Sonning Penny Savings Bank: The trustees of the Sonning Penny Savings Bank met on Wednesday March 4th at the Sonning vicarage and later announced alterations to the rules of the bank. The interest rate would be a half-penny per each completed calendar month upon every pound paid in. Moreover, not more than £8 can be deposited within any year and should the cash balance of a depositor reach £10 interest would cease.

May 1874

Indian Famine: The famine, which had caused devastating impact upon India's Bengal region, was graphically reported. The dramatic failure of essential food crops had plunged some twenty-six million inhabitants into a state of starvation. Comparison was given that this number roughly equated with the total population of England, Scotland and Wales. The Indian Government had purchased large amounts of rice for the stricken people, but it was made clear that support by donations from Britain were urgently needed. A collection had been made in St. Andrew's and the sum of £30 14s was subsequently forwarded to the Lord Mayor of London to be added to the Mansion House Fund.

School Accounts 1873: The income attributed to the Sonning, Woodley and Dunsden schools amounted to £367 6s 3d. After expenses the in-hand balance was just 11d.

June 1874

Flower Show at Woodley: 'A show of flowers, fruit and vegetables, will be held at Woodley in August or September, at which all living in the district of Woodley and Sandford are invited to take part. The Rules and Regulations, together with a list of Prizes, will be published later.'

Royal Berks Hospital: 'The annual collections for the Hospital, were made at All Saints' Church on May 10th, amounting to £8 5s 7d and at St. Andrew's Church on May 17th, amounting to £31 1s 6d.'

July 1874

In response to the continuing article upon *Sonning's Natural History*, a reader had provided terms for a collection of some species of birds which included: *depping* of sheldrakes, *badelynge* of ducks, *congregation* of plovers, *exaltation* of larks and a *charm* of goldfinch.

September 1874

Sonning Dispensary: The Dispensary and its rules of membership were explained in detail. Two classes of membership were offered; these were referred to as *First Class* and *Second Class* and were dependent upon the annual income of the member. The scale of annual subscription, which ranged from 9s 6d to 12s 0d, took into account whether the membership related to a single person, a husband and wife with two children or a husband and wife with all of their children. Details of the available medical attention were included and it was noted that in the previous year more than 300 cases attended on the dispensary account. The surgeon's salary was given as £50 a year, he undertaking to provide all necessary drugs and appliances.

October 1874

Woodley & Sandford Cottage Garden Society: The main contribution was a report from the first annual exhibition of the newly formed society. Prizes were awarded in various classes for vegetables, fruit and flowers. Further prizes were awarded in a *Women's and Children's Work* class where there was a condition that no dressmaker or tailoress might enter; the first prize was won for the making of a working man's shirt.

Harvest Thanksgiving: 'The annual Thanksgiving for the late abundant harvest was held throughout the parish. Collections were made for the schools amounting to £38 0s 8d.'

November 1874
Woodley Cricket Club: Information concerning the cricket club, which was formed at the beginning of the year, noted that Woodley CC had won three matches of the five they had played during the first season.

Better Times: An address by the Rev. F. W. Robertson to the working men of Brighton was reproduced. During the speech he commented upon the future prospects for England and the English working man. The final passage of Robertson's oration was an emotional call which appeared to have some resemblance to King Henry V at Agincourt:
'The heart of England is waking to her words, which is hard to rouse to strong emotion, but the pulses of which, when once roused, are like the ocean in its strength, sweeping all before it. This is not death. This is not decay. The sun of England's glory has not set. There is a bright long day before her yet. There are better times to come.'

December 1874
Rev. Richard Palmer: The death of Robert Palmer's younger brother Richard at the age of 78 was announced with a four page tribute by Rev. Hugh Pearson. On the death of his brother Robert, Richard Palmer had taken occupation late in 1872 of Holme Park, Sonning, where he died on Sunday October 25th.
(see Palmer family tree – page 22)

Rural Deanery of Sonning: 'A change has recently taken place in the ecclesiastical arrangements of the Diocese, by which Sonning has been removed from the Deanery of Henley-on-Thames, and has given its name to a new Rural Deanery. When Bishop Wilberforce re-arranged the Diocese, he made the Henley Deanery to comprise parishes in the three archdeaconries of Oxford, Berks and Bucks. An Act of Parliament passed in the last Session, provides that henceforth no Rural

Deanery shall be in more than one Archdeaconry. Ours had therefore
to be broken up. The Bishop has united the Deanery of Henley with
the Deanery of Nettlebed and has also constituted a new Deanery of
Sonning, under the Rev. Hugh Pearson. This Deanery contains
Wargrave and Remenham and all the parishes which were formerly
under the peculiar jurisdiction of the Dean of Sarum, of which the
Vicar of Sonning used to be Rural Dean.'

January 1875

The first issue of 1875 commenced with a review of the old year and
good wishes to the readers for the year to come. It was noted that 1874
would be remembered for the result of the February general election
when Mr. William Gladstone's Liberal ministry was replaced by Mr.
Benjamin Disraeli's Conservative party. It was further mentioned that:
'In spite of many gloomy forebodings from all quarters, the harvest of
last year, almost over the world, was one of great and unusual
abundance.'

All Saints' Church: 'This church has received the gift of a most beautiful
painted window in memory of the late Miss Crawshay. The window is
the large West one of three lights. The glass is the workmanship of
Messrs. Hardman of Birmingham.'

February 1875

St. John's Woodley: 'A great addition has been made to the beautiful new
church at Woodley. An organ has been erected in the church and was
opened on Sunday, January 24th. It is a fine, and thoroughly well
constructed instrument, with two rows of keys, and of ample sufficient
power for the church. The front pipes are beautifully painted and
illuminated, and add much to the rich effect of the chancel.'

A forceful article, *Compulsory Education* by Professor Fawcett, appeared
detailing many of the inconsistencies that were present in England's
rudimentary education system. The vast educational discrepancies
between cities and rural areas, as well as occupational variations, were
discussed. An example clearly gave force to many of the points raised by
Fawcett: 'A lad employed in a textile factory has to attend school until
he is 14, unless at 13 he has attained a certain standard of education;

but a child employed in agriculture, (and is not the mind of a child employed in agriculture equally worthy of the care of the State?) may be taken away from school at eleven, although he has attained no standard of education at all.' Fawcett further emphasised that once a boy had reached manhood he wished that they be: 'rid of the absurdity that a man be respected and valued not because in his daily work he wears a black coat while another man a corduroy jacket; but according to his duty in life and success in the trade or labour by which he obtains his livelihood.'

April 1875

St. Andrew's Organ: Mention was made that the church organ had received: 'a thorough cleaning, nothing of the kind having been done since it was placed in its present position in the Tower, and advantage was taken of the opportunity to add a new reed stop, called a Clarinet, to the great organ. The effect of this stop is as nearly as possible that of the orchestral instrument of the same name. It is beautiful for the playing of solo airs, taking, as it does, the part of the human voice.'

School Inspections: The schools were inspected by the General Inspector of Schools for the Diocese of Oxford. 'Sonning Boys' School: The School is in a very satisfactory condition. Discipline and tone of School excellent. Sonning Girls' School: The paper work, writing and spelling very good, as also discipline. All Saints' School: Religious knowledge very fair, writing very good. Woodley School: Religious knowledge in the first class commended, reading and writing fair.'

August 1875

St. Andrew's Church Memorial Window: The window in memory of the late Bishop of Winchester had been recently installed in the east wall of the vestry and the following comments by Rev. Pearson were printed: 'We hardly like to express an opinion as to the merits of the new window, both because it is extremely difficult to form a fair judgment of such a work of art without longer consideration than we have yet been able to give it, and also because painted windows improve so very much by time. We may say however generally that the window is rich and harmonious in colouring, and that the subjects are well and reverently treated.'

November 1875

Club for Working Men: 'It is proposed to establish a club for Working Men in the Village of Sonning. The object of these Institutions is to provide for working men advantages similar to those which the clubs in London and our larger towns provide for another class of person. A house for this purpose is most generously provided by Miss Palmer, in which two rooms will be set aside for the club.' The rules and the conditions for membership of the proposed Sonning working men's club were printed in this issue and included were the following requirements:

1. The rooms shall be open to men of 18 years of age, on payment of an admission fee of one shilling and a subscription of two shillings a year.

2. The Managing Committee shall consist of seven members.

3. The Committee shall meet the first Tuesday in every month.

4. A Committee member shall be appointed for each night, to see that the rules are observed.

5. Bad language or unruly behaviour shall be sufficient cause for removal from the room and if persistent by expulsion from membership.

6. No gambling of any kind shall be carried on.

7. The rooms shall be open every evening (except Sunday) from 6.30pm and closed punctually at 10pm.

8. Coffee and beer may be provided for the use of the members. The quantity of beer supplied to any member in one day shall be limited to two pints.

December 1875

Working Men's Club: Further details of the club were announced which included the hope that it would be opened during December. The two objectives of the club were mentioned: 'One to afford recreation and amusement, and the other, to give the opportunity of reading and instruction by means of a library and reading room. There must be recreation and entertainment, but it will not do to have nothing but these. If it were so the result would be that the more intelligent men would keep away.'

River Thames Flooding: Severe flooding had occurred during November and was recorded as: 'the highest flood known for more than sixty years.' At Sonning Lock the water on November 16th had reached 3ft. 5in. above the high water mark.'

January 1876
In his summary of 1875, Hugh Pearson commented upon the excessive rain during the summer and autumn, and the massive flooding which had occurred in Sonning and many other parts of the country: 'Notwithstanding the ungenial season, we have great reason to be thankful for the harvest, which, if not quite up the average, was well got in, and has proved plentiful. The failure in the potato crop is the greatest loss we have sustained.'

Pearson announced that during 1876: 'Arrangements are being made for constituting All Saints' Church, in the Liberty of Eye and Dunsden, into a separate ecclesiastical district. The whole of Dunsden, with the exception of the part already attached to Kidmore, will thus be included, and the incumbent will be styled the Vicar of Dunsden. The whole of Sonning Eye will still belong to Sonning.'

The Parish Magazine: It was noted that at the opening of its eighth year, sales of the magazine were steadily increasing, and circulation had extended to all parts of the parish. The extent of the magazine had remained as six pages for several months, with the page size and format unchanged from the initial issue.

Reredos: Mention was made of the new reredos in the process of being completed in St. Andrew's Church, together with decorations and four sculptured figures of the saints: Andrew, Peter, John the Evangelist and an Angel, all being carved by Mr. Nicholls of London.

February 1876
Working Men's Club: The club at Sonning was officially opened on Monday January 3rd. The members had assembled at six o'clock for the opening. In addressing the meeting Hugh Pearson was quoted as saying: 'He saw no reason why under the management of a Committee of its own members, and carried on with good feeling, and spirit, and with a determination to observe the rules in a business-like way, an institution of this kind might not succeed as well as a club in London, or a Working Men's Club in any of the great towns, and though some might think that it would not retain its interest for long, he yet hoped and believed that it would be a lasting institution in the parish.'

April 1876

Temperance and Abstinence: In a précis of a speech by the Bishop of
Salisbury, Hugh Pearson commended the bishop when he had: 'spoken
strongly in favour of temperance, as distinct from total abstinence.'
Moreover, the bishop's comment: 'that he must lift his voice against the
exaggeration involved in the attempt to make total abstinence the rule
of all who called themselves Christian people,' was particularly warmly
welcomed by Pearson, who emphasised that it was: 'a pleasure to think
that we have so high a sanction for the principle on which our Working
Men's Club is established.'

Sonning and Woodley Coal Clubs: It was noted that subscriptions to the
Sonning club, will be received at the Sonning Girls' School at twelve
o'clock, and the Woodley club, at Woodley School, at four o'clock on
the first Monday in each month from May to November.

May 1876

School Inspection: An inspection of the local schools was followed by a
report from the Diocese Inspector who commented: 'I inspected the
schools in Sonning on April 5th. I do not think it necessary to make a
separate or detailed report of the examination. The progress of the
children is entirely satisfactory, both in religion and secular knowledge.
Their conduct and discipline and the general tone of the schools are
excellent.'

June 1976

Sonning Working Men's Club: The fledgling club continued to prosper
and at a general meeting held on April 4th the following proposal was
unanimously carried: 'That the Rev. Hugh Pearson be solicited to
accept the office of President of the Club', which Hugh Pearson
accepted with pleasure.

Woodley Clothing Club: 'The club consisting of about 50 members has
for many years been carried on successfully in Woodley, through the
kindness of Miss Palmer. It is now proposed to enlarge the club, and to
increase its field of usefulness, by enabling any inhabitant of Woodley,
who may wish to do so, to become a subscriber.'

August 1876

Sonning Penny Savings Bank: 'The list of depositors for Sonning and Woodley, for the half-year, shews in names 133, in money £156 16s 2d. Interest has been credited to depositors at the rate of two and a half per cent, amounting during the present half-year to £1 2s 2d.'

October 1876

Harvest Thanksgiving: Services were held in Dunsden, Sonning and Woodley churches. It was noted that: 'All three churches were as usual beautifully decorated by the care and labour of the kind friends, to whom we have been so often indebted.'

Woodley Clothing Fund: 'It is proposed to employ the money remaining in hand from the fund in providing needlework for the children of Woodley School. The articles of clothing, when made, may be purchased by the children at half the cost price, the other half being given to them as payment for their work.'

Almsgiving: A forceful article supported the case for withholding the giving of alms without first justifying the need: 'The custom of giving alms without due enquiry, to everyone who seek relief, is now universally condemned by all who have the real good of the poor at heart. Indeed there are very few who can feel justified in supporting a practice, which must tend to the loss of self respect and not to the decrease of poverty. People need sometimes to be reminded that it is their duty to try to help themselves before they consider seeking help from others.'

November 1876

Education Act: Details of the Education Act, which was to come into force on the first of January 1877, were printed. Under the provisions of the Act education would cease to be a privilege and become a right. All children between the age of five and fourteen would receive an elementary education, and restrictions were to be imposed whereby no child shall be taken into employment before the age of ten. Further conditions were included which related to parents and the employers of children whereby breaches of these conditions would be punishable with fines.

January 1877

The review of the old year mentioned the severe winter conditions that extended to late April with deep snow still on the ground so late as Good Friday, April 14th. However, by the beginning of May the weather had changed and brought very warm conditions which then lasted for the best part of the summer months. It was reported that the harvest was reduced in quantity but was of the finest quality.

All Saints' Church, Dunsden: The separation of All Saints' Church from the mother parish was accomplished in 1876, but it was noted that: 'there is still a connection with our friends on the other side of the river, by means of the magazine to which we invite their contributions.'

February 1877

Smallpox: A serious outbreak of smallpox had occurred in London and: 'everyone's thoughts had been directed to the subject.' A letter, which raised the matter of who first developed a vaccine for smallpox, was received by the magazine's editor from a Mr. Edmond Warre of Eton College. Warre had read an inscription on the tombstone of Benjamin Jesty (1736-1816) which claimed that it was he who first introduced cowpox by inoculation in 1774. Edward Jenner, a medical doctor who publicised his findings in 1796 via a medical paper, is generally regarded as the rightful claimant. Jesty, who was a Dorset farmer, appeared not to publicise his findings and perhaps did not receive the acclaim he deserved.

Floods: Severe local flooding was again reported: 'The rains began at the end of November and have continued ever since with but few intervals of more that twenty-four hours. The Thames had risen to 3ft. 1in above the high water mark and the road between Sonning Bridge and Playhatch had been under water for most of the last six weeks.'

March 1877

Mothers' Meeting at Woodley: 'The tea which is annually given on Shrove Tuesday to the members of the Woodley Mothers' Meetings, took place on February 13th. The day was unfortunately rainy, but in spite of the bad weather 40 members were present.'

Concerts: Three concerts were reported upon in this issue. Included was the programme of music for each performance to which the audience gave a hearty appreciation. The annual concert of the Sonning choir took place in the Sonning schoolroom during the evening of Monday February 5th. A further concert was given by members of the choir in the Dunsden schoolroom on Friday evening February 9th. These two concerts were followed by the Woodley choir with a performance in the Woodley schoolroom on Monday evening, February 12th.

April 1877
Notwithstanding the excessive rain and flooding noted in the February issue, a report in this April issue refers to the exceptional mildness of the past winter: 'The mildest that has been known for many years. To shew the infrequency and slightness of the frosts experienced, we may remark that even in exposed gardens rose trees have never ceased growing, ferns have retained quite a summer appearance and broccoli has been cut during the whole winter; scarlet geraniums also left in the open ground have remained perfectly green and healthy.'

June 1877
William Laud: Archbishop Laud was the subject of an article appearing in this issue. Laud mentions in his diary that while staying at Hurst, he went over to preach at Sonning: 'Anno 1623, Aug 31ˢᵗ I preached at Sonning with my Lord of Bristol.' William Laud, the son of a clothier, had been born in Reading in 1573 where he attended the free school until the age of sixteen. Having risen to become Archbishop of Canterbury and a Commissioner of the Treasury he became unpopular by his tyrannical conduct and was eventually tried and executed by beheading on Tower Hill.

August 1877
School Feast: 'We were most fortunate in the weather for our School feast, on Tuesday, July 17ᵗʰ. It was fine all day, although cloudy, and the absence of the sun was no loss at all to those who took part in the games. There were 285 children from Sonning and Woodley; and thanks to all our kind friends, there was a plentiful supply of entertainments.'

Home Missions: 'Subscriptions and donations in aid of the Society for Providing Additional Curates in populous places for 1877 amounted to £15 2s 6d.'

October 1877

Sonning Penny Savings Bank: The list of depositors as at the half-year showed 115 names with payments received of £140 2s 5d. Compared with the last report this was a decrease of five depositors. The fund value had a balance of £171 7s 3d. The interest rate had remained at two and a half per cent.

Indian Famine: 'On Sunday, September 2nd, a collection was made in Sonning Church for the Relief of the Sufferers by Famine in India. It amounted to £40 10s, and was forwarded to the Mansion House.'

Woodley and Sandford Cottagers Horticultural Society: The fourth annual show of the society had been held during September in Mr. Adey's meadow. It was noted that: 'The exhibition improves each year and is evidence of the good which such societies do amongst the cottagers.' There were 61 exhibitors and 371 entries in various classes. Mention was made of fruit and flower collections and a super of honey, all having been provided.

January 1878

The review of 1877 was dominated by the war raging in Eastern Europe which had broken out in the last spring, between the Russian Empire, aided by several Balkan countries, and the Turkish Ottoman Empire. It was reported that Russia had made a number of gains and that the prospects for Turkey were very "gloomy". There was expressed some relief: 'that England has taken no part in the struggle, and cherish the belief that for our country, the new year, like its predecessor, may be a year of peace.'

April 1878

Fatal Accident on the Thames: This news item recorded an explosion aboard a Thames steam tug: 'A calamitous accident took place on the *Spitfire* with the bursting of the tug's boiler near Sonning Lock on Monday March 18th. Two persons, the steersman and a boy, lost their lives. Another man and a boy were also on board, but happily escaped without injury. The barge ran upon the bank some distance above the scene of the accident and sank. The shock of the explosion was felt all over the village and parts of the steamer, wood and iron, were hurled into Holme Park. The body of the poor boy fell on the towing path, He was buried in St. Andrew's churchyard on the following Thursday.'

Coal Clubs: Details were provided of the Sonning, Sonning Eye and Woodley clubs: 'Subscriptions must not be less than 1s. per month for every family, or 6d. per month for families receiving parish relief and for single lodgers. A premium of 5s. would be given to all families subscribing throughout the year and 2s 6d to every lodger subscribing throughout the year.' It was further noted: 'It is hoped that all parishioners will now become members of the Coal Club, as there will henceforth be no annual gift of coal.'

May 1878

Thames Accident: 'Following a long search the body of the steersman, Charles Green, who was killed by the explosion on the *Spitfire*, was found at the lower weir near Sonning Mill on Friday April 12th. He was buried in our churchyard close to the grave of the poor boy who lost his life in the same accident.'

[*The grave of Charles Green and that of the boy, John Collier, are located within the northern area of the Sonning churchyard.*]

Sanitary Inspection: A report from the Wokingham District Sanitary Inspector included the following comments: 'Sonning, there is but little call to remark in this particularly clean village. I think, however, money would have been well expended had my suggestion been carried out with reference to bringing water down from a spring by pipes to the centre of the village. The well water of the village is, however, fairly satisfactory as to quality. Cobbler's City, Woodley, this hamlet has been improved by the abatement of several nuisances, and one old obstinate case of overcrowding has been got rid of. Several cottages have been repaired.'

August 1878

New Dunsden Well: A new well had been sunk, to the depth of one hundred and fifty feet, at Dunsden Green and had been opened for use during June. The well, located on land given by Sir Robert Phillimore, received the following comment in the magazine: 'Those who live on low ground can, perhaps, hardly realise how great a boon is an abundant supply of pure water at a higher elevation.'

October 1878
The Mothers' Meetings: 'The Meetings will be held as usual in Woodley School, during the winter months, on every Thursday from 2pm to 4pm.'

Cottagers' Horticultural Show: 'The fifth annual exhibition of the Woodley and Sandford Show took place on Wednesday, September 4th. The show each year becomes more popular, as proved by the number of entries in the various classes, there being no less than 420 entries this year, against 371 last year.'

December 1878
History of Reading: A two-part article upon the history of the town, commenced in this issue by concentrating upon Reading Abbey and its connection with royalty and nobility in past centuries. Notable events within the article included the founding of the abbey by Henry 1 in 1121 and visits by a number of English sovereigns; Richard 1, John, Henry 111, Henry V11, Henry V111 and Edward 1V, the latter thought to have first openly acknowledged his marriage to Elizabeth Woodville during a visit to the abbey.

January 1879
Parish Magazine: The accustomed review of the previous year commenced by reminding readers that the *Sonning Parish Magazine* had: 'completed ten years of its life and it has now become one of our established institutions, and all doubtless appreciate the many advantages it confers upon our parish.'

Russo-Turkish War: The review noted that the Russo-Turkish War had recently been brought to an end resulting in Turkey losing to Russia considerable influence in the Balkan region. Concern was felt in Britain for the expansionist aspirations of the Russian Empire, which had become a powerful force in Eastern Europe. It was further mentioned that to secure the safety of Britain's Indian Empire, war had been declared against the Ameer of Afghanistan towards the end of November.

Royal Death: The death of one of Queen Victoria's daughters, Princess Alice occurred during December 1878 and was referred to within the review.

The Harvest: 'Following a genial summer, we are thankful to say that the harvest was a favourable one, especially in our neighbourhood, and was, on the whole better than any we have experienced during the last few years.'

April 1879
The Coal Clubs: 'The Sonning Coal Club had 98 subscribers from May to December 1878, the money collected was £65 15s. At the Woodley Coal Club there were 121 subscribers with collected money of £45 and the premium amounted to £26 12s 4d.'

Soup Kitchen: A charity soup kitchen was opened at Sonning during the most severe weeks of the winter, and 225 gallons of "good soup" were given away to those in most need of it. The expenses were met by subscriptions from the inhabitants of Sonning.

June 1879
Church of St. Bartholomew: The church, in the Liberty of Earley, was consecrated by the Bishop of Oxford on April 30th. It was noted that: 'This is the fourth church that has been built within the mother parish of Sonning in the course of the last six and thirty years.'

Intercessions for Missions: 'Tuesday, May 20th, was appointed for this year as the day for Intercession on behalf of foreign Missions of the Church. The Offertory at Sonning on Ascension Day, May 22nd, amounted to the sum of £6 10s.'

School Accounts: Expenditure during the year 1878 relating to the Sonning and Woodley schools amounted to £419 9s 1d.

August 1879

Girls Friendly Society: A report was included upon the annual fete of the Sonning and Wokingham branch of the society, which was held in Earley on July 8th. Ninety-eight members from Sonning, Twyford, Wokingham and a further six parishes attended. The society began in 1875 with the object of providing a friend for every working girl in England; whether at home, in service, employed in a shop, the work room, the laundry or the factory. It was stated that during the four years of its existence the society had: "spread all over England".

September 1879

Violent Storm: An account of the severe storm which struck most of southern England during the night of August 2nd and 3rd was the main entry in this issue: 'For four hours the thunder and lightning were incessant, and the lightning, having the appearance of a sheet of fire, will be ever impressed on the memory of those who watched it. We have great reason to be thankful that we were spared the terrible hail which fell in many parts of the country at the same time, and though the deluge of rain caused much distress and damage in the houses of our friends, which we truly lament, yet no one was seriously injured so far as we can learn. It lasted longer and was altogether more alarming than any storm that has visited this place in the remembrance of any of its present inhabitants.'

Diocesan Spiritual Help Society: 'A collection for the society was made in Sonning Church, in compliance with the Bishop's Pastoral letter, on July 18th, and amounted to £17 2s.'

December 1879

School Fire: During the night of November 6th a fire broke out in the school at Woodley: 'It was first discovered about twelve o'clock when flames were seen issuing from the class-room windows. Within little more than an hour's time from the alarm being given the Twyford Strollers Fire Brigade, with their new engine worked by steam, came to the rescue. It is impossible to speak too highly of the manner in which the engine was worked, or of the wonderful rapidity with which in the middle of the night the brigade was gathered together and appeared on the scene of the disaster. As it was, the class-room, containing all the books of the school, and a lending library, numbering nearly four hundred volumes, were utterly destroyed.'

The Royal Vaults in St. George's Chapel, Windsor: This two part article provided an interesting account of monarchs, consorts and other royalty whose remains rest in these vaults. It was explained that the burial place of King Charles 1, following his execution, required permission and the first choice of Westminster Abbey was refused. Ultimately, approval was given that his remains could be interred at Windsor.
[*Within this article the year of Charles 1 execution and burial is given erroneously as 1648, the actual year was 1649.*]

Harvest Thanksgiving: 'The Thanksgiving Service was held at Woodley Church, on Sunday, November 2nd, when the amount of £2 14s 5d was collected for the Schools of the Parish. Services were held at Sonning Church on November 9th, the collections for the Schools amounting to £15 19s 5d.'

January 1880
It was noted that the year 1879 was remarkable for the: 'almost unparalleled inclemency of the weather from January to December. The inevitable result of so much cold and wet during the seasons of spring and summer, was a disastrous harvest.'

Afghanistan and Zulu Wars: Comment was made of two wars which were being waged: 'England has unfortunately been engaged in war both in Africa [the Zulu War] and Asia [Afghanistan] and, not withstanding brilliant successes, cannot as yet be considered out of trouble in either quarter. It is impossible for us at present to form a precise opinion as to the eventual results of our campaigns in Afghanistan, but there is no reason to doubt that the stability of our rule in India will be increased by the manifest determination of the English people to protect the distant frontiers of the Empire.'
[*England is often referred to during this period, although in many such references Britain would be appropriate.*]

The Society for the Propagation of the Gospel in Foreign Parts: The annual collection in Dunsden church amounted to £4 10s 11d.

February 1880

Susanna Caroline Palmer (1804–1880): The obituary of Caroline Palmer was spread over nine pages of the February and March issues. She was the last surviving Palmer sibling of the generation which had included Robert, Richard, Henry and Laura. Caroline had been responsible for continuing the Palmer benevolence received in Sonning and the local area. *(see: Palmer family tree – page 22 and portrait – page 50)*

Dunsden Coal and Clothing Clubs: 'These two Clubs continue to do a most useful work and to be well supported. Always appreciated they are more than ever valued on the occasion of the exceedingly severe winter through which we are now passing. The united payments of the members amount to £150.'

April 1880

Sonning Church Organ and Choir: In a reference to St. Andrew's Church, Pearson explained that the finishing act of restoration had taken place: 'It has been obvious that the position both of the organ and choir was very inconvenient, and that if any method could be devised for bringing them together, the efficiency of the services would be greatly increased. This has been accomplished by the admission of the choir into the chancel, and the removal of the organ into the south chancel aisle.'

The Duchess of Marlborough's Fund: 'The collection in Sonning Church, on February 29th, in aid of this Fund for the relief of the distress in Ireland, amounted to £33.'

August 1880

Choir Excursion: 'An excursion to Hastings for local choirs, organised by the Rural Dean, Mr. Brown, of Wokingham, took place on Monday, July 19th. The choirs of Sonning, Dunsden and Woodley, numbering 90 in all, joined the party, and dined together at the "Swan" Hotel. The day was beautiful throughout, and the expedition most enjoyable.'

September 1880

Schools Entertainment: 'The annual entertainment of both the Sonning and the Woodley schools was given on Friday, July 30th. The number of

SUSANNA CAROLINE PALMER, of Holme Park,
1804 –1880

*Reproduced from September 1910 issue, in a series of portraits
"Benefactors of Sonning".*

children present amounted to 350.   There was, as usual, no lack of presents kindly given by friends to enliven the games; the weather, of which there had been great fear, continued fine throughout the day, and everything went off as happily as possible.'

The page extent of the magazine now varied between issues, from a minimum of four pages to as many as ten, when a particularly extended article was included.

December 1880
An extensive article *A Trip to "The May"* concerned a visit to an island situated off the North Berwick coast. The May had once belonged to the Abbey of Reading: 'About 1128, when King Henry 1 was founding the great monastery of Reading, his brother-in-law, David, King of Scotland, in order to gratify him, affiliated the Priory of The May to the new English establishment.'   However, in the late thirteenth century the Priory of May was eventually bought for the sum of 1,100 marks from the Abbot of Reading by the Bishop of St. Andrew's in Scotland, William Wishart.

Sonning Deanery Society of Change Ringers: 'The last monthly meeting of the Society was held in our Belfry on Wednesday evening, November 10th. There was a large attendance of members from both Belfries in Wokingham, from Wargrave, and from Arborfield. A plain course of Grandsire Triples was rung by the ringers from St. Paul's Wokingham, and 120 Grandsire Doubles were successfully got through by the Wargrave ringers, and by a mixed band.'

March 1881
The Great Snowstorm: Hugh Pearson gave a detailed account of a storm which occurred on Tuesday January 18th: 'The only sign of its approach was the sudden and rapid fall of the barometer just before the gale began. Early in the morning the wind rose, from the north-east, and by midday the tempest was at its height. The snow was whirled across the sky in eddying flakes. There was no pause for twenty-four hours; it snowed all through the night, and for some hours the next day. When at last the storm had spent its force, a strange scene appeared; the village was almost buried, the snow lay eight or ten feet deep in all the

lanes, there was no communication possible with Reading or Twyford except on foot, wagons were snowed up, and locomotion was well-nigh suspended.' Various eye-witness accounts of the storm were quoted and its comparison with earlier storms. The thaw was followed by flooding which was noted in this March issue as "gradually subsiding". Past snow storms were recalled within the article and compared with this fall of 1881. Within living memory the snow of 1836 and 1855 were mentioned also 1814. In comparing the snow of 1855 with that of 1814 the late Robert Palmer had been quoted as saying the fall of 1814 was 'much heavier than in 1855.'

Prayer Book Presentation: 'A beautiful gift of a large folio Prayer-Book, richly bound, which is to be used at the reading-desk, has lately been made to Sonning church by the Rev. R. Hart-Davis, Vicar of All Saints' Church, Dunsden.'

April 1881
Confirmation Service: A service was held in St. Andrew's Church on Monday, February 28th. 'We had in all 154 candidates, 60 from Sonning, 35 from Woodley, 29 from Dunsden and 30 from Earley. It was an impressive and interesting sight, the singing was excellent and there was nothing throughout to mar the solemnity of the service. There was a larger number of male than female candidates; all seemed serious and in earnest, and gave good promise for the future.'

May 1881
Confirmation that a National Census had taken place on the night of April 3rd was followed by a brief history of the census in the United Kingdom and a number of other countries.

Details of the local population were printed. In 1841 Sonning Town Liberty contained 550 inhabitants and in 1881 the number was 494. The author of the article, Hugh Pearson, mentioned: 'To this population we have to add, as belonging to the present Parish of Sonning, 96 persons in the liberty of Woodley, residing on this side of the railway line and 167 in Sonning Eye. We must not be surprised if on a wet Sunday our Church looks rather empty, it holds something like 600 persons.'

June 1881

St. John's Church, Woodley: 'It is with much satisfaction that we are able to announce the completion of the arrangement by which St. John's Woodley is constituted a District Church.' The *London Gazette* of May 10th, signified the assent of the Queen in Council, and in the opinion of the Ecclesiastical Commissioners: 'it is expedient that banns of matrimony should be published, and that marriages, baptisms, churching and burials should be solemnized or performed at the said Church of St. John the Evangelist.'

August 1881

School Inspections: Sonning and Woodley schools were inspected on July 6th and 7th. It was reported that: 'the Boys' School Sonning had passed a remarkably good examination. In each class the answering was both keen and accurate, and in the first class special intelligence was manifested. Girls' School, Sonning; The answering was good, and the written work exceedingly neat and accurate as a whole. The tone of the School is remarkably good. Infants School Sonning; The answering of the children was very fair generally. Woodley School; The School has improved considerably. There is a little unevenness in Standards II and III, but in the highest and lowest classes the answering was very general, and at the top of the School it was very good.'

November 1881

The Sonning Church Bells: 'We were somewhat dismayed in the summer at hearing that our bells were in serious danger of being cracked, in consequence of their having never been turned, so as to let the clappers wear both sides equally. When Messrs: Mears and Stainbank, the bell-founders in Whitechapel, came to examine the belfry it appeared that the old frame was worn out, and that the ringing floor was also in a most dangerous state. The bells have been placed in a new frame of English oak; new stocks have been fitted to seven of them and an entire new floor has been laid in the bell-chamber.'

Sonning Working Men's Club: 'The Quarterly Meeting was held on September 29th. It was well attended by the members. More books were recommended to be purchased for the library, as also a good atlas for the centre table.'

December 1881

Sonning Church: 'Our Church has lately received a valuable present. Two new chandeliers, the work of Messrs. Hardman of Birmingham, have been put up in the nave, and the Church is now well lighted in every part. We offer our grateful thanks to the kind friends who have presented us with this costly and beautiful gift.'

Sonning Penny Bank: The list of depositors for the half-year ending June 1881 totalled 93 with cash deposited of £132 17s 7d. Compared with the last report there was a decrease of one depositor. The bonus rate was noted as: '1d. on every 4s. up to £8, and 1d. on every 6s. above £8.'

January 1882

The review of the previous year by Hugh Pearson commenced by commenting upon: 'The strange and rapid succession of deaths which had taken place in the world of literature and politics.' The names mentioned were George Eliot [Mary Ann Evans], Thomas Carlyle, Lord Beaconsfield [Benjamin Disraeli] and the Dean of Westminster, Arthur Stanley. Also mentioned were the assassinations of the Emperor of Russia and of the American President, James A. Garfield.

[*It was unusual for Hugh Pearson to refer to the passing of national and international personage, for it was but a few weeks hence that his own death would occur.*]

Extreme Weather Conditions: The extremes of weather we experienced during 1881 commenced with the tremendous snowstorm of January 18th. By July the temperature during that month was: 'equal to the greatest heat felt in Bombay during the whole of 1880.' The hurricane which struck on October 13th and 14th caused great destruction: 'In Pound Lane eight or nine large trees were blown down, one of the finest elms in Holme Park and two venerable poplars at the weir.'

February 1882

Change Ringing: 'On Wednesday evening, the 18th of January, a band of eight Reading men, members of the Oxford Diocesan Guild of Church Bell-ringers, rang on Sonning Church bells a peal of 5,040 grandsire triples in three hours and twenty-one minutes. This we believe is the first complete peal ever rung on our bells, and the first by a band of Reading men for 150 years.'

May 1882

Regrettably, there is no copy of the May issue of *Sonning Parish Magazine* within the parish archives. The issue will no doubt have carried the sad news of Reverend Hugh Pearson's death at the age of 64 years. He died on Thursday, April 13th in the vicarage which had been his home for forty years. Undoubtedly, Pearson had been a massive influence on the parish and a wide area beyond. (*see: portrait – page 56*)

[*An account of Hugh Pearson's life was recorded by W. R .W Stephens (the Prebendary of Chichester and Rector of Woolbeding, Sussex) in his "Memoir of Hugh Pearson" included within "Memorials of the Church and Parish of Sonning" by Hugh Pearson and published by Blackwell, Reading 1890.*]

June 1882

Whilst this issue was understandably dominated with references to the late Hugh Pearson, the first entry announced the appointment of his successor: 'We are sure that the inhabitants of this parish have received with pleasure the news that the Venerable Alfred Pott, Archdeacon of Berks, Vicar of Clifton Hampden, has been appointed to the living of Sonning.'

The Master of Balliol College, Oxford had preached a sermon dedicated to Hugh Pearson on Sunday, April 23rd. The unabridged sermon was printed on three and a half pages of this issue.

Rev. Hugh Pearson Memorial: 'At a gathering of relatives and friends of the late Canon Pearson, held on Monday, the 22nd inst. it was resolved, on the motion of Lord Coleridge, Lord Chief Justice of England, "That a Memorial of Hugh Pearson, in the form of a recumbent figure, be placed in Sonning Church, under the sculptured arch between the Vestry and the Sanctuary". An executive committee was named to select an artist, and to superintend the carrying out of the projected memorial, which it is estimated, may be achieved at a cost not exceeding £1,000. Of this sum, more than one half has been already promised.'

July 1882

The Ven. Alfred Pott, Archdeacon of Berks, was inducted into the living of Sonning, by the Rev. J. T. Brown the Rural Dean at a special service held on Thursday, June 15th, at 5 o'clock.

HUGH PEARSON, M.A.,
Born 1817; Curate of Wythyham, Sussex, 1841;
Vicar of Sonning, 1842–1882; Rural Dean, 1864–1876;
Canon of Windsor, 1876; Died at Sonning, April 13th, 1882.

Reproduced from October 1910 issue, in a series of portraits
"Benefactors of Sonning".

Hugh Pearson: This July issue comprised sixteen pages of which fourteen were devoted to a tribute to Hugh Pearson by W. R. W. Stephens, together with reminiscences by many of his friends.

Pearson Memorial Fund: It was recorded that further sums, making a total of £987 0s 6d, had been subscribed for the sculptured memorial of Canon Hugh Pearson.

August 1882
Royal Berkshire Hospital: 'The annual collections were made at Sonning, on Sunday, July 9th, amounting to £39 16s 3d. The collections at Dunsden were made on the same day and amounted to £18.'

School Inspection: The Sonning schools were inspected on June 6th, by Rev. Lenny the Diocesan Inspector. In his report Mr. Lenny stated: 'Boys' School, maintains its high character both for attainments and discipline. Girls' School, I was very pleased with this School. The children answered very intelligently, and Mrs. Ford shewed herself to be a very painstaking teacher and good disciplinarian. Infants' School, there is a marked improvement in this School since I last visited it'.

Dunsden School: The Rev. Du Port, H.M. Inspector, made his annual examination of the Dunsden School on Thursday, June 22nd and made the following comment: 'We are glad to be able to say that the Report is again an encouraging one.'

September 1882
Sonning and Woodley Schools: 'The annual School Feast was held on Tuesday, August 8th, in the grounds of Holme Park, on the kind invitation of Mr. and Mrs. G. Palmer who entertained most hospitably about 300 children and their friends. Thanks to our many friends, there were plenty of prizes and toys, and nothing could be more pleasant and successful than the whole day.'

[*Following the death of Susanna Caroline Palmer in 1880 the Palmer estate passed to her nephew the Rev. Henry Golding (1816-1897). Golding added his mother's maiden name to become Golding Palmer and took up residence at Holme Park with his wife Mary Isabella (nee L'Estrange Ewen 1831-1916).*] see: Palmer Family Tree – page 22

English and Foreign Printers: The author of the article (M. J.) explained that he had been: 'endeavouring to discover the precise relationship of Christopher Barker (c1529-1599), the Queen's Printer, to Sonning and Hurst worthies.' The article which comprised some four pages, explained in some detail the contribution that Barker made during the formative period when printing was introduced into England. However, the attempt to connect Barker with Sonning remained tenuous. The author traced Barker's career and his contribution to improving the quality of printing in England, and its standing, compared with the leading foreign printers of his day. Although William Caxton is recognised as being "the father of English printing", Barker did make a significant contribution to the further development of the trade. He was born into a well connected family and his appointment as the royal printer, which included responsibility for printing the Bible, greatly helped his recognition.

October 1882

Woodley and Sandford Cottage Garden Show: 'The ninth and certainly most successful Show was held on Tuesday, August 29th, in Mr. Adey's meadow at Woodley. The growth of the Society since its formation in 1874 has been rapid. On the present occasion there were than 144 exhibitors, twelve in excess of the greatest number in any previous year.'

November 1882

Services for Harvest Thanksgiving: 'Services for the Harvest were held in St. Andrew's Church, on Sunday, October 8th. The collections, which were on behalf of the Sonning schools, amounted to £15 19s 8d.' The Thanksgiving Services at All Saints' Church, Dunsden were held on Sunday, September 24th: 'to Almighty God for His blessing upon the fruits of field and garden, and for the restoration of peace.' The collections made on behalf of the parish school, amounted to £14 15s.

Pearson Memorial Fund: The Rev. Hugh Pearson memorial fund was confirmed to be standing at £1,192 3s 0d

December 1882

Parish Magazine: It was noted: 'The magazine will be continued in its old form and at its old price during the coming year.'

Archdeacon Alfred Pott: The new incumbent, Alfred Pott, had taken the opportunity, via the magazine, to address the parishioners of Sonning and explain the programme of services and events planned for the coming year. His address commenced: 'There has been a much longer interval than I could have wished, between my institution to the vicarage and my permanent residence among you; and since I have been in residence the calls in different directions have been so many, and my family anxieties so frequent, that regrettably as yet I have made personal acquaintance with very few amongst you. I trust that in the next few weeks some at least of these hindrances may be removed.'

CHURCH SERVICES.

SONNING.—Daily, 8.30 a.m.   Holydays, 11 a.m.   7 p.m.
   ,,   Sundays, 11 a.m.   6.30 p.m.
   ,,   Holy Communion, 1st and 3rd Sunday,   11 a.m.
             ,,   2nd and 4th Sunday,   8.30 a.m.
DUNSDEN.—Sunday, 11 a.m.   3.30 p.m.
WOODLEY.—Sunday, 11 a.m.   3 p.m.

BAPTISMS AND CHURCHINGS.

The Afternoon Service at Sonning having been dropped, it is thought desirable to fix a given Sunday in the month for Baptisms and Churchings. The Second Sunday in the month after the Children's Service, appears to be the most convenient time. But Baptisms can be fixed for any other Sunday Afternoon, by giving due notice to the Sexton, not later than 10 a.m. on Sunday morning: and women may be Churched before the Service on any day (except Sunday morning) on which the Church is open, Sunday or Week-day.

CHILDREN'S SERVICE.

The Children's Service, which has been suspended for some months past, will begin again on the Second Sunday in February, at 3 p.m.

HUGH PEARSON MEMORIAL FUND.

The following Subscription have been received:—
        Mrs. Bird - - - - - - £1   1   0

WOODLEY WORKING MEN'S CLUB.

It is proposed to establish a Club or Coffee House for Working Men, at Woodley. The need of such an Institution has long been felt. It would form a centre where friends might meet and pass an hour or two rationally and pleasantly together when the day's work is done. In fact a strong desire for some years past has been expressed that Club Rooms might be opened. There seems now to be every probability that a sufficient numbers of member will join to ensure a fair prospect of success.

Miss Ellen Dashwood has generously offered the ground floor of one of her cottages at Headley (Cobblers' City), free of rent for the use of the Club. There will be two rooms, a Reading Room and a Smoking Room.

The rules of the Club will be modelled for the most part upon the rules of the Sonning Club. Refreshments in the form of coffee, tea, and bread and butter, will be served to members at a moderate price, to be determined by the Committee.

It is hoped that the Rooms will be ready some time in January. The names of the Committee and the rules of the Club will, all well, be printed in the next number of the Magazine. A general meeting will be called together in the Schoolroom at Woodley, a few days before the opening of the Club, at which all interested in its welfare are invited to be present.

The Rooms cannot be fitted up and furnished, nor the Club supported, without some little outlay and expense. It is sincerely hoped that kind friends in the neighbourhood will help towards founding and maintaining this little centre of village life which has for its object the promotion of friendly intetcourse and good will.

Donations in money, gifts of furniture, or the promise of annual subscriptions, will be gladly received, until the Committee be formed, by the Rev. E. A. Gray, and the receipts will be duly acknowledged in the Magazine. Daily or Weekly Newspapers, Magazines, &c., which any kind friend may be disposed to forward for the use of the Club, will be most welcome.   E. A. G.

DONATIONS PROMISED.

The Rev. H. Golding-Palmer £10 0 0 | The Rev. E. A. Gray £5 0 0

THE LAW OF MARRIAGE.

An attempt has been made for some years past, and will no doubt be renewed this year, to alter the old Marriage Law of England. Hitherto the Law of the Land has followed the Law of the Church, and a widower has been always forbidden to contract a marriage with his Deceased Wife's Sister. In many countries such marriages are allowed, and some persons have contracted such marriages in England, although they are entirely unlawful, and a man might at any moment desert a wife so married, and marry another. An attempt will be made to make these unions lawful, and so bring the Law of the State into collision with that of the Church. In this Diocese Petitions are being signed against this change, of which a copy is appended. It may be permitted to add that your late Vicar,

Text page: January 1883. (21.5 x 14cm)

CHAPTER TWO

1883 - 1899

C hanges had not been made to the appearance and main format of the magazine since its inception. Although contributors to the content of the magazine were either referred to by their initials or were anonymous, it was clear that Hugh Pearson was, until his death in 1882, by far the main contributor and editor in all but name. Pearson had clearly stamped an indelible mark on the magazine and his successor, Alfred Pott, would now be responsible to ensure that the publication would continue to flourish under his leadership.

The magazine had now become an established means of providing information about clubs and societies, such as coal and clothing clubs. It was also a most helpful means of appealing to readers' generosity to support causes approved or sponsored by the church.

January 1883
The précis of the old year was confined to the passing of two notable churchmen: 'Another year has been numbered among the past. To the church at large it has been a very marked year; the Archbishop has been taken to his rest – one of the ablest among the many able men, who have held that high position. A loss yet nearer home has fallen upon this parish, in the removal to his rest of him, who for so many years carried on among you so loving and faithful ministry. There is much for us all to look back upon as Christian men, who have a life to live and a death to die.'
[*Archbishop of Canterbury Archibald Campbell Tait (1811-1882) died 3rd December.*]

Woodley Working Men's Club: In this issue was a proposal to establish a club or coffee house for Woodley's working men: 'Miss Ellen Dashwood has generously offered the ground floor of one of her cottages at

Headley (Cobblers' City), free of rent for the use of the Club. There will be two rooms, a Reading Room and a Smoking Room. The rules of the Club will be modelled for the most part upon the rules of the Sonning Club.'

February 1883
Dunsden Entertainment Evening: 'On Thursday evening, December 21st, a mixed entertainment of music, reading and acting was given in the Dunsden Schoolroom. There was a good attendance. The actors performed their parts with the greatest spirit, and the well-known farce of "Box and Cox", was fully appreciated.'

Dunsden Working Men's Club: 'A public meeting was held in the schoolroom at Dunsden, on Tuesday evening, January 2nd, to consider the question of opening a Working Men's Club at the house hitherto known as the "Rising Sun". The club was opened on January 8th, with 55 members. The club is open to men above 16 years of age, on payment of 1/- per quarter. Coffee, tea, ginger beer, &c, are provided.'

April 1883
'A lady working in the East of London has asked us to send her some flowers for distribution among her poor people, and the sick people in the Infirmary of the Marylebone Workhouse are also most grateful for similar gifts. A box will be sent to each place alternatively, every Monday, and all sorts of flowers, even bunches of daisies, will be thankfully received, and should be sent to the Vicarage before 12 a.m.'

June 1883
Sonning Bell Ringers: 'The Ringers will be gratified with the following report, received from Mr. Haworth, the Diocesan Instructor in Change-Ringing – Not much practice for some time, but able to ring Grandsire Doubles, 120 changes. It pleased all concerned when, before the instructor left, a course of Grandsire Triples, 70 changes, was rung for the first time.'

July 1883
Sonning Church Hymn Book: 'Another edition is now with the printers and will shortly be published and contain a number of new Hymns.'

Sonning Penny Bank: The forty-fifth report stated that 88 members had deposited £138 3s 8d. This was a decrease of eight members since the previous reported period. The fund had a balance of £145 1s 3d. and a bonus of £2 8s 5d. had been credited to the depositors account during the last half-year.

August 1883

Choir Excursions: 'An excursion to London, for the special purpose of seeing the Fisheries Exhibition, took place on Monday, July 16th. The choir boys of Sonning had a separate treat on Friday, July 27th. Magdalen College and Christ Church, Oxford, were first of all visited; the party then going by steam-launch to Nuneham, and walking from there to Clifton Hampden, where tea was served in the Vicarage Garden.'

September 1883

Dunsden School: 'The first Examination of the School under the New Code, was made by the H.M. Inspector on Wednesday, June 27th. It is pleasant to be able to record that the result, looked forward to with more than usual anxiety, was again an encouraging one.' The Dunsden school accounts for the last year were printed and indicated that the total receipts amounted to £200 17s 3d. which included a government grant of £64 1s 6d.

October 1883

St. Andrew's Hymn Book: 'There has been some delay in the issuing of our new hymn book, but it is hoped that before All Saints' Day (November 1st), it will be ready for general circulation. It is an exact reprint of the old book with an appendix of additional hymns, taken mainly from "Hymns: Ancient and Modern". The appearance of the book will be identical with that of the old one. The price of the new book will be one shilling and three pence. Those who have the old book in use will be able to procure the appendix separately for three pence.'

November 1883

Woodley Football Club: 'During the past month a Football Club has been formed at Woodley. There are many who find it a pleasant thing to meet together for a good manly game on a Saturday afternoon, and now that the cricket season is over the need has been felt of something to take the place of the weekly cricket match. Mr. Wheble has kindly allowed the practising and matches to take place at Bulmershe.'

December 1883
The magazine had started to contain more news items at the expense of the serialised articles which were a feature of the Pearson editorship. Quite clearly an increasing number of sports, social clubs etc., were being formed which provided an ideal opportunity for the new editor to include reports upon their activities.

Parish Nurse: A news item which no doubt was well received throughout the parish, concerned the appointment of a parish nurse: 'For some time past a great want has been felt of a nurse for the infirm and sick. It is hoped that before this month's magazine is in the readers' hands, a nurse will have been engaged and be in full work. The cost will be about £50 annually, and towards this cost a number of promises have been given.'

Additional Curates Society (Home Missions): 'We collected on Sunday, November 11th, for the Society. The total given was £5 5s 3d.'

January 1884
The Pearson Memorial: The memorial was installed in St. Andrew's Church on Saturday, December 22nd, 1883. The following are extracts from the article which appeared in this January issue: 'After many months of waiting we have seen the memorial to our dear friend at length placed beneath the arch dividing the Sacrarium from the Vestry. A portion of the screen has been removed in order to give light on both sides of the figure. The figures supporting the head are two angels, one with a harp, the other with the model of a church, representing music and architecture, which were Canon Pearson's favourite arts. The whole is sculptured out of one solid block of Carrara marble. The stone is generally very pure and beautiful; there is a slight discolouration on the south side, from which no marble is ever quite safe. The sculptor was Mr. Thrupp of the Marylebone Road, London. The architectural details were arranged by Mr. Nutt of Windsor.'

March 1884

Our Village Nurse: Confirmation of the appointment of a parish nurse, which had been commented upon in the December 1883 magazine, was included in this issue: 'After the experience of three months we are entitled to say that our Village Nurse is a success. Mrs. Coggins has acted under the direction of the Parochial Clergy and Mr. Brooks [the Sonning doctor], and both are fully satisfied with her work. Almost all our parishioners have subscribed towards the cost. During the past three months she has (in addition to the general superintendence of the old and infirm) nursed sixteen cases, one being a paying case. She has paid 228 visits, and sat up 15 nights.'

Woodley Working Men's Club: 'Two Entertainments were given by the Singing Class of the Club on the evenings of Friday and Saturday, February 15 and 16. The programme was a varied one, and the clever and amusing performance of the Woodley Amateur Minstrel Troupe was, in particular, thoroughly appreciated by the audience.'

April 1884

Dunsden School: 'The School Inspector of the Diocese paid a visit on Wednesday, March 12th. In spite of the serious drawback of sickness, which had necessitated the closing of the School for nine weeks during the past year, the result of the Examination was very creditable to the children.'

Dispensary Accounts: 'All persons resident in Sonning and Woodley should become paying members of the Dispensary. Free orders will be given very rarely, and only in cases of extreme need.' Details of the accounts from Lady Day 1882 to Lady Day 1883 appeared in this issue. The only payments listed were to Mr. Brooks [the Sonning doctor] amounting to £58 11s 6d. Income was via members' payments and subscriptions and totalled £55 2s 6d.

June 1884

Woodley Coal and Clothing Clubs: The 1883 accounts of the coal club and clothing club were published. Receipts from members of the coal club amounted to £56 6s 0d and contributions totalling £23 1s 8d were received from all donations. One hundred and one members had paid

PRESENTATION TO THE REV. J. L. COTTON.

During the past month we have lost from amongst us the Rev. J. L. Cotton, who has gone to his new home at Flordon in the Diocese of Norwich, carrying with him all the best wishes of his old friends at Sonning. On the evening of Thursday, February 7th, many of the parishioners met in the School-room to witness the presentation of an offering to which all the parishioners had contributed. The testimonial consisted of a beautiful Tea and Coffee Service in silver of the Queen Anne pattern, and in addition, of a handsome Drawing-room Clock. Mr. Golding-Palmer spoke on behalf of the Parish, dwelling upon the valuable services rendered for some years past by Mr. Cotton,—upon the gratitude with which those services would always be remembered, and upon the readiness with which all classes had come forward to assist in testifying to that gratitude by the present offering. Mr. Cotton, in acknowledging the testimonial, spoke of the happiness which he had experienced during his residence here, —of the sorrow which all in common had experienced in the year 1882,—and of his conviction that their loss at that time had done mnch to bind all classes in this Parish closer together. He trusted yet from time to time to see much of his Sonning friends.

Mr. Cotton left us in the course of the following week.

THE COMING MONTH.

Ash-Wednesday will have passed before March begins,—but our Special Course of Lent Sermons commences with Thursday, March 6th. The list of Preachers has been already distributed in the Village, and the names are again printed in the Calendar. The Service on Thursday evening will be as last year, viz.—shortened Evensong, Sermon, Commination Service from the *Miserere*.

During Lent, Morning Prayer on Wednesdays and Fridays will be at 11 a.m.

At Woodley there will be (D.V.) Special Lent Services on Wednesday Evenings during Lent, at 7.30 p.m.

HISTORY OF SONNING.

Mrs. Jervis has kindly contributed a continuation of the History of Sonning, a portion of which appears in our present issue. In connexion with this history the following is communicated by T. Walrond, Esq., one of the Literary Executors of the late Dean Stanley.

" A certain celebrated Architect of the reign of James I., Henry " Spene, writes among his accounts" (quoted in Walpole's Anecdotes of Painting, 11.32), " Formerly I made a little tomb of white marble, " being an eagle with an escutcheon on his breast, set up at Sonning " in Berkshire for £7." The "little tomb of white marble" is still to be seen in the North Chancel Aisle. It purports to have been erected by Sir John Williams to the memory of his brother Charles. The date is 1652, many years after the death of James I.

OUR VILLAGE NURSE.

After the experience of three months we are entitled to say that our Village Nurse is a success. Mrs. Coggins has acted under the direction of the Parochial Clergy and Mr. Brooks, and both are fully

Text page: March 1884. (21.5 x 14cm)

into the coal club, with a minimum monthly subscription of one shilling. Clothing club income in 1883 included monthly payments of £65 15s 0d from the one hundred and ninety-five members. A sum of £19 6s 6d had been received from subscriptions and interest.

August 1884

Dunsden School: The Dunsden School was examined by H.M. Inspector on Tuesday, June 17th, and it was reported that: 'There is every reason to be satisfied with the result. Notwithstanding that the School was closed for nine weeks together, owing to an outbreak of scarlatina.'

Woodley School: H.M. Inspector examined Woodley School on June 12th, and his report made the following comments: 'Mixed School – The general working seems to have been very zealous, and no doubt by another year this will be a thoroughly good School. Infants' Class – Evidently zealous work has been done among the Infants, with fairly good general success, considering the condition in which these little ones were found.' The amount of grant earned was £74 2s 11d.

September 1884

Choir Excursion: 'Our choir, men and boys, all went to Brighton on Wednesday, July 23rd. They were accompanied on the excursion by Mr. J. B. Palmer, Mr. Gregory and two of the Misses Pott. All went well and the weather was also favourable. The number who were able to avail themselves of the excursion was 34.'

Temperance Sermon: 'The annual Temperance sermon will be preached (without special collection) on the evening of Sunday, September 14th, by the Rev. Dr. Leighton Coleman, Secretary of the Church of England Temperance Society for the Diocese of Oxford.'

November 1884

Telegraph Communication: In 1870 the Post Office had taken over control of the telegraph system from both the railway and private telegraph companies. The service had reached Sonning in 1883 and provided a remarkable advance in communication for people living in the parish. The introduction of the service drew this comment in the magazine: 'It is just twelve months since our Post Office was opened for

Telegrams. In that period nine hundred messages have been sent and sixteen hundred have been received – far exceeding our most sanguine expectations.'

January 1885
Within the comments concerning the previous year, it was noted that an unusually high number of deaths had occurred in Sonning. In 1883 four deaths had occurred but in 1884 the number has risen to fourteen: 'The difference is very striking. There has been no epidemic sickness, but many of the aged have dropped off. Generally throughout England this beautiful warm dry season has not proved a healthy one; on the other hand the plague of cholera has, through God's mercy, been kept from our land.'

Woodley Concert: 'On Friday Evening, December 5th, a concert was given by the Woodley Singing Class in the school-room at Woodley, on behalf of the Working Men's Club. The room was crowded and the concert was in every way a success.'

March 1885
New Sonning Pulpit: 'During the past month, our new pulpit, forming part of the memorial to Canon Pearson, has been erected. The carved work both in the pulpit itself and in the canopy is very beautiful. The whole work has an additional interest from the fact that Sonning hands have been employed upon it. Around the base runs the motto *Pasce oves* – Feed my sheep. The centre of the canopy shews the figure of the cross with rays spreading on all sides.'

May 1885
Sonning Dispensary Accounts: The accounts were published for the year ended 1 April 1885. Payments totalled £72 0s 0d. and the income was £64 9s 6d. A deficit of £10. 9s 5d. was carried forward.

September 1885
Choir and Sunday School Excursion: The Sonning choir and members of the Sunday school had taken day trips during July; these were referred to as "Choir and School Treats": 'On Tuesday, July 28th, our choir made their annual expedition, and they were accompanied by Mr. Gregory,

Mr. J. B. Palmer and several members of the Archdeacon's family. The excursion this year was to Cowes, by way of Southampton water. The weather was favourable and all went well. On Thursday, July 30th, the Sunday School had a trip down the river in a house boat. On their return the annual Sunday School prizes were distributed on the Vicarage lawn.'

October 1885

St. Andrew's Church Repairs: 'The north aisle of our church has for some years shewn symptoms of weakness, the columns leaning outwards and the inclination being on the increase. Under the advice of Mr. Woodyer, strong transverse iron ties have been fixed during the last month in the nave roof, which it is hoped will prevent the mischief going further. It may be necessary hereafter to rebuild the pillars which are at present of a somewhat weak material.'

Haggerston Work Club: For many years this local club had regularly made clothes which had been sent to the sisters of Haggerston Priory. The garment for October was a child's warm frock.

November 1885

General Election: Details were printed of the general election which was to take place during the month of November. There were to be vast changes to the voting system at this election which would enable far more of the population the right of a vote. Those eligible to vote were urged in this issue to use it, but not to be misled by the names of the parties, Conservatives, Liberals, Radicals, rather to 'think of the policy of the men who bear the names.'

[*The Liberal Party led by William Ewart Gladstone was returned with the most seats but did not achieve a majority. The Irish Nationalist Party held the balance of power which resulted in a further general election being called during the following year. The 1886 election returned another minority government, the Conservative Party led by Lord Salisbury, which governed with the support of the new Liberal Unionist Party.*]

January 1886

Review of 1885: In reviewing the previous year it was noted: 'There had been twelve baptisms at Sonning Church during 1885, four marriages and sixteen burials. Of the burials three lost their lives by drowning, one was an interment from Reading and one came from the Union Workhouse.' It was also mentioned that: 'During the last ten years as many as seven have been found drowned in the river.'

February 1886

Offertory Accounts: The following accounts from the year 1885 were included in this issue:

Sonning Accounts – Offertories and collections £111 16s 0d. The total remittances were £112 4s 9d. The recipients included Reading Hospital, Central African Mission, giving of alms to the poor of Sonning and Woodley and also the giving of meat, wine and clothing.

Dunsden Accounts – Offertories and collections £33 13s 9d. The total remittances were £35 18s 7d. The recipients included relief to sick, Reading Hospital and Dunsden School.

Woodley Accounts – Offertories, collections and donations amounted to £51 5s 9d. The income was given to recipients who included the Hospital, Woodley School and the poor.

March 1886

New Font for Sonning Church: 'In March last when the beautiful pulpit now in Sonning Church was put up in memory of our dear friend and vicar, Hugh Pearson, the old pulpit which dates from the restoration of the church in 1852, was removed to All Saints' Dunsden. One other gift yet remains to be mentioned. Mr. James Dolphin has lately presented us with a font designed to harmonise with the pulpit, by Mr. Nutt, architect to the Dean and Chapter of Windsor.'

July 1886

School Inspections: The Diocesan Inspector paid his annual visit to the Sonning schools on June 8th. 'The Boys' School, the results were satisfactory, the Higher Division did very well. Girls' School, they have again passed a satisfactory examination. Infants' School, they answered well in parts of the examination, in some respects going beyond the usual standard.'

August 1886

Sonning Bread Charity: By a bequest of six pounds annually under the will of Mr. Clifford of Aldermaston the poor of Sonning, who receive no alms from the parish, were to receive bread on St. Thomas's day. It had been recognised that recently the bread had been given to many who were not really poor. The Sonning Dispensary was in need of more funding and this caused an application to the Charity Commissioners for leave to divert the bequest to the benefit of the Dispensary: 'The Medical Charities, the Dispensary and the Parish Nurse are greatly in need of help, the expenditure annually exceeding the income. It is probably that to one of these the Clifford Charity will in future be applied.'

[*It was later confirmed that the Dispensary would receive the bequest for the ensuing year.*]

September 1886
The Shiplake, Dunsden and Harpsden Cottage Garden Society: The second annual show was held on Monday, August 2nd in Crowsley Park. Prizes were awarded in thirteen divisions, these included vegetables, fruit, flowers, supers of honey and the making of garments.

December 1886
Sonning Parish Nurse: 'We are now entering upon the fourth year of her work, and each year has shewn more and more the value of her services. Our rules remain unaltered, having been found to work well.' The subscriptions and donations for the previous twelve months amounted to £60 11s 6d. Expenditure comprised of £40 6s payment for salary and £10 10s rent.

Haggerston Work Club: 'We have given no particular subjects during the last year, but have left it to the kindness of members to send whatever they like. At present the number of articles sent is very small, but we hope that all who can, will send us some things this month.'

February 1887
Sonning Dispensary: Following confirmation within the December 1886 issue that the rules would remain unaltered, it was now confirmed that a change of one of the rules relating to the Sonning Dispensary had been agreed: 'The subscriptions must be paid in advance punctually, on the first Monday in every quarter before 12 noon, to the Collector, and no patient can be admitted to the Dispensary who does not show the

Collector's receipt. No person can make use of the Dispensary whose subscription is in arrears. Any person in arrear for three months will be struck off the list and cannot have his name replaced except on special application to the Vicar, after paying up all arrears due.'

March 1887

Queen Victoria's Golden Jubilee: Celebrations were to take place to mark the fiftieth anniversary of the Queen's reign: 'During the past month collections have been received from our Sonning and Woodley people towards the Women's Offering to the Queen on the occasion of her Jubilee. The collection made in Sonning amounted to £6 7s 5d. and in Woodley £3 0s 8d.'

Dunsden Church: 'On the Feast of the Purification a very beautiful Stained Glass Window was put up in one of the Lancets on the Northern side of this Church. The subject is the Raising of Lazarus. The name of Mr. Pace is familiar to many of our readers as that of the artist of the window in St. George's Chapel, Windsor.'

Dunsden Clothing and Coal Clubs: 'These Clubs continue to do useful work. The thanks of the Members are due to the Subscribers, and to Mr. Charles Reading, who has very carefully gone through all the cards and accounts.' The accounts of the Dunsden clothing, coal and school shoe club were printed, together with the accounts of the Dunsden penny bank.

June 1887

Long Reigns of English Sovereigns: 'Her Majesty ascended the Throne at the age of eighteen in the year 1837 – and on Monday, June 21st, completes the fiftieth year of her reign. There are those yet living who remember the Jubilee of the Queen's Grandfather, King George III, in the year 1810; besides these, two English sovereigns only have had a reign exceeding fifty years, Henry 111 was on the Throne from 1216 to 1272 and Edward 111 from 1327 to 1377. Our own services of Thanksgiving for the last fifty years will be held on Sunday, June 26th. A special service has been drawn up by the Archbishop of Canterbury. Tuesday the 21st, is announced as the day for a General Holiday.'

Sonning Cricket Club: Agreement had been reached to found a cricket club in Sonning, the first match was played on Saturday, May 7th, however, no result of the game was published. The rules of the club were printed and the following is an abbreviated version:

1. The Club is called The Sonning Cricket Club
2. Details of election of committee etc.,
3. Notice that an Annual General Meeting will be held
4. All parishioners of Sonning being eligible to become members, also non residents if proposed and seconded by Sonning parishioners.
5. Residents of Sonning must be members of the club in order to play. Members can introduce a friend, not being a resident, to play in games or matches.
6. Annual subscriptions being 2/6d for over 18 years and 1/- under 18 years of age.
7. Details of practice nights etc.
8. No cricket to be played on Sundays or Good Friday.
9. List of disciplinary rules.
10. The prohibition of all alcoholic drink on the ground during practice nights and no alcoholic drink to be sold on the ground at any time.

July 1887

The Jubilee Celebrations: A report upon Sonning's celebration of Queen Victoria's Jubilee included: 'The Jubilee was observed in Sonning on Thursday, June 23rd. The old people dined together in the school and the women and children had tea in Holme Park. In memory of the Jubilee each child received a medal with a portrait of the Queen in relief. A display of fireworks was kindly provided during the evening by the Misses Dashwood.'

Payne's Charity: 'The Charity will be given away, as usual, on St. James' Day. The dole is divided between Sonning and Dunsden, and consists of Ten Half Crowns given away in each Parish. The Dunsden portion will be distributed by Mr. Hart-Davis.'

August 1887

Royal Berkshire Hospital: 'On Sunday, July 3rd, the annual Collections were made in Woodley Church for the Royal Berkshire Hospital. The amount of the sum collected was £3 6s 6d. During the past year no less than eight in-patients and seventeen out-patients have visited the hospital from Woodley.'

A Letter from the Queen: Following the collection made in Sonning and Woodley by "Women of England" in recognition of the Jubilee, the following letter had been received and included in this issue:

Windsor Castle, June 22nd. 1887
I am anxious to express to all Women of Great Britain and Ireland how deeply gratified I am by their very kind and generous present. I thank them most warmly for it, and shall value their gift of the Statue of my Beloved Husband very highly as a touching remembrance of this interesting and never-to-be forgotten day and of their great loyalty and affection.
　　　　　　"Victoria, R. and I."

Woodley Jubilee Memorial: It was determined that the Woodley memorial of the Queen's Jubilee should take some permanent form and it was finally settled that a village recreation ground, if possible, should be obtained. The Rev. Henry Golding-Palmer agreed to lease a field in his ownership, at a greatly reduced rent, to be used for this purpose.
[*The recreation ground, initial known as the Jubilee Recreation Field is situated north of Headley Road, Woodley.*]

October 1887
Sonning Mortuary: The construction of a mortuary on Sonning church land was announced: 'By the time that our October number is issued our Mortuary will have been almost or altogether completed. In design we have endeavoured to assimilate our new building to the old Church; and its situation is alike conveniently near to the river and to the churchyard. The first purpose of the building is to receive the bodies taken from the river, for the proper reception of which no provision has existed. The position of our Sonning Lock in relation to Reading leads to many bodies being floated down to us, especially in flood time.'
[*The mortuary which was built in the St. Andrew's churchyard, later formed part of the St. Sarik Room, built in 2000 to commemorate the millennium.*]

The Children's Fresh Air Mission: 'During the summer of 1886 several parties of London children were boarded in cottages at Dunsden. The plan was on the whole so successful that it was determined to continue it this year. It was most amusing to listen to their quick eager chatter, uttered with true cockney intonation. They knew no real difference between wheat, barley and oats; turnips, swedes and mangold wurzel were to them all alike – cabbages.'

December 1887
Sonning Cricket Club: A report upon the first season of the newly formed Sonning Cricket Club noted that 12 matches had been played, of these Sonning CC won 9 and lost 3. 'Thanks to the energetic committee and owing especially to the kindness of its President, The Rev. H. Golding-Palmer, all difficulties in the choice of a ground and its preparation for play were smoothed over.'

January 1888
In addition to the Queen's Jubilee, the parish notes for the year of 1887 referred to the establishment of a juvenile branch of the Church of England Temperance Society, and the erection of the mortuary: 'a building very much needed, as the experience of many years testifies.' Comment was also made concerning the unusual weather conditions: 'The season has been marked by a long continuance of drought, such as has been unknown in England for many years past. In many places this long period of drought has been followed by extensive outbreaks of epidemic sickness – from which God's mercy has preserved our village.'

March 1888
Our Village Entertainments: Two functions were reported: 'On Friday, February 10th, Mr. Randall Parsons, Rector of Sandhurst, gave a lecture on Early Church History, beautifully illustrated with a magic lantern. On Monday, February 13th, the members of the Sonning choir gave their annual concert in the Boys' Schoolroom, under the direction of Mr. Gregory, organist of Sonning.'

Woodley Coal and Clothing Clubs: 'The number of members in each of these Clubs is a large one. At the present time the number of subscribers on the books of the Clothing Club is 229, and on the books of the Coal Club, 105. During the last year the monthly payments of members in the Clothing Club amounted to £79, and in the Coal Club to £59. It is creditable to the thrift of the place that so large a sum as this has been saved during a single year.'

May 1888

The Woodley Jubilee Recreation Field: The Golden Jubilee project had been opened and received the following comment: 'There is no doubt that the Recreation Field has already made a considerable addition to the attraction of Woodley, and as time goes on the beauties of the field will undoubtedly increase.' A cricket pavilion had been built, although the grass on the intended cricket pitch had yet to be established before matches could be played upon it.

Dispensary Accounts: The income and expenditure for the year ended April 1st, 1888 showed members payments, subscriptions and charity contributions which totalled some £75. The expenditure of £71 9s 6d included a salary payment of £70 to the doctor, Mr. Brooks.

July 1888

School Inspection: The Sonning schools were examined in religious knowledge on Tuesday, June 5th, by the Bishop's Inspector. The report stated that in the Boys' School: 'The various standards have passed a good examination. The knowledge of Scripture, though good on the whole, was not quite so satisfactory as that of other subjects.' Girls' School: 'This school has done excellently on the whole. The knowledge of Scripture is sound and satisfactory. The Infants' answered clear and well.'

September 1888

Sonning Cricket Club: Detailed scorecards were printed from all five matches played during the season; resulting in three Sonning wins, one defeat and one drawn match.

Our Holiday Children: 'During the last three months we have had a continual succession of children down from London, sent by the London Children's Country Holiday Fund. They have come from two parishes in Haggerston, and the Harrow Mission, Edgware Road, and altogether have numbered 110; the ages varying from 3 to 13. Those who always live in the country can hardly realise what this short holiday means to the poor children born and bred in the dirty streets and alleys of London, and it is wonderful to see the change that a fortnight's fresh air and good food will make in these poor little ones.'

November 1888
China Mission: 'Our friend and fellow-parishioner, Rev, Herbert Knox, left England on Friday, October 19th, for his work in China. He will carry with him our best wishes in that work, and many of us will remember him in our prayers.'

Haggerston Work Club: 'We should like to remind our kind workers that we hope to send up a box of clothes at Christmas time, and, if possible, we should like it to be a larger box than last year. Miss Pott will be glad to receive any things that people like to make, and all sizes and all sorts are acceptable.'

Sonning Cricket Club: Detailed results of cricket matches, including scorecards, played by the club had been included within a number of issues during the summer months. In this issue were listed the results of all matches played during the last season and the batting and bowling performance of each member of the team.

January 1889
The review of 1888 included comments upon the health of the local community: 'The year upon the whole has been, thank God, a healthy one with us, spite of an outbreak of measles, far less severe with us than with many of our neighbours. Our number of deaths, six only, is distinctly below the average.'

New Parish Rooms: Progress upon the construction of new parish rooms was given: 'We had hoped to have seen (the rooms) completed and opened within the year. But we have been disappointed through the delays, which seem always to attend building operations. We shall hope to have the building in use by the early spring. We are indebted in the main for this most valuable addition to our parish organisation to the bequest of our late vicar. The rooms, when completed, will meet a want which we have long felt.'
[*The building was named The Pearson Hall – see April 1889 issue.*]

March 1889
The Bishop's Pastoral: 'According to the usual rules in this Diocese, the Bishop has issued his Pastoral Letter on behalf of the Education

Society. This society makes grants for building and enlarging schools, for providing books and apparatus, and has general charge of examination in Religious Knowledge. At the present moment it is greatly in need of funds – and we look to the Pastoral Letter now issued for an adequate supply for the next three years. In Sonning, where the maintenance of the schools costs the parishioners so little, there ought to be a liberal response towards helping the poor parishes of the Diocese.'

Sonning Club Accounts: The accounts for 1888 listed income totalling some £45, including members subscriptions and the sale of beer. The expenses were £43 17s 3d.

April 1889
The Pearson Hall: 'Our new Parish Room, will, we hope, be completed sufficiently for use by Easter Day. We propose to open it by the name of "Pearson Hall" on Easter Tuesday. The ladies of Sonning propose to entertain at tea as many of the parishioners as the room will hold.'

May 1889
Opening of Pearson Hall: 'After many delays, our Pearson Hall is at last complete and was formally opened on Tuesday April 23rd. The Hall will be available for any and every purpose connected with the Parish – Concerts, Lectures, Missionary Meetings, Bands of Hope, Bible Classes, Choir Practices – will, it is hoped, all find their home here.'

Our Flower Mission: 'We hope to send our weekly baskets of flowers up to London this year, as we have done in previous years. The first will go on May 6th. All flowers are welcome, and should be sent to Mrs. Brooks every Monday morning.'

June 1889
Pearson Hall Entertainment: 'A concert held on April 25th, was the first public performance in the new Pearson Hall, and consequently excited an unusual amount of interest. The room was quite full and presented a very pretty appearance, the arrangement of the stage being particularly effective. The concert was followed on April 29th by an entertainment of quite a different nature, though equally good in point of merit.

Those in the Parish who through lack of room were unable to be present on the occasion of the opening of the Hall, received an invitation to be present at a conjuring performance by Signor Besoni. The Hall was completely filled, the number being estimated at not less than 350.'

October 1889

Recovery of a Drowned Man: 'For the third time during the present year our mortuary doors have been opened, to receive the body of a drowned man. On Sunday, September 15th, a body was taken out of the water above Sonning Lock. He was identified as a Reading man, but how he came into the river there was no evidence to shew. He was buried in our churchyard on Wednesday, September 18th.'

Our Church Drainage: 'We find that there has been hardly any part of the foundations of the Sonning Church that have not suffered from the settlement of water. We hope that the thoroughness of work now nearing completion will do much to ensure the stability of the fabric in the future. All the rain water from both sides of the Church will in future be carried into a large tank near the Mortuary; and this will provide a valuable store of water for the Church.'

November 1889

Our Band of Hope: 'Our Juvenile branch of the Church of England Temperance Society resumed its meetings in the Parish Hall on Friday, September 27th. The branch numbers 70 members. We contemplate forming an adult branch in the course of the winter.'

Woodley Football Club: 'The football season has begun and the Woodley eleven has already played two matches. We trust that it will maintain the very creditable position which it won last year,' There followed a match list for the 1889-1990 season which included matches against teams from Reading, Maidenhead, Bracknell, Wokingham etc.,

December 1889

The Bishop of Reading: 'For the first time in the history of England the town of Reading has had the honour of giving its name to a bishop. The ceremony was held on All Saints' Day when The Ven. James Leslie

Randall, Archdeacon of Buckingham, was duly consecrated Bishop Suffragan of Reading, in Westminster Abbey,'

Cookery Lectures: 'A series of lectures on cookery was commenced on Tuesday, November 12th, principally through the instrumentality of Miss Ellen Dashwood. These lectures have hitherto been very well attended.'

Magic Lantern Lecture: 'On Tuesday, December 10th, a lecture on church history, illustrated with a magic lantern, will be given by the Hon. and Rev. Randall Parsons, Rector of Sandhurst. Admission free.'

January 1890
Review of the year 1889: 'We have great reason for thankfulness for the general healthiness of Sonning during the past year. At the same time there have been the usual of occasional and chronic illness, and the services of our parish nurse have been in constant requisition, to the very great comfort of the sick poor. Among improvements which we have been able to carry out in the parish, we note specially the Pearson Hall, the value and use of which grows upon us every month. The second great work undertaken has been the complete drainage of the church, without which one side of the fabric would have been in imminent peril.'

February 1890
Epidemic of Influenza: 'Sonning has not been free from this prevailing scourge of sickness. At this time of writing several local people are suffering from it, but mostly, thank God, in a mild form.'

New Window in St. Andrew's Church: 'New glass has been inserted in the large church window over the children's seats. The window is, as we think, one of singular beauty – the drawing accurate and the colouring subdued, and not too dark. The figures represent the two great musical saints, S. Gregory and S. Cecilia.'

April 1890
Our School Inspection: The Sonning schools were examined on March 13th, by the Diocesan Inspector of Religious Knowledge. The report

mentioned that in the Boys' School: 'Religious instruction has been pains-taking and intelligent.' The Girls' School received the comment: 'A very satisfactory Examination has been passed.' The Inspector commented that the infant children were: 'very carefully taught, and the order and behaviour are excellent.'

June 1890
Whitsuntide at Sonning: 'During the last week of the month of May we enjoyed the most brilliant weather – and Sonning was full of visitors. Our church services were arranged in the same way as last year, except that we added in the afternoon a Flower Service, the flowers afterwards sent up to the poor in London. Our communicants numbered – early 42 and later 54.'

Missionary Sale: 'There will be a needlework and fancy articles sale in the Pearson Hall, on July 2nd, for the Missions of the Church in China.'

July 1890
Hospital Collection: 'The collections in Church on Sunday, June 8th, amounted to £16 18s 4d, which was remitted to the Hospital in the following week.'

The Diocesan Conference: 'This being the year of Election to a new Diocesan Conference in Oxford, a meeting was held on May 31st to appoint Lay Deputies for the election in the Sonning Deanery. Mr. Witherington and Mr. Wiggins were nominated and elected.'

September 1890
Choir Excursion: 'On Thursday, August 14th, the choir had their annual excursion and Southsea was again chosen, giving the shortest railway journey, together with the longest time at the sea-side. Portsmouth was reached about 10.30am; those interested in cricket had the good fortune to see the match being played on the Portsmouth ground between the Australians and Members of the two Universities. Some others went across to the Isle of Wight, all met up at the Esplanade Hotel for tea. Returning from Portsmouth at 6.40pm, Reading was reached after a pleasant journey and by 10 o'clock the whole party had returned to Sonning.'

October 1890

Mission to China: 'A great Missionary Conference was held in Shanghai in May, and proved a most remarkable gathering. About four hundred and fifty missionaries were assembled. They send extremely solemn and moving appeals to Christians at home; one of these appeals calls for many hundreds of ordained men; another pleads for hundreds of lay evangelists; a third, sent forth by the lady missionaries present, appeals for Christian women; and the fourth definitely asks for a thousand additional missionaries within five years of this time. "We make these appeals", as they go on to say, "on behalf of three hundred millions of unevangelised heathen, we make it with all earnestness, as men overwhelmed with the magnitude of the work before us".'

Our Mothers' Meetings: 'In previous years we have had separate Mothers' Meetings in Sonning Eye for women on that side of the river; but for the future we propose having only one meeting for the whole parish. The river makes too great a division already, and we hope that our united Mothers' Meetings may be a step towards drawing the two sides of the Village more together.'

December 1890

London Church Appeal: 'On Sunday, November 23rd, Rev. G. Berkeley, Vicar of All Hallows, Southwark, came to plead the cause of his poverty-stricken parish containing some 6,000 people in South London, and to ask for funding help for the completion of his church. Mr. Berkeley was extremely gratified at the substantial help given for the House of God at All Hallows by his friends in Sonning, whose offering on the day was £14 12s 0d.'

January 1891

The review of 1890 reflected upon a damp and cheerless summer where the actual amount of rain was well below average – resulting in the river and springs being quite low. There was a great deal of sickness in the parish, which received the following comment: 'The influenza (so called) really a form of oriental fever, was very generally prevalent during the early months, and disease of the throat and chest very prevalent towards the year's close. From the influenza our own parish suffered less than many of our neighbours.'

Pearson Hall: The opening of the Pearson Hall had attracted a wide range of uses, such as concerts, club and society dinners and a variety of meetings. Since the opening of the Pearson Hall most issues of the magazine included a report upon one or more functions which had been held at the venue. Within this issue the following comment was made: 'The Pearson Hall has been in constant requisition for purposes of all kinds. The great value of this building is becoming more apparent every month.'

Dunsden Coal and Clothing Clubs: 'There are now 134 members of these two clubs, who have made their weekly payments with praiseworthy regularity.' The accounts for the year ended September 30th, 1890 showed that the clothing club had received a total of £85 in members payments and donations, and had paid out all of the income, the far greater amount spent on purchasing of clothing. The coal club's income of £88 was all spent on coal purchasing.

March 1891

Great Western Railway: The two broad gauge rail lines which had been favoured when the Great Western Railway Company had opened Sonning Cutting in March 1840, were now to be replaced with four lines of the narrower gauge. Major reconstruction of the Sonning Cutting was needed which included reducing the angle of the banking. The initial acute angle of this banking contributed to the landslide on Christmas Eve 1841 which resulted in a number of fatalities. The announcement of the widening work was printed in this issue: 'A large number of railway labourers are now being employed on the Great West Railway in widening the line, and are just beginning the great Sonning Cutting, which is considered a work of special difficulty. This work will hardly be completed in two years.' A fund was commenced to maintain a lay missioner to work among the men and their families. The role included responsibility for holding services, arranging evening school etc., for those workers who were employed on the stretch of line between Taplow and Reading.

Diphtheria: 'Since the great frost broke up, the village has been visited with an outbreak of Diphtheria, but the character has been mild, thank God, and has been confined entirely to girls.'

Haggerston Work Club: 'Our annual Box of Clothes which were made by the members of the Work Club, was sent up during January, and contained 68 garments. The following letter, written by Sister Elizabeth to acknowledge its arrival, will interest many of us. She writes – Your splendid parcel has just been unpacked and is most delightful, we shall find good use for all the nice warm things. I don't think we ever had such a demand for clothing before. The distress here is awful, the bitter cold, and the price of coals adding to the misery. We get crowds of such hungry children to our dinners three times a week, and have always to send some away. The other day, having fed 72, there was a little dinner left for two big ones or three little ones, and they must decide who it should be. After a little hesitation they said "three of the littlest " and the big boys picked out the three smallest children, pushed them in, and went away themselves. Please thank very warmly all the kind friends who have worked for us.'

April 1891
The Outbreak of Diphtheria: The comments upon the diphtheria outbreak which appeared in the March issue was followed in this issue with a further report: 'Our village has during the last month been suffering from a trying visitation of that subtle and difficult throat disease called diphtheria. In one case at least, perhaps two, the issue has been fatal. Some of us recollect the first visitation of this disease in England – it was at first called the "Boulogne throat", having been thought to have come from that place. Every precaution has been taken to prevent the malady spreading.'

Sick Nursing: 'A course of lectures on sick nursing shall be given in the Pearson Hall during April and May. The subjects of the lectures will be – the sick room, the nurse and nursing, children's diseases, infectious diseases, outward applications and emergencies.'

June 1891
Diphtheria: The last reference to the epidemic of diphtheria in Sonning was recorded in this issue: 'We may hope that by the time our June issue is in the hands of our readers, the diphtheria will be really at an end, but it is a very insidious disease and difficult to deal with. Every possible means to check it has been taken in Sonning. The Girls'

School will have been closed for nearly three months, to the great inconvenience of both parents and children. Drainage and water has been carefully examined, buildings and sick rooms disinfected and patients supplied with all necessities. Our obituary for this spring shews at least three deaths, perhaps four, traceable to this origin. It has been generally an unhealthy time, influenza in a malignant form being very prevalent in our large towns.'

Dispensary Account: 'It will be seen that the Dispensary and the Nursing account both indicate an adverse balance, notwithstanding the liberality of our subscribers. Both Charities are so important, and both have done such good service during the recent period of illness, that we should be most unwilling to see either dropped. It will perhaps be necessary to have a collection in Church on behalf of our Medical Charities in the course of the summer.'

September 1891
The page extent of the magazine had varied quite considerably over a number of past years, from four pages to occasionally twelve pages, and was to continue fluctuating well into the twentieth century.

The Church Warming Apparatus: An early form of central heating was installed in St. Andrew's Church and commissioned in time for the oncoming winter weather: 'The work of laying the new warming apparatus in the church is now completed. The apparatus has already been tested with most satisfactory results, a sufficient degree of warmth is being obtained in a period of less than two hours, and this too, under circumstances not altogether favourable. On Friday, August 23rd, all those who had been employed on the work were invited to a supper at the Pearson Hall. The party broke up at 9 o'clock after a very pleasant evening.'

Sonning Choir Excursion: 'The Choir had their Annual Excursion on Wednesday, July 29th. Partly in consequence of the general uncertainty of the weather, Brighton was chosen for this year's outing, and the choice proved fortunate, as the rain in the latter part of the day was continuous. In spite, however, of all drawbacks, the journey and the different amusements of Brighton were much enjoyed.'

October 1891.

Free Education and Thrift: The 1891 Elementary Education Act provided a government payment of school fees to a maximum of ten shillings per year for each child over three and under fifteen years old attending public elementary schools: 'As a result of an Act of Parliament passed during this year the payment of School Pence by parents has been remitted in our own and in most other village schools. For the future the State undertakes these payments. It is hoped that the money thus saved may find its way into our Penny Bank or Post Office Savings Bank, as some little provision in the future.'

Sonning Churchyard: Guidance was given in an article concerning the need to maintain St. Andrew's churchyard in an acceptable condition, such comments continue to be relevant to the good upkeep and standard of the consecrated ground: 'Our churchyard has the very serious drawback of being intersected in every direction by public paths, and each of these are important thoroughfares from one part of the village to another. It were greatly to be wished that those who use these pathways would recollect that they are passing through consecrated ground and that there is a degree of reverence due to the churchyard as well as the church itself. This is not always the case. It will be necessary during this coming autumn to do something towards clearing away some of the superfluous shrubs and some of the wooden monumental rails, which are very dilapidated and have entirely lost their inscriptions. It may here be noted, that where it is desired to plant anything over the graves of the departed, such shrubs should *not* be of a kind likely to grow to any large size, as the time must come when it is necessary to clear them away. On this account a rose bush or low flowering shrub is much better than box, cypress or yew. With regard to temporary memorials placed on the graves, at funerals or immediately after, *real* flowers, either in wreaths of otherwise, are the only allowable decorations. Anything *unreal* is out of place. Artificial flowers made of metal or porcelain, and enclosed in glass, should always be avoided. It is a practice borrowed from France and not to be encouraged.'

November 1891

Parish Nurse: 'In consequence of ill health, Mrs Coggins has been obliged to resign her situation as parish nurse. At a meeting of subscribers to the fund held on October 15th, it was resolved to appoint a nurse in the place of Mrs. Coggins. It was also resolved to raise a fund towards assisting Mrs. Coggins during the next few months.'

December 1891
Woodley Penny Bank: 'During the last month a Penny Bank has been opened in Woodley in connection with the Post Office Savings Bank. Payments amounting to one penny and upwards will be received at the Woodley School-room on Mondays at twelve o'clock.'

Sonning Working Men's Club: 'The following Lectures will take place during the ensuing winter. Wherever practicable, the lectures will be illustrated by means of a magic lantern and slides. December – *On Books and Reading*, January – *Astronomy*, February – *Reading Abbey and Monastic Life*, March – *Village Antiquities*, April – *Land of the Rising Sun*.'

February 1892
Influenza: An influenza pandemic which was first identified in Russia during the late 1880's, and eventually swept across Europe, was responsible for many deaths in Britain. Comments in this February issue emphasise the local concern in Sonning and the wider area: 'The new year has been marked by much anxiety and in many families by great sorrow. The mysterious complaint, which for the want of a better name, the Italians named influenza, has been universal. In Sonning Town we have had many cases, but hitherto, thank God, no deaths. In Dunsden and Woodley the loss has been greater. The rapid illness and death in the Royal Family has been greatly felt all through the land.'
[*The royal victim of influenza was Prince Albert Victor, Duke of Clarence and eldest son of the Prince of Wales – later King Edward V11.*]

March 1892
Both coal and clothes clubs of Sonning and Woodley had continued to be well supported, and were encouragingly reported upon in this article concerning the Woodley clubs: 'A still increasing number of members in these clubs bears witness to the welcome with which they are received and also it is hoped to the good that they are the means of conferring amongst the people of Woodley. During 1891 there were 106 contributors to the Coal Club and 264 to the Clothing Club.'

National Census: The 1891 census indicated 106 inhabited houses in Sonning Town with 231 male and 284 female residents. It was noted: 'Generally speaking, the villages within England are diminishing in population, whilst the towns are largely increasing in population.'

May 1892

Parish Nurse: 'With regard to the Nursing Fund, the place of Mrs. Coggins has been supplied by Mrs. Giles, who has been in full work during the winter and early spring. It has been necessary to provide her with furnished rooms and the cost of furniture will add somewhat to the expenses of this year.'

National Census: The 1891 census of Woodley recorded 135 inhabited dwellings and a population of 374 males and 313 females. The Total number of parishioners increased by 32 compared with 1881 census.

July 1892

The General Election: The 1892 election was held during July, prior to voting the following advice was printed in this issue: 'Try and look upon a vote as a trust, not as a privilege – a trust can be exercised for the good of your country, not for any selfish class interest or for the sake of party. Do not believe all you hear or read – do not believe any promises of party orators. Many promises are made unscrupulously and will certainly prove disappointing. Do not try to influence others, or be influenced yourself by lower or meaner motives.'

[*No party was returned with an overall majority and Gladstone again formed a minority Liberal government, aided by Irish Nationalist support.*]

September 1892

Exhibition of Village Industries: The exhibition, which was held in the Pearson Hall, was open to all the residents of Sonning. Prizes were to be awarded in a number of classes – best made man's shirt, patchwork quilt, best dressed doll, best washed baby's frock, baked apple dumpling, wood carving, best blacked boots, darning and patching etc.,

October 1892

Harvest Thanksgiving: 'The collection at the Thanksgiving Services on Sunday, September 25th raised £13 for the Agricultural Benefit Society.'

Woodley Flower Show: The nineteenth annual flower show was held in the Recreation Ground at Woodley on Wednesday, August 24[th.] 'The weather was beautifully fine. There were a large number of visitors, and in every way the Show was a great success. The Exhibition was held in one large and three smaller tents. The arrangement of the flowers, fruit, vegetables and needlework was admirably made.'

December 1892
Extension of Sonning Churchyard: 'The ancient churchyard of Sonning was enlarged some thirty-five years since by the addition of a portion of Bone Orchard. The new part is now almost full, and through the liberality of Mr. Golding-Palmer, we are enabled to add a piece of nearly the same size that was added previously. The wall at the south end is being removed, and we hope to have the new ground ready for consecration in February. The expenses to fall upon the Parish will be the cost of Conveyance, the removal of the wall, and other items of fencing, and the levelling and laying out of paths and ground.'

The Sewing Class: 'Under the management of Mrs. Brooks, the Sewing Class will be resumed Monday, December 5th, at the Pearson Hall, and continue every Monday at 5.30 p.m. during the winter. All children over nine years of age are asked to belong and attend regularly.'

January 1893
Parish Nurse: 'Since Michaelmas there has been no Nurse in the Parish. Fortunately there have been no cases of sickness. Nurse Giles left us at her own desire and the difficulty of finding anyone suitable for our village has been considerable.' Mrs. Coggins health had recovered and she agreed to resume her village nursing role, but with a somewhat reduced time commitment.

February 1893
Sonning Dispensary: 'It has been the custom for many years for people who have been ill for many days to send for the doctor late at night. Mr. Brooks must ask his patients to let him know if they wish to be seen (between the hours of 9 and 10.30 in the morning); otherwise they cannot be visited that day. In cases of sudden illness an exception will be made and they will be attended to at once.'

April 1893

Sonning Cricket Club: 'The Annual Entertainment, consisting this year of Vocal and Instrumental Music, and the Farce entitled "My Lord in Livery" will be performed in the Pearson Hall on Thursday, April 6th, commencing at 7.30.'

Sonning Working Men's Club: 'The 17th Annual Club Meeting was held at the Club Rooms on January 27th. The Committee have the pleasure to present a favourable report. The prosperity of the Club is shewn by the numbers who frequent it and by the increased number of names on the books, which is 42. This beats the record for the previous six years.'

The Gregory Memorial Window: 'The Window to the memory of Mr. Gregory, has just been fixed in the North Aisle of the Sonning Church. The figures are those of St. Ambrose and St. Osmund, both intimately connected with the history of Church music. The window is the work of Mr. Kempe of Nottingham Place.'
[*William Gregory (1834-1892) was the Sonning church organist who is interred in the Sonning churchyard.*] (*St. Andrew's Church - Record of Burials etc.,* 2012)

June 1893

Sonning Glee Society: 'This Society gave its first concert on August 20th, on the success of which all members are to be heartily congratulated, especially the conductor. The piece which seemed to be most appreciated was the part song, entitled "Prophundo Basso", which was most humorously rendered.'

Flower Service: 'The first Flower Service of the season was held on Trinity Sunday, when the children brought 120 bunches of beautiful flowers, which were afterwards sent to various London Hospitals.'

July 1893

Royal Berkshire Hospital: 'The Annual Sermons were preached on Sunday, May 25th and the collections made amounted to £19 10s 6d. In addition, a considerable amounted was collected by means of boxes circulated throughout the Parish, whereby all who were prevented from making their offerings in Church were afforded an opportunity of contributing to the fund.'

September 1893
County Council Exhibitions: 'We congratulate Mr. Watson upon the success of one of his pupils in the competition for the Scholarships. The Council offered twenty Scholarships of £25 each for the open competition among boys of Elementary Schools. A. G. Pembroke will join the Reading Grammar School in September.'

October 1893
Contagious Diseases: The diphtheria pandemic had continued to be prevalent in Britain but appears to have relented in Sonning and nearby villages by late 1893. However, scarlatina had also been active and concern for the spread of these highly contagious diseases brought about the following report in this issue: 'We are thankful to say that there has been but little spread of diphtheria in the Eye, or of scarlatina in Sonning Town. All mothers should be aware that they are bound by law to notify every case of contagious disease in their home to the proper authorities, and are also liable to penalties for allowing children to go out before all infection is at an end. In the case of Scarlatina contagion is much greater when the patient is recovering and the skin peeling than in the early stages of the illness.'

December 1893
Sonning Cricket Club: 'The home-bringing of the Reading and District Challenge Cup, won this year by Sonning, was accorded quite a joyous welcome on its arrival in the village on Friday evening, October 27th. It was met at the lower gates of Holme Park by a procession of the members of the club and the villagers, nearly all of whom carried Chinese lanterns. The houses all along the route taken were decorated, and the street in many places was festooned with lanterns.'

January 1894
A review of the previous year included mention of a new water supply for Sonning: 'that was opened in the autumn, which we trust may be a source of increased health and comfort to the village.'

Almanac: 'An 1894 sheet almanac for the use of the parish has been prepared by Mr. Mowbray of Oxford. Copies at one penny each, can be procured at the Vicarage.'

March 1894

Exhibition of Village Industries: 'The Exhibition is fixed for Wednesday and Thursday, April 4th and 5th. All exhibits must be sent to the Pearson Hall on Monday, April 2nd. Last year one or two classes were very poorly represented, chiefly the washing and the fret saw. This is a defect that should be remedied this year, and we hope to see, not only these two, but also all the other stalls well filled with good exhibits.'

Woodley Coal and Clothing Clubs: 'In 1893 there were 286 members of the Clothing Club and 109 members of the Coal Club.' Members of the clothing club contributed £95 to the income with a further £18 received from donations. The coal club income amounted to £85 of which the members contributed £62 and donations £23.

June 1894

Parish Councils: 'Our readers have no doubt heard a good deal about the Act of Parliament passed last session, establishing Parish Councils, and altering materially the constitution of the Board of Guardians. Generally, we may say it restricts the Parish Vestry to strict church purposes, and the Churchwardens' office will be henceforth really what the name imports, the Warden or Guardian of the Church.'

July 1894

Parish Councils: 'Since the issue of our June number we learn that the Parish of Sonning Town will have six members allotted to it, and Woodley (which has a much larger population), seven. Eye and Dunsden is in the county of Oxfordshire, and, therefore, under the jurisdiction of the council and that County. It will be well for those interested in parochial work to seriously consider which of our fellow-parishioners it would be preferable to choose for the Council. Men of business habits and who will attend regularly seem essential. Men or women from all classes of society are eligible.'

September 1894

Sonning Schools: An abbreviated report upon the visit of Her Majesty's Inspector was included: 'Boys' School – The third standard has not a very sound knowledge of grammar, but in all other respects the boys have passed an extremely good examination. Girls' School – The girls are in excellent discipline and have acquitted themselves with credit in reading and arithmetic, but their spelling is only pretty good. Infants' School – This is a delightful little school and excellent in every respect.'

December 1894

The 1894 Flood: 'Dwellers in the Thames Valley will long remember the great flood of 1894. A fortnight of showers, everywhere saturating the subsoil, and filling up the water channels, followed by a deluge lasting the greater part of twenty-four hours, produced a flood unparalleled in the memory of the oldest. Hence it came about that on Friday and Saturday, November 16th and 17th, the Thames at Sonning Lock stood 4 feet 2 inches above high water level, and in the *Reading Mercury* of Saturday, November 17th, is reported "The Thames rose twelve inches during the night". The extent of ground covered by water may be more easily grasped by others if it is stated that it stretched in one unbroken sheet from the Vicarage lawn to Aberlash and Sonning Mill. In the kitchens of Aberlash were four inches of water, and in the Mill were two feet.'

January 1895

The two major events of 1894, the November flood and the creation of parish councils, were highlighted when reviewing the previous year: 'The most remarkable feature in the history of last year was the very heavy rainfall in November, and the consequent flood, which reached its highest point on the seventeenth day of the month. It is noticeable that the four great floods of the century have all reached their highest point on either the sixteenth or seventeenth of November. The year will also be remembered for the election of the first Parish Council, which took place on December the 17th. The first meeting of the New Council will be held in January, and we all will look forward with interest to the results of this latest form of local government.'

February 1895

Nursing Lectures: 'With a view to giving our readers timely notice it may be mentioned here that a course of lectures on nursing will begin in the Pearson Hall in March. The first lecture will be given on Wednesday, March 6th. All necessary particulars will be duly notified by Miss Ellen Dashwood.'

March 1895

Parish Council (Sonning Town): 'The first meeting of the Sonning Parish Council was held on January 1ˢᵗ, in the Pearson Hall. Mr. Knox was elected Chairman. The assistant overseer, Mr. Hamilton was appointed Clerk, his salary to be settled at the next meeting. The second meeting was held on January 30ᵗʰ; it was decided to give the clerk £8 per year, in addition to the £15 which he receives as Assistant Overseer.'

Sonning Parish Accounts 1884: A list of fourteen charity accounts, for the previous year, was printed in this issue. The parish magazine account was included and indicated a trading shortfall during the past year of £2 13s 6d and a carried forward deficit of £12 3s 8d.

June 1895

The magazine had increasingly become a most useful and accepted means of reporting the activities of a wide range of clubs and societies, many of which were using the Pearson Hall as a venue for meetings and entertainment. The affairs of the recently formed parish council were well documented, and the magazine was clearly a helpful means of bringing the work of the new council to the notice of local residents.

The Unusual Season: 'May, during the past year, has been marked by most unusual vicissitudes of temperature. Intense and unusual heat, reaching its highest point on Sunday, May 12ᵗʰ, when the thermometer in the shade reached 85 degrees, followed by bitter cold searching wind within four days. The rainfall meanwhile has been very slight.'

July 1895

Behaviour during Services: 'Our ritual in Sonning Church is of the most simplest. However, there is one point in which we would welcome an improvement. We have been asked by several members of the congregation to encourage the practice (common in most churches) of the congregation rising in their seats, when the clergy and choir enter the church, and remaining quiet in their seats until the clergy have left. We heartedly commend this practice, especially after the celebration of Holy Communion. The noise of people leaving the church, before the holy vessels have been removed from the tables is unseemly. A few minutes given to private prayer at such time would be good.'

The Parish Nurse: 'It has been thought desirable to reprint here the rules under which the nursing fund is administered. It has been alleged that cases have occurred where the nurse has been called away from the houses of the poor people to give help at those of a higher class. Such allegation has not a shadow of foundation in fact.' The following is an abbreviation of the rules:

1. The Nurse will attend ordinary cases of sickness among the poor of Sonning and Eye.

2. She will conform absolutely to the directions of the doctor.

3. Cases of women in confinements are exceptional, and can only be taken when the Nurse's other duties allow.

4. When attending any case of contagious disease, she cannot nurse at another house at the same time.

5. If not employed in attending to the sick poor, her services may be engaged by persons of a higher class.

6. Scale of payments for confinements and those of a higher class of society.

September 1895

The General Election: 'The election is now over, with all its strife and misrepresentations. In this division of the county of Berkshire we have been saved a great deal by the blessing of an uncontested return.'

[*Lord Rosebery had succeeded to the premiership during the previous year, following William Gladstone's retirement at the age of 84 years. The election took place between 13 July and 7 August. Under the leadership of Lord Salisbury, the Conservative party, in alliance with the Liberal Unionists, achieved a large majority over Lord Rosebery's Liberal party.*]

Church Flags: 'Two new flags have been purchased; a Royal Standard for the Queen's Birthday etc., and the Union Jack for other festivals.'

November 1895

Our Endowed Charities: 'So much confusion has arisen on this subject arising from the difficulty of understanding the recent Act of Parliament, that it seems desirable to publish in full the decision of the Charity Commissioners on the subject. It is understood that the ancient Parish of Sonning consists of four separate Liberties, or Poor Parishes, each having their own Parish Council, *viz*, Sonning Town, Earley, Eye and Dunsden, Woodley.' There followed details of the administration requirements under the new Act where one or more of these liberties had an interest in the existing charities (the Clifford, Barker, Blagrave and Payne charities were listed).

Our Church Collections: 'The amount collected for Harvest Thanksgiving on St. Michael's Day amounted to £15 1s 8d, which has been remitted to the Royal Agricultural Benevolent Society.'

January 1896
Archdeacon Pott: The issue contained just four pages of which the major portion was used to print a letter from Archdeacon Alfred Pott. Having mentioned various matters, including the appointment of a new schoolmistress and the changes in the trusteeship of parochial charities brought about by the new parish council, Pott made the following personal comments: 'I must express my regret that continued and increasing ill-health in myself and in my family has seriously interrupted my own ministrations among you during the past year. Those ministrations I shall sincerely hope to resume ere long. I should like also to recognise my debt to those who have so kindly and efficiently supplied my place.'

March 1896
Our Mortuary: 'The Mortuary was built some years since on a portion of Glebe Land. It has now been conveyed in Trust to the Vicar and Churchwardens in perpetuity, the deed having been executed by the Bishop and Archdeacon. This has been done without the intervention of the Parish Council. The Mortuary in future stands on the same footing as the Churchyard. The Bishop has considered Consecration needless, as no interments can ever take place in that ground.'

May 1896
The Fire at the Club House: 'A fire broke out about 6.45pm on Easter Tuesday (April 7th), which at one time threatened all that end of the village. The shed being of combustible material and contents burned very rapidly, and by the exertions of some of our people, aided by the engine from Holme Park, was extinguished before the flames laid hold of the Club house itself.' As a result of the fire an approach was made to the Parish Council drawing their attention to the need for immediate steps to be taken to improve provisions against fire in the village.

June 1896

The Late Fire: 'A subscription has been raised towards providing hose of sufficient length to carry water up to the highest buildings in the Parish. The exact position of the hydrants has also been indicated, so that there will in future be no difficulty in finding, when required, the nearest source of water. The expense of these very important improvements will be defrayed by voluntary subscription.'

Our Schools: 'We received during Friday, May 15th, what is technically termed "a visit of surprise" from one of Her Majesty's Inspectors of Schools. These visits which may occur on any School-day, have generally taken the place of formal fixed Inspections. We have had no report but have no reason to doubt that in all three schools the Inspection was satisfactory.'

Woodley Penny Bank: 'The number of depositors in 1895 was 134. The money paid into the Bank during the year amounted to £37 12s 4d. The total amount of the money standing to the credit of the members of the Penny Bank on January, 1st, 1896 and invested by the Treasurer in the Post Office Savings' Bank, was £24 15s 9d.'

September 1896

Sonning Brass Band: 'The committee and all others connected with the Sonning Brass Band wish to thanks all of the subscribers for their generosity in helping them to start the band. Our very best thanks are due to Mr. Witherington for placing his coach-house at the disposal of the Committee for practice until the room at Play Hatch is finished.'

December 1896

Our Church Hymn Book: 'It will be remembered that in the year 1882 a new edition of the old Sonning Hymn Book was printed, with an appendix added. This second edition of 1,000 copies is now wholly exhausted. We propose on Christmas Day to begin the use of "Hymns: Ancient and Modern", a manual very largely in use all over the English Church at home and abroad. Copies of Hymns: A and M in all sizes and at all prices, may be obtained of most booksellers, and we have arranged at our own Post Office for the sale of copies of three of the most useful varieties, at the price of two pence and upwards.'

January 1897

The Earthquake of December 17th: 'We are not visited with severe shocks of earthquakes in England, although experts tell us that our country lies in the direct line where they might be expected. On December 17th, about 5 a.m., a shock passed through a considerable part of the country, being felt more severely in the western counties, Gloucester and Hereford. The disturbance was, however, sensibly recognised in the Thames Valley area, and in our own village. Persons were awakened at Holme Park and the Vicarage. At Twyford and Wokingham it was yet more distinct.'

February 1897

Sonning Choral Society: 'An excellent and successful Concert was given on Wednesday, January 13th, by the Sonning Choral Society. The Concert opened by a duet, well rendered by Miss Cox and Mr. Boseley, and later on two duets for four persons on two pianofortes was much appreciated, and one, "The Marionettes," was encored. The fantasia on "National Melodies" made a spirited finale to the Concert.'

April 1897

Sonning Churchyard: Following comments in the October 1891 issue, concerning the upkeep of the Sonning churchyard, it was reported in this issue that a number of the old wooden memorials within the churchyard were badly deteriorating and will have to be removed. It was pointed out that wooden memorials were now rarely erected, and that stone and marble were easier to obtain and would be far more durable.

June 1897

Woodley Penny Bank: 'During the year 1896 the number of contributors paying into the Woodley Penny Bank was 132. The payments during the course of the year amounted to £32 7s and the sum withdrawn was £36 18s 3d. At the beginning of this year the amount standing in the Bank to the credit of the members and invested in the Post Office Savings' Bank was £24 4s 2d.'

July 1897

Our Nursing Fund: It was reported in this issue that a meeting was to be called to consider the future of the fund. This was seen to be necessary due to the following news and comment: 'After some years of very active and useful service, Mrs. Coggins finds it impossible to continue her work, owing to failing health. The possibility of continuing the Charity at all must depend upon the liberality of subscribers.'

August 1897

Mrs. Coggins: A presentation was made to Mrs. Coggins in recognition of the nursing services she had given to Sonning residents over many past years and the following appreciation was printed: 'Most of us know how patiently, tenderly and skilfully she has tended the sick and old, under many difficulties, often when she herself hardly equal to any exertion.' The presentation to Mrs. Coggins, of proceeds from a cash collection, amounted to £20 3s 0d.

The Nursing Fund: 'It has not yet been found possible to provide a suitable successor to Mrs. Coggins. All enquiries have been made, but the probable expense will be considerably larger than our present subscriptions will cover. If the institution is to continue we must ask for larger contributions.'

Queen Victoria's Diamond Jubilee: The Jubilee was celebrated on Sunday, June 20th, although Tuesday, June 22nd was declared the day of national celebration. Local activities which took place included a party in Banda Park for the residents of Dunsden: 'To each household was given half-a-pound of tea, to the men and grown lads an ounce of tobacco, and to each child a jubilee mug and a bag of sugar-plums.' It was noted that similar festivities were held in Woodley and Sonning.

The Jubilee Gate: 'As a permanent memorial, it is proposed to improve the entrance to the Churchyard at the south (Sonning Lane) end, by the erection of a standing porch, and moving the present gate to the commencement of the new addition to the Churchyard. The plans are not quite complete, nor is all the money yet raised.'

October 1897

The Nursing Fund: 'For some months past we have had no parish nurse, to the great loss of the old and sick in the Parish. A General Meeting will shortly be held, of which due notice will be given, to consider the

best means of reviving this institution. We shall never again get such splendid work at so small a cost as that done by Mrs. Coggins. The expenses of her successor cannot be put at less than £50 per year.' No further reference to this nursing service was made. However, a new nursing service was later established.
(see: April 1900)

Woodley and Sandford Cottage Garden Association: The annual show was held at Woodley's Recreation Field on Wednesday, August 25th. The *Reading Mercury* newspaper commented: 'The Woodley and Sandford Cottage Garden Association which is one of the oldest horticultural societies in this district – having existed for a quarter of a century – can claim to have placed before the public one of the most attractive of the numerous shows held in the Reading district this summer.'

November 1897
The Woodley Church Clock: 'A General Meeting of the parishioners and of the subscribers to the fund for the erection of the Church Clock was held in the Schoolroom on Monday evening, October 4th. A tender from the firm of Thwaites and Reed, 15 Bowling Green, London, for the supply of the Clock, exclusive of builders' and carpenters' expenses, for the sum of fifty guineas, was considered and accepted. It is hoped that the Clock will be heard striking in the parish soon after the beginning of the New Year.'

The Pearson Hall: 'The applications for the use of the Hall have become so numerous that it is now necessary for all of our Parishioners to understand that such applications should be made, as long as possible before the day, on which the Hall is needed.'

December 1897
Rev. Henry Golding-Palmer: The death of Henry Golding-Palmer which occurred during the month of November was recorded in this issue. He had occupied Holme Park, and was the main landowner of the parish, for seventeen years. Moreover, Golding-Palmer was a substantial benefactor for many local causes which were undoubtedly the poorer for his passing.
(see: Palmer family tree – page 22)

January 1898

The Year of 1897: 'The old year has been one of mixed joy and sorrow; a year marked by a great national festival, marked also by great changes and losses near our own doors in Sonning. The death of Mr. Palmer in November must lead to the break up of the Holme Park in its entirety, and will very largely affect many interested in Sonning. The number of burials altogether has been in excess of our average, so that our Jubilee in Sonning has been characterised by its own special sorrows.'

Our Jubilee Memorial: 'Our new entrance gate, facing Sonning Lane, will, we hope, be fixed by December 31st. The contractors have found more work in Mr. Greenaway's design than they had anticipated, and have disappointed our expectations as to the time of completion.'

February 1898

The Loss of the Golding-Palmer Benefaction: An open letter from Alfred Pott explained the financial loss that had been caused by the death of Henry Golding-Palmer. Pott indicated his intention to convene a parish meeting to discuss the financial consequences following the loss of such a benefactor, upon whom many local charities relied so heavily. Among the causes that would particularly suffer greatly were the schools, church expenses, the Pearson Hall, the dispensary and the coal club. The letter emphasised the seriousness of the loss of this financial support. It further pointed out the likely need, that the parishioners would be required to play a full part in financing the shortfall, unless some of these important causes were to be put in jeopardy.

Sonning Churchyard: 'We would call the attention of some families to the way in which some of the memorials in our Churchyard are falling out of the perpendicular, owing to the failure of the soil beneath.'

March 1898

The Jubilee Gate: 'After many delays the gate is complete. The work and materials are alike excellent, and the whole gives a character and dignity to this approach to the Churchyard which has been hitherto wanting. At the same time we have carried out a much needed alteration on the side of the Churchyard path leading from the entrance gates. The old wire hurdles have been superseded by a rustic fence, in character with the other boundaries of the Churchyard, and the new fence has been carried up where the close paling stood, so as to throw the old and new parts into one. A new and sufficient drain has been carried across the whole width of the cemetery, into the barrel drain running along the north wall.'

Sonning Organ: 'The Archdeacon has received a very munificent offer from Mr. Mathews to undertake at his own cost some very extensive improvements in our organ, The instrument very much needs such repairs. These will include the transfer of the keyboard to a site on a line with the Choir, a change which will be very helpful to the Organist.'

April 1898
The Pearson Hall: 'It is now necessary to make some regulations as to a charge for the use of the Pearson Hall in the future. For all Parish and Council Meetings, Classes, Missionary Meetings, Temperance Meetings and the like, the use will be free, as in the past. For any Clubs or Associations having incomes, for Social Gatherings, Dances Etc., there will be a charge.'

June 1898
Our Almshouses: 'By the recent death of Mr. Golding-Palmer, the last Trustee of the original foundation has been taken from us. The Charity Commissioners have drawn up a new scheme for future management. When confirmed by the Commissioners, the new Trustees will lay down new rules for the inmates of the Almshouses, which will be communicated to each of them.'

Woodley Church Clock: A clock was installed on the face of the belfry chamber of Woodley Church and was started on Thursday morning, April 28th. It was noted: 'The thanks of the people of Woodley are due to the many friends who have lent so helpful and generous a hand towards the conferring of this boon upon the Parish.'

July 1898
Apprenticeship Fund: 'There is a small sum belonging to this Charity for apprenticeship. This will amount at the end of July to a little over £16.

Any person living in Sonning Town or in Dunsden may apply, on behalf of a son, to the Archdeacon. It will be necessary to satisfy the Trustees as to the character of the boy, and the nature of the intended apprenticeship. Apprentices, according to the terms of the will, must be chosen from the Free School of Sonning.'

Woodley School: An examination took place on Thursday, June 2nd by the Diocesan Inspector of Schools for the Rural Deanery of Sonning: 'The School has passed a good examination in all the departments. The infants were especially bright and intelligent. The tone and discipline of the whole School was excellent.'

August 1898

Sonning Lock: 'As usual our Lock was gaily decorated with Chinese lanterns on the evening of the last day of Henley Regatta, and fully justified its reputation for taste. The number of boats which passed through the Lock to and from Reading was smaller this year than usual, as so many visitors took train or went by road to Henley, where an immense number of boats were to be had. All Sonning will be glad that Mr, T. Sadler gained the second prize for his pretty Lock.'

Sonning Boys' School Library and Reading Room: 'The Reading Room and also the Library have been of a great value to the School since their institution. Any suitable books and magazines would be very welcome, and a boy would gladly call for either or both on receipt of a note left at the School or Schoolhouse.'

October 1898

School Feast: 'On September 9th, the annual School Feast was held by kind permission of Mrs. Wade Palmer in Holme Park. The weather was very favourable, and the games were continued till after sundown.'
(See Palmer family tree – p.22)

New Bier for St. John's Church: A mobile bier, with rubber tyres, at a cost of seventeen pounds, had been commissioned for the use of the church. A fee of one shilling was to be charged for use of the bier by any Woodley resident, and two shillings and sixpence for anyone from another parish.

Sonning Working Men's Club: A meeting of all the members of the club was held in the Pearson Hall on Thursday, September 8th.   A letter was read from Mr. Reeve, acting as agent for Mrs. Wade Palmer, offering to continue the use of the club house at an annual rental of £5.   Two resolutions were passed:

'1. That Mrs. Palmer's offer be accepted with thanks.

  2. That on and after January 1st. 1899, the present subscription of Ordinary Members be doubled, and be at the rate of two shillings each quarter.'

December 1898

Sonning's New Bier: It was reported that the church had received the gift of a bier, having the same design and by the same supplier as the bier recently made for St. John's Church, Woodley.

January 1899

The page extent of the magazine continued to vary quite considerably, with an issue of just four pages in January and twelve pages in the following month.   The format, with some minor changes in layout, was still very similar in appearance to the first issue published some thirty years earlier.

The Year 1898:   Comments made concerning the old year mentioned long periods of drought which had been experienced locally, as well as elsewhere in England.   The year had been altogether healthy, other than outbreaks of whooping cough and measles which had occurred during the late autumn period.

Dorcas Society: It was reported that the society had made fifty four garments which had been distributed before Christmas.   Parcels had been despatched to a number of good causes including Guy's Hospital, London for distribution to the poor.

March 1899

Church Organist: The appointment of a new organist for St. Andrew's Church had taken place and Mr. Boggiss had begun his work on the first Sunday in February.   It was mentioned that: 'Mr, Strickland had kindly undertaken to assist Mr. Boggiss for the first six months in training the choir.'

Woodley Clothing and Coal Clubs: The accounts for both of these clubs were printed. Clothing club: 264 members subscribed £90 3s 5d with further income from interest and donations totalling £18 2s 5d. The clothing suppliers included established Reading retailers: Heelas, McIlroy, Jackson, Milward, Burberry and Bull. Coal club: a total of 107 members had paid into the fund £62 14s 6d with further income received of £24 11s 1d from the Robert Palmer bequest and in addition interest was also included of 13s 8d.

May 1899

Church Annual Accounts: The annual accounts of the St. Andrew's churchwardens listed receipts of £188 0s 0d. This amount included income from church lands and a rent of £50 from Simonds & Co., in respect of the Bull Inn.

June 1899

The Blue Coat School: In 1666 Sir Thomas Rich of Sonning gave the sum of £1,000 to maintain six poor boys at the Aldworth Hospital Charity School in Reading (later known as Reading Blue Coat School); three of the boys were to be chosen from the parish of Sonning. Consequently, the following notice was printed in this issue: 'There will be a vacancy in the Blue Coat School after the summer holidays. The applicants must be Sonning Town boys, and over eleven years of age. They must also be qualified to pass the Fourth Standard.'

September 1899

Flower Service: 'At the service held on July 23rd, seventy-eight bunches of flowers were presented, which were then sent to the Marylebone Workhouse Infirmary.'

Harvest Thanksgiving: 'Harvest has been very early this year. The Annual Festival will be held on Sunday, September 10th. The collection will be given, as usual, to the Royal Agricultural Benevolent Institution.'

Missions to Seamen: 'Sermons were preached on behalf of this Society according to our annual custom, on Sunday, August 13th, morning and evening, by the Rev. G. E. Wilson. The collection amounted to £13 6s. which was remitted to the Society.'

October 1899

Woodley Church Heating Apparatus: The heating system at St. John's Church, which was installed when the church was consecrated in 1873, now required replacing.   The contractor was Messrs: Callas of Reading.

November 1899

Presentation to the Archdeacon.   Within this issue the announcement was made of Alfred Pott's retirement: 'On Monday, October 2nd, the Archdeacon received from a large body of the parishioners a very beautiful Service of Plate for the table as a memorial of Sonning.   The gift was presented in the name of the subscribers by Mr. Witherington.'

Archdeacon Alfred Pott's Valediction: In a moving letter of appreciation to the parishioners, Alfred Pott asked that his successor, Henry Barter, might receive the help and support from the parishioners that he had received throughout seventeen years of his ministry.   Within the letter he also mentioned the important additions and improvements to the church that had been carried out during his period in Sonning: 'We have added a new pulpit in memory of my predecessor, and the building itself has been strengthened, perhaps saved from very serious disaster, by a new and complete system of drainage, and security of the Central Nave has been ensured by a system of iron ties, which have quite answered their intended purpose.   Outside the building we have been enabled to increase the Churchyard, through the liberality of the late Mr. Golding-Palmer, and on the other side to add a much needed Mortuary, to prevent the desecration of bodies taken from the river.   This last building now forms part of the Churchyard itself, having been consecrated by the Bishop.'   Pott continued by mentioning the excellent condition of the schools and the great improvement in the church music including the rebuilding of the organ.   In conclusion he thanked the various churchwardens and others for their support during his ministry and all the parishioners who had contributed to the wellbeing of St. Andrew's Church and its activities.

A word to our Readers: 'By the time that this number of the Magazine is in your hands, the Archdeacon will be on the eve of leaving Sonning, and Mr. Barter will be taking possession.   The new Rector will not receive formal Institution and Induction until a month later on, owing to the inconvenient provisions of a recent Act of Parliament; but for all practical purposes Mr. Barter will be in possession. The regulation of our Magazine, if continued, will pass into the hands of the new Rector, and any necessary alterations will rest with him. I only note here that the cost of the Magazine has every year considerably exceeded the receipts, owing to the very low price at which it is sold.'

The African War: The following comment was included concerning the Boer War which commenced on October 11th. 1899: 'The month of November is likely to be marked by much suffering and sorrow, arising from the unhappy war in South Africa. We probably all think that the war has not been of our own seeking, and was necessary in the interest of the British Empire.'

December 1899
Rev. Henry Barter: This issue included comments by the vicar designate of Sonning for the kind initial reception he had received from parishioners and confirmed that Sunday services will continue in the present form.

The Parish Magazine: 'It is most unsatisfactory that this Parish Magazine should be sold at a considerable loss, and it would be still more unsatisfactory to put a stop to its circulation. Probably at the price of one and a half pence it would be nearly self-supporting, and an effort will be made to carry it on at that price, and to preserve its character as a useful record of all past events in the parish, as well as a convenient medium of notices of future arrangements.'

THE PAST MONTH.

Our Registers.

Burials.   SONNING.

Nov. 30.—Ann Flower, aged 83 years.
Dec. 1.—William Liddiard, aged 30 years.
  „ 21.—Elizabeth Leach, aged 81 years.
  „ 22.—Stephen Rothwell, aged 74 years.

Baptisms.   DUNSDEN.

Dec. 10.—Frederick, son of Wm. Herbert and Emma Louisa Marcham.
  „ 10.—Mabel Eliza, daugter of John and Annie East.
  „ 10.—Frederick Henry, son of Emmanuel and Martha Ann Gibbs.

Marriages.

Nov. 18.—Henry Edward Tayler to Lilian Ruth Strong, both of
    Dunsden.
Dec. 23.—Charles Barnes to Eliza Kate Chandler, both of Dunsden.
  „ 26.—Henry Ranson, of St. Botolph's, Corbridge, to Elizabeth
    Hawkins, of Dunsden.

Burials. Dec. 27.—Esther Price, aged 14 years.
    „ 28.—Hannah Maria Amor, aged 54 years.

In 1899.—Baptisms, 14 ; Marriages, 7 ; Burials, 5.

Baptisms.   WOODLEY.

Nov. 26.—Ann, daughter of Edwin and Elizabeth Long.
  „ 26.—Emma Maud, daughter of Edwin and Elizabeth Long.
  „ 30.—Dorothy Joan, daughter of William and Elizabeth Medcalf.
Dec. 3.—Fred and Frank, twin sons of Henry and Mary Saunders.
  „ 3.—George Llando, son of Thomas and Jane Moore.
  „ 3.—Phœbe, daughter of Francis William and Eliza Hiscock.

Burial. Nov. 27.—Hannah Redman, aged 66 years.

WOODLEY REGISTERS, 1899.

Baptisms, 22 ; Marriages, 5 ; Burials, 9.

———

The Vicar was duly instituted by the Bishop of Oxford at the Diocesan Registry on Friday, Dec. 15th, and on the following Tuesday he was inducted into possession of the Church and Vicarage by the Rev. E. A. Gray, who was asked by the Archdeacon of Berks to represent him.

The Rev. F. E. Robinson, the Master of the Diocesan Guild of Bellringers, brought a band of experienced ringers to the tower on Saturday, Dec. 16th, and gave us the pleasure of listening for an hour to the music of the Stedman method rung with great precision. Unfortunately, the peal was not completed, but we hope before this is in print to have heard a five thousand on the Sonning bells.

Text page: January 1900. (22.5 x 14.5cm)

CHAPTER THREE

1900 - 1913

W ith the sun setting on the Victorian era vast changes were about to occur in the next few years, both for good and ill. The beginning of the new century was but a year hence when a change at the helm of the *Sonning Parish Magazine* took place. However, the new vicar's tenure, which commenced with his induction to St. Andrew's Church in the last few days of 1899, was to be brief. During the short period of the new ministry the appearance of the magazine was retained very much in the style and format which had existed throughout the first three decades of publication.

With the dawning of the twentieth century came massive technological changes. The horse driven carriage would give way to the combustion engine, whilst the beginning of powered flight and the development of military equipment and weapons would have a great impact on a vast number of people. Within industry, printing was no exception to the development that would take place; the typesetting of *The Sonning Parish Magazine*, which in 1900 was still likely to have been composed by hand, was within a few years to be revolutionised with the introduction of mechanical casting of lead type controlled by typing onto a keyboard.

January 1900
The New Vicar: The official appointment of Rev. Henry Barter to the Sonning ministry was recorded in this first magazine issue of the year 1900: 'The Vicar was duly instituted by the Bishop of Oxford at the Diocesan Registry on Friday, December 15th, and on the following Tuesday he was inducted into possession of the Church and Vicarage by the Rev. E. A. Gray [the Vicar of Woodley] who was asked by the Archdeacon of Berks to represent him.'

Boer War: News of casualties, due to the fighting in the South African Second Boer War, was being regularly received in Britain and charitable giving for the dependents of those killed and maimed was well supported: 'Collections were made in Sonning Church on Sunday, Christmas Eve, for the widows and orphans of those killed in the Transvaal War. The sum of £18 15s 0d was sent to the Lord Mayor.'

February 1900

Sonning Sewerage Work: 'At a special meeting held of the Rural District Council of Wokingham on January 9th, several tenders for carrying out the Sewerage Works at Sonning were received. The tender accepted was from Mr. McCarthy Fitt, of Oxford Road, Reading, and it is expected, should the weather be favourable, that the work will be commenced in February.'

March 1900

Mothers' Union: 'Mrs. Barter has been requested by the Diocesan Committee of the Mothers' Union to endeavour to form a branch for the Parish of Sonning. The M.U. is under the patronage of the Bishop of Oxford and his Archdeacons. There are 158 branches in the Oxford Diocese, six in Sonning Deanery, with 6,539 Members and Associates. The aims, objects and constitution of the Mothers' Union will be explained at a meeting to be held in the Pearson Hall on March 15th.'

The Floods: 'To one who has lived at some distance from the banks of the river for the last 38 years, the ways of Father Thames seem wonderful and mysterious. He has not as yet been able to equal his performances of 1894, but has succeeded in invading a few cottages in Sonning Eye, to the great discomfort of their occupants. The direction of the valley, which is here a continuation of the Kennet bed, causes him to rise higher on the Oxfordshire than the Berkshire bank. February has kept up its character of "Filldike" with fifteen inches of snow and abundance of rain, and we now look forward to the proverbial peck of March dust which is worth a king's ransom.'

April 1900

Anonymous Letters: Henry Barter was moved to include the following announcement in this issue: 'It is necessary for the Vicar to explain that no notice will in any case be taken of anonymous communications on any subject. Whether letters or postcards, they will be at once destroyed, as far as possible without being read. If any parishioner wishes to make any suggestion, or has any grievance, and will communicate personally or by signed letter with the Vicar, he is willing to give such a matter due consideration. An anonymous letter is like a stab in the dark, which is a favourite method of attack in some countries, but not among Englishmen.'

Sonning Nursing Association: 'It has been decided to establish at once an Association for providing Nurses for sickness and accidents. A few rules are now under consideration and will shortly be printed and sent to every house. Annual subscriptions are invited, and subscribers will have the services of the Nurse at greatly reduced rates. In the case of farm labourers the annual subscription of 2/- will secure the *free* services of the Nurse for sickness and accident.'

May 1900
Parish Nurse: 'The parish nurse, Miss Creighton, arrived on Monday before Easter, and has already been found very useful in two cases. She is living at the Vicarage until a suitable lodging can be found for her. It is highly desirable that those who intend to subscribe to the Nursing Association should do so as soon as possible, as it must depend upon the amount received whether it will be possible to retain the services of the nurse.'

Mission to the Jews: 'A collection was made on Good Friday in the alms box for this Mission. The amount being 10s was forwarded to the Kilburn Mission to the Jews.'

June 1900
Parish Staff House: 'The Vicar has great pleasure in announcing the generous gift on the part of the Misses Dashwood, of funds for building a house as a residence for the teachers of the Girls' and Infants' Schools and the Parish Nurse.'

Sonning Cricket Club: 'The Cricket Supper took place on April 25th. Sixty sat down to an excellent dinner provided by Mr. Allnatt.'

The Banner of Faith.

FEBRUARY, 1901.

BAD EXAMPLE

BY
HELEN SHIPTON,
AUTHOR OF "JUD," A FIERY FURNACE, &c

CHAPTER II.

CRANSTEAD was unfortunate in one respect. Though a fair-sized village, it had no church of its own. It belonged to Fairmead parish, and Fairmead Church was a mile away, and the clergyman there was old and in feeble health. He did his duty conscientiously in his church and in his own immediate neighbourhood; and he thought, and quite truly, that the Cranstead people ought not to let the distance of a mile hinder them from attending the services. But he did not know them very well, and they did not know him well enough to find it natural to go to him in all their difficulties. So he did not know that there was anything specially wrong about Frank Wetherall, though it often grieved him to think that many of the young men, both in Cranstead and Fairmead, drank more than they ought. And it did not occur to John Martin, though he went to church regularly, to tell Mr. Proctor of his trouble about his assistant, and to consult him as to whether anything could be done.

As for Frank, it was not altogether out of weakness that he went and got tipsy on that Saturday night, knowing well that it would end in his having to leave an employer from whom he was sorry to part.

He *could* have kept sober that night, he knew; and they might even have gone on for another month or so pretty comfortably. But to himself

A title page example of a monthly inset, the thirty-two page "The Banner of Faith", copies of these insets were supplied for inclusion in local parish magazines. (1901)

Mafeking: 'The news of the Relief of Mafeking reached us on Saturday, May 21st, and it was celebrated here as elsewhere with great joy. Flags were flying from the Church tower and from most of the houses, the bells were rung, and in the evening a torchlight procession went round the village and was greeted everywhere with enthusiastic shouts. On Sunday, after Evensong, the National Anthem with effective variations was played by Dr. Boggiss.'

[*The siege of a British garrison at Mafeking during the Second Boer War had lasted for seven months; it had been regularly reported in Britain and had gripped the attention of many of the British population. The arrival of the news of "the relief of Mafeking" was a signal for widespread rejoicing throughout much of Britain.*]

August 1900
New Sonning Church Books: 'Sixty Prayer Books with Hymns: Ancient and Modern, bound in red basil and stamped with the words, Church of S. Andrew, Sonning, have been placed in the Church for the use of children or any member of the congregation. If care is taken they ought to last many years.'

Sonning Church Font: 'It was found that the chain by which the cover of the Font was attached to a compensating weight above the gutters of the Church roof, was nearly destroyed by rust. There seemed immediate danger of an accident, which would have done much damage to the font cover or the roof, or both. The chain and weight have now been replaced by the order of the Churchwardens, by a windlass and steel chain, which easily but slowly lifts the heavy weight when required, and has at once lifted a heavy weight of anxiety from the Vicar's mind.'

November 1900
The Parish Magazine: The following announcement, which clearly threatened the future monthly publishing of this magazine, was printed in this issue: 'Notwithstanding the efforts that have been made to meet the wishes of subscribers by fuller details of parochial events, the circulation of the Magazine, which is sold far below cost price, has not increased. It will not, therefore, be continued beyond the present year, but in order to preserve a record that may be of interest to some persons, and to provide for publication of parochial accounts, a paper of the same size as this Magazine, but without any periodical bound up

with it, will be issued at the end of each quarter at one and a half
pence, or 6d. for the year. This will avoid any want of continuity in the
parochial records, and it will be at any time possible, if a general wish
for it is expressed, to revert to monthly publication.'

[*The 'bound-in periodical' referred to would have been one of the monthly insets
published for inclusion in local parish magazines. Within the archives of the Sonning
Parish Magazine are copies of a monthly periodical 'The Banner of Faith' (dated 1901)
which was likely to have been the inset referred to by Henry Barter.*]

(*see: page 112*)

December 1900

The Parish Magazine: Thankfully, the magazine received a reprieve and
survived to continue providing information and interest articles to the
residents of Sonning, Woodley and other villages in the area: 'The
question of the continuance of the Magazine has been much in the
Vicar's mind during the past month, and he now proposes to continue
it for another year, printing only 100 copies, and thus somewhat
reducing the probable loss. When it is necessary to print more than
two pages the Calendar will be omitted or curtailed.'

January 1901

The New Century: This first issue of the twentieth century began with
the following expression of hope and good wishes for the future from
Henry Barter: 'We wish our readers all happiness in the Century just
commencing. We must all be ready to move with the times, and to
welcome and encourage the progress of the rising generation. We must
be ready to try, and, after due trial to adopt, all methods of work and
organisation which may be helpful, so long as they are consistent with
loyalty to our Church.'

February 1901

Death of Queen Victoria: After a reign of over sixty-three years Victoria,
Queen of the United Kingdom and Ireland, Empress of India, died on
January 22nd 1901 at her home, Osborne House on the Isle of Wight in
the eighty second year of her age. She was succeeded by her fifty-nine
years old eldest son the Prince of Wales, who took the title of King
Edward the Seventh and thus heralded in the Edwardian period into
Britain.

The heavy black bordered announcement under the heading of *The Mourning Nation*, which appeared in this issue of the magazine, conveyed the deep sadness felt due to the death of Queen Victoria: 'We have given expression to our sorrow in the muffled sound of the bells, in the solemn music of the Church Services, and on the day of the Funeral we shall be uniting in Memorial Services with the prayers and thanksgivings which will go up from the hearts of the people of England and of their friends all over the world. God has given us a Queen whose goodness and wisdom have no parallel in the history of nations, and now that He has taken her to Himself we know that He will still bless us if we strive to walk in His laws.'

Sonning Nursing Association: 'The Association was started in the spring, and the nurse, Miss Creighton, began her work on April 9th. Since then she has nursed eleven cases of various severity and duration, some having required night and day nursing, and four of which ended fatally. Besides these she has paid occasional visits where required, and is always ready to attend to anyone who wishes for her assistance and skill. Those whom she has nursed speak of her kindness and attention.'

April 1901
The Sonning Church Bells: 'Time and incompetent workmanship had combined to cause much to be desired in the "go" of our bells, and an expert has been called in to remedy some of the defects. The work will be completed before Easter.'

Woodley Mothers' Union: 'A tea was provided for the members of the Mother's Union on Wednesday, March 20th, in the Schoolroom. Between 30 and 40 mothers were present. A very kind and helpful address was given afterwards by Mrs. Clayton, and at the close of the meeting five new members joined the Society. There are now 50 mothers in Woodley who are members of the Society.'

May 1901
Exhibition of Animated Pictures: 'On Monday, April 15th, the Rev. Grey Neville, the Vicar of Waltham St. Lawrence, exhibited with his Magic Lantern a most admirable display of animated pictures and of very beautiful views of Japan. The schoolroom was well filled, and the

spectators most thoroughly enjoyed the beauty and marvels of the pictures shewn to them.'

Woodley Penny Bank: 'The number of depositors during 1900 was eighty-six. The amount subscribed was £32 0s 8d. and the amount withdrawn £31 8s 4d. The deposited balance in the Post Office Savings Bank at the beginning of 1901 to the credit of the depositors was £17 3s 9d.'

June 1901
The Rev Henry Barter: The unexpected death of the vicar, Henry Barter, was reported in this issue: 'A great sorrow has fallen upon the Parish of Sonning. After a very brief illness, Henry Barter, the Vicar of the Parish, entered into rest on Friday morning, May 24th. During a recent visit to London to attend Convocation he had caught a severe cold, which was followed by pneumonia and pleurisy; but owing to the great strength of his constitution hopes of recovery remained strong until the last. The news of his death came as a sudden and great shock to all his friends and parishioners.'
[*Henry Barter (1835-1901) was interred in the churchyard at Sonning, as was his wife, Elspeth Catherine Barter, nee Moberly (1843-1938).*]

July 1901
Death of Miss Dashwood: The death was announced of Isabel Emily Dashwood (1828-1901), who had assisted for many years in providing help to the most needy in Sonning and Woodley. She had taught at the Woodley School, and played a prominent part in the founding and maintaining of a number of local clubs and societies.

Temporary Vicar: 'The duty at Sonning Church on Sundays is being taken for the present by the Rev. W. Slater, Chaplin of Christ Church.'

August 1901
The New Vicar: The following entry in *The Times* announcing the appointment of Ernest Edward Holmes as the new vicar of Sonning was reproduced in this issue of the magazine: 'Owing to the recent vacancy in the See of Oxford the appointment to the Vicarage of Sonning, which is in the patronage of the Bishop, has lapsed to the Crown for this turn. On the recommendation of the new Bishop, the First Lord

of the Treasury has submitted to the King the name of the Rev. E. E. Holmes, Honorary Canon of Christ Church, Oxford, and the King has been pleased to approve the appointment.'

September 1901

Woodley and Sandford Cottage Garden Association: 'The twenty-eighth Annual Show of the Association was held in the Recreation Field at Woodley during the afternoon of Wednesday, August 21st. The Show, notwithstanding the dryness of the season, was a very excellent one. There was a large entry of exhibits, their number 620, comparing very favourably with that of the majority of preceding years.'

Sonning Schools: 'The Government School Inspector paid our Schools an unexpected visit on June 19th, and his Report was received on July 2nd. Boys' School: Very good discipline is pleasantly maintained, and the progress that the boys are making does much credit to the Master. Girls' School: The discipline is kindly, and the teaching painstaking, and the general progress of the girls seems satisfactory. Infant School: The School well maintains its reputation for bright, sympathetic and successful teaching. The staff of the Boys' School should be at once strengthened, so as to meet the requirements of Article 73 of the Code.'

October 1901

The New Vicar: 'Canon Holmes was Instituted by the Bishop of Oxford on Wednesday, September 4th, "read himself in" at 3pm on Sunday, the 8th: and was Inducted by the Archdeacon on Monday, September 9th.'

Home-Coming of Colonel Deare: 'Flags were hung across the street and suspended from windows. The reason was a patriotic one, it was to accord a hearty welcome to one deservedly much respected and esteemed inhabitant, Colonel Deare, who has just returned after eighteen months absence, invalided home from the campaign in South Africa. At about 3pm the carriage was sighted at the top of Sonning Lane, and on its arrival there, loud cheers burst forth from a large and thoroughly representative number of the Sonning inhabitants. The horses were speedily taken out and the carriage dragged triumphantly by willing hands to the Colonel's home. On the Saturday evening a procession of torchlights, lanterns and an improvised cannon went through the village to the gallant soldier's home. Amidst cheers, the Colonel came out and expressed his very great gratitude to his friends in Sonning.'

December 1901

Parish Council: 'The Quarterly Meeting of the Parish Council was held in the Pearson Hall on November, 18th, at 7 p.m. It was agreed to pay the nominal sum of one shilling a year to the Thames Conservancy for permission to place a footboard at the bathing place.'

Sonning Church Curate: 'The Vicar has been much disappointed in having to wait for the help of his Curate, the Rev. F. Symes-Thompson, who was taken ill on the day he arrived in Sonning. Mr. Symes-Thompson overworked himself at High Wycombe, and was obliged to take a much needed rest.'

Rev. F. Symes-Thompson: 'The Vicar has just heard with great regret that Mr. Symes-Thompson is forbidden to do any work until after Christmas.'

January 1902

The Parish Magazine: Ernest Holmes, used this first issue of 1902 to address the readers of the magazine, and in particular to explain changes that had been made to the presentation of the publication. The page size had been substantially increased to 9.25 inches deep x 7.25 inches wide (235 x 185 mm). It would appear that the change of size was made to accommodate the dimension of the new monthly inset that was now included. The title of the inset was *Goodwill*, edited by Canon Scott Holland one of the canons of St. Paul's Cathedral. The parish magazine comprised of only four pages, and the front page maintained a very similar appearance to the original design which included the line engraving of Sonning Church. With a far wider page size the layout of the magazine now adopted a two column width with a heading for each article. This gave the magazine an appearance rather more akin to the daily newspapers of the day. (*see: page 120.*)

Ernest Holmes stated his wish not to cease publishing the magazine with these comments: 'I should be very sorry to drop the Magazine, as it is practically our only record of parish events, and how valuable such a record is can be seen in the history of Sonning written by Canon Pearson in the back numbers of the Sonning Magazine.' Clearly, the magazine continued to be published at a financial loss, a situation which was found to be unsatisfactory, and if not solved might well cause the publication to cease.

Cottage Gardening: Mr. Hudson of the Deanery Garden, offered to provide three prizes for the three best cottage gardens in Sonning village. The competition would be judged on the "beauty of the cottage from the road". The first prize was £5 and a copy of the book *The Century Book of Gardening*, the second prize was the same book without cash and the third prize a copy of *Gardening for Beginners*.

March 1902

Whilst there appeared to be an intention to contain the page extent of the magazine in order to save cost, surprisingly, the number of pages now increased and fluctuated from six to as many as ten pages for a number of future issues.

Sonning and Woodley Cottage Nursing Association: 'The Secretary has arranged with a capable nurse to attend cases when required. The Nurse will live in the patient's house and look after the patient and family for a period, as a rule, not exceeding three weeks. It has been decided to combine Sonning and Woodley under the same Association. Will all those who wish to subscribe and have not already done so, kindly send their subscriptions to Mrs. Robinson, the White House, Sonning.'

April 1902

Sonning Lads' Club: A class of lads, which consisted of a small group of Confirmation candidates, had been started. It was reported that from this group had been formed a Sonning Lads' Club which would meet in the Pearson Hall on Monday evenings. The club to be a recreational club for young men of the village.

Confirmation: 'At the Confirmation held in Sonning Church, thirty-two candidates from Woodley were presented to the Bishop of Oxford.'

minster Abbey, when the King will be crowned by the Archbishop of Canterbury, and the Queen by the Archbishop of York, and it is hoped that all who can attend the Service before going up to the field will do so.

On the Sunday evening following the Coronation Day, the three Choirs of Sonning, Woodley, and Dunsden, will unite in a Service of Praise in the Mother Church at 6.30.

Mr. Hobbs, who is, we are all glad to know, rapidly getting better, has kindly promised to be responsible for the bonfire on the evening of the Coronation Day.

Mrs. Wade-Palmer has kindly promised to give a Coronation medal to each of the School children.

Mrs. Deare has undertaken to give a tea to the inmates of the Almshouses.

SONNING CORONATION SPORTS.

JUNE 26TH, 1902.

PROGRAMME.

1.—100 Yards.　Boys under 12.
2.—　　,,　　Boys over 12 and under 15.
3.—　　,,　　Girls under 12.
4.—　　,,　　Girls over 12 and under 15.
5.—　　,,　　Handicap.
6.—Sack Race.　50 Yards.
7.—Hurdle Race.　120 Yards.　　　　[back.
8.—Threading the Needle Race.　50 Yards out and
9.—Tug of War.　Sonning v. Sonning Eye.
10.—Bicycle Race.　One Mile.
11.—50 Yards Handicap.　(Ladies).
12.—Egg and Spoon Race.
13.—Best Decorated Bicycle.　Ladies and Children over 12.
14.—Hat Trimming Competition.
15.—Veterans' Race.　(Men).
16.—50 Yards Handicap.　(Women over 50).
17.—Half-Mile Handicap.　(Men).

CHILDREN'S ENTERTAINMENT.

The Boys' Schoolroom was filled with children from both Schools at a capital evening's entertainment, which Mr. Harries kindly arranged for them. No fewer than 120 different scenes were exhibited and described with the help of a magic lantern, and pictures illustrating a trip through Canada, incidents and places connected with the Boer War, English and Boer Generals, &c., brought distant events closely home to the children, who thoroughly entered into and appreciated the Diorama. The Canadian Pacific Railway, the Rocky Mountains, hunting buffaloes in the Wild West, Canadian farming, the Falls of Niagara, scenes in Venice and Madrid (including a Spanish bull fight), the Battles of Modder River, Colenso, Magersfontein, and the triumphant entry of Lord Roberts and Lord Kitchener into Pretoria and the Relief of Ladysmith by Gen.

Buller, seemed to interest the spectators greatly, and a final burst of cheering and the National Anthem brought a happy evening to a close, as an excellent likeness of King Edward VII. was thrown upon the sheet.

COTTAGE GARDEN PRIZE.

We would remind our readers that Mr. Hudson has kindly offered a prize of £5 for the best kept Cottage Garden in Sonning. This prize will be awarded in August, and Colonel Deare and Mr. Plum have kindly promised to act as Judges. Mr. Hudson's desire to encourage cottage gardens will, we are sure, be much and practically appreciated. In awarding the prize, the Judges will chiefly consider flowers, vegetables, and general floral effect, and the best kept garden as a whole.

CENSUS, 1901.

Sonning Town		442
Liberty of Woodley and Sandford		987
Liberty of Eye and Dunsden ...		943
Parish of Sonning.		
In Sonning Town		442
In Liberty of Woodley & Sandford		84
In Liberty of Eye and Dunsden ...		147
		673
Parish of Woodley		614
Parish of Dunsden		582
Liberty of Woodley and Sandford.		
In Woodley		614
In Earley		289
In Sonning		84
		987
Liberty of Eye and Dunsden.		
In Dunsden		582
In Sonning		147
In Kidmore		214
		943

DEBATING SOCIETY.

Owing to want of space the account of the last debate, on "The Sunday Question," must be held over until next month's Magazine.

LECTURE ON THE "NAVY AND THE NATION."

A lecture, entitled "The Navy and the Nation" (illustrated by lantern slides), was given in the Pearson Hall, on April 23rd, by Mr. H. T. C. Knox, late Lieut. R.N., and the Hon. Sec. of the Navy League. Canon Holmes occupied the chair.

Text page: June 1902. The increased page width provided the opportunity to create a two column page design. (23.5 x 18cm)

May 1902

Sonning Drainage: A local government board enquiry was convened in the Pearson Hall into an application by Wokingham Rural District Council: 'for sanction to borrow £1,000 for purposes of sewerage and sewerage disposal for the Liberty of Sonning'. Following an extensive report which occupied some four columns of the magazine, it was stated that the meeting terminated and the inspector proceeded to view the works. No further mention of the application appeared.

The Sonning Lads' Club: 'The Club is always well attended, the punch ball and boxing gloves, being always in request. It has been decided to hold a Boxing Competition on May 19th, open to all from Sonning.'

June 1902

1901 Census: The Census declared the population of the whole Liberty of Woodley and Sandford to be 987. The population of the Parish of Sonning was 673. (*see: page 120*)

Coronation of King Edward VII: Some details were included of extensive celebrations which were planned to take place in Sonning to mark the forthcoming event. A service was to be held in St. Andrew's Church and a coronation sports programme was planned with a large number of competitions for children and adults.

July 1902

The King's Illness: 'Very sad news reached us on Tuesday last. The King was ill and the Coronation was to be postponed. The whole nation will sorrow with the King and Queen [Alexandra], and we must hope and pray that their, and our, sorrow may be turned into joy by the news that his Majesty is making a good recovery.'

[*The King had been afflicted with a serious life threatening condition. The operation included the draining of an abdominal abscess, and took place on a table in the music room at Buckingham Palace. The King conferred a knighthood upon the surgeon immediately prior to the medical procedure.*]

The content of the magazine had become markedly more broadly based and was likely to appeal to a wider audience. Sports and social club reports were becoming more prominent, whilst the interest of the church was still well represented.   The inclusion of "Letters to the Vicar" was a new introduction to the magazine, and no doubt encouraged readers to become more involved in the publication.   It was noticeable that several editorial changes had taken place, and had occurred contemporaneously with the beginning of Holmes' ministry.

Peace: 'Late on Sunday night, June 1st, the inhabitants of Sonning were started out of their inland quiet by a noise which left no doubt in the minds of even the least nervous that the village was on fire.'   So commenced the report upon the reaction in Sonning when news that the Second Boer War had ended.   The celebrations that followed were exuberant, and included the prolonged ringing of the church bells.

[*The Second Boer War, which ended on May 31st, 1902, resulted in defeat for the Boers and the end of Dutch supremacy in South Africa.   Britain had lost some 22,000 officers and men and the conflict had cost Britain £222,000,000.*]

August 1902
The line engraving of St. Andrew's Church, which had appeared on the title page of the magazine, was now replaced with a printer's half tone reproduction from a photograph of St. Andrew's Church.
(*see: page 124.*)

Sonning Cricket Club: The scorecards from five matched which had been played during the summer were reproduced.   The matches were played against teams from Leighton Park, Caversham C.C, Hurst C.C, Mr. Joyce's XI, and Waltham C.C.   Of these matches Sonning won two and lost three.

September 1902
Coronation Day: The Coronation of King Edward VII eventually took place on Saturday, August 9th.   Various commemorative activities had been arranged in Sonning, Dunsden and Woodley and were reported upon in this issue.

Sonning Coronation Celebrations: 'At 7a.m. a Coronation Peal of bells rang out the news that it was Coronation Day.   At Noon a large congregation met in the Parish Church to use the Official Coronation Service and to sing the National Anthem.   At 1p.m. some 450 residents from Sonning and Eye assembled in the field kindly lent by Mr. Hobbs, and sat down to dinner which did Mr. Allnatt's catering powers great credit. The band played selections of music during the meal. Everything went as well as possible, and everyone was as pleased as possible. The sports were first-rate, the fireworks were admirable, and the bonfire made a grand end to the day.'

Coronation Festivities at Woodley: 'After a special service in the Church at half-past one, at which there was a very large congregation, headed by the band and followed by the children, a long procession made its way to the Recreation Field. There, in the course of the afternoon an excellent tea was provided, and a series of races and sports and pastimes aroused much interest. Night began to draw on, and then, just at the right moment, followed a most excellent display of animated pictures, which were shown on a large screen suspended in the open air. As the darkness deepened rockets were to be seen ascending from towns and villages in many different directions.'

Dunsden Coronation Rejoicings: 'The proceedings of the day opened with Service in the Church at 12 o'clock. The festivities began in Mr. Deare's meadow at two o'clock, when 260 adults sat down to dinner in a spacious tent. The sports came next, and together with dancing and country games were the great attraction of the day. No more enjoyable day has ever been spent in the parish. After their tea each child received a copy of "King Edward's Realm" and an illuminated box of chocolate.'

Proposed Sonning Flower Show: Consideration was being given to the commencement of a flower show in Sonning and various possibilities had been proposed. One suggestion was for Sonning to join the existing Woodley and Sandford Flower Club. In addition to a report upon a Sonning meeting convened to consider the matter, an exchange of letters was printed, between Rev. Ernest Holmes and Mr. J. Parsons, secretary of the Woodley and Sandford Cottage Garden Association, whereby agreement was reached that the matter of including Sonning into the existing flower club should be a matter of further serious consideration.

This image of St. Andrew's Church on the front page of the August 1902 issue was the first photographic reproduction to be printed in the magazine. (23.5 x 18.5cm)

October 1902

Home from the Front: The third soldier from a Sonning family returned from the South African war on Sunday, September 15th. Col. Deare and Mr. Hubert Witherington had already been welcomed home, and now Mr. Ivor Rose. 'The Church bells announced his arrival, and prepared us for the cheers that came from Sonning Lane as the horses were unharnessed and his friends dragged the carriage to the Red House.'

November 1902

Annual Flower Show: Agreement was reached between Woodley and Sonning to include Sonning in the existing flower show, and that it would be called the Woodley, Sandford and Sonning Flower Show. The annual show was to be alternatively hosted by Sonning and Woodley.

January 1903

The Nursing Fund. Accounts of the fund were printed in this issue and indicated that the total income had been £34 1s 0d and expenditure of £27 0s 3d had been incurred, resulting in a surplus of £7 0s 9d. On behalf of the villagers, grateful thanks were extended to Mrs. Robinson, the honorary secretary, who was responsible for the administration of the nursing fund.

The Almshouses: 'It is well from time to time to remind ourselves of the origin of the Sonning Trusts and of the conditions attached to them. It does not seem, for instance, to be well known that the appointment to the Sonning Almshouses rest entirely with the owner of Holme Park, and that (unless it lapses to the Vicar) the other Trustees have no voice in the appointment'.

Dunsden Ladies' Hockey Club: 'The Club was started in November 1901. During the first season nineteen members joined, from whom a Captain and a Committee were elected. Two matches were played towards the end of the season, in which the Dunsden eleven were beaten. Six more members were added to the Club during November 1902. The games are played by the kind permission of Mr. Cane in his field every Saturday, beginning at 2.45pm.'

February 1903

Obituaries: The death was announced of two ladies who had been well known to the residents of Sonning: Mrs. Pott, the wife of Alfred Pott the one time vicar of Sonning, had died in late January. Mention was made of the ill health that Mrs. Pott endured during most of her seventeen years of residency in the Sonning vicarage. Mrs. Catherine Mary Elliott, the sister of Canon Hugh Pearson, had also died in late January, and was buried in the Pearson family vault in the Sonning churchyard.

Canon Pearson's Brother: An article reproduced from the *Reading Mercury* newspaper, concerning Henry Hugh Pearson, appeared in this issue. Henry Hugh Pearson, was the brother of Canon Hugh Pearson and had been recognised as an accomplished composer (*see: March 1873*). Within the article it is noted: 'The family name was originally spelt Pierson, and to this form Henry Hugh Pearson reverted when making Germany his home, discarding also the English Henry and Hugh in favour of Henri Hugo.'

St. John's Church, Woodley: The vicar of St. John's, the Rev E. A. Gray, included in this issue details of the replacement of old worn out hymn books which had been replaced by "Hymns: Ancient and Modern". A collection in St. John's Church, which was augmented with a generous gift from Mrs. Golding-Palmer, enabled the purchase of prayer books, new psalters for the choir, a set of six dozen hassocks as well as the hymn books.

March 1903

Musical Entertainment: 'A very popular and successful entertainment was given in the School-room at Woodley on Friday Evening, February 6th, in aid of the Woodley Schools. The programme was a varied one and was warmly appreciated by a large audience.'

May 1903

Working Men's Club: 'The legal difficulties in connection with the conveyance of the land on which the Pearson Hall stands have been overcome, and plans are already in course of preparation for the proposed new Club. It is hoped that the work will commence next month. The Club will include an excellent billiards room with lounge (wanted, a billiards table), a good reading room, and a third room for bagatelle board etc., and will we hope prove a great boon to the village.'

Club Dance: 'The dance in the Pearson Hall, on Easter Monday was a great success, and full enjoyment was got out of the evening. The "gate money" went towards the funds of the Club.'

New Stained Glass Window: 'The window most kindly and generously presented by Mr. Knox, in remembrance of the Coronation of the King, has been set up in its place in the Woodley Church. The position which it occupies is on the south side of the Chancel, directly over the seats of the Choir.'

July 1903

The Summer Floods: The severe flooding which occurred during the summer, drew the following comment from the magazine's editor: 'Not since 1809 - it is said, has there been such a summer flood as in June 1903. It is bad enough for those whose houses and grounds are close to the river, but their lot is a happy one compared with that of the farmers, whose land is under water and whose hay seems to be hopelessly ruined.'

August 1903

Cyclist Church Parade: A report appeared concerning a large number of cyclists who had assembled at St. Andrew's where they attended an afternoon service on Sunday June 28th. The article went on to explain the development of the bicycle from the "bone-shaker", which was introduced into England in 1868, to the: 'light and swift machine which now forms so prominent and practical a part in the business and pleasure of English life.'

Cricket Match at Holme Park: 'By the kind invitation of Mr. Wertheimer a pleasant afternoon was spent on Wednesday in Holme Park. An eleven got together by Mr. Wertheimer played a team composed of local cricketers, and managed to beat the latter by the narrow margin of seven runs. Tea and other refreshments were partaken of, under the welcome shade of a large elm.'

September 1903

Woodley and Sonning Flower Show: An extensive report gave an account of the thirtieth annual show of this association, held at Holme Park, Sonning on the afternoon of Wednesday August 19th by kind permission of Mrs. Wade-Palmer. The report was introduced with the following comment: 'Most of our readers will have seen the report of the Flower Show in the *Reading Mercury* of August 22nd, but as the Magazine is the chronicler of the history of the Parish we repeat the account for future reference.'

October 1903

The Recent Gale: 'In spite of its sheltered position Sonning did not escape the terrific gale which sprang up so suddenly on the evening of Thursday, September 10th. No less than eight trees fell and obstructed the roads in various parts of the Holme Park Estate. A large limb from one of the old elms in the churchyard also fell across the path onto the Deanery wall.'

Bursting of the Sonning Weir: 'No little excitement was caused on Sunday, September 13th, by the bursting of the weir adjoining the lock island. The large oak beam which has held the "rimers" in their place for the last twenty-five years suddenly snapped owing no doubt to its decayed condition. The Thames Conservancy with commendable promptitude arrived and by the Monday evening fixed up a temporary structure in its place.'

Sonning Parish Library: A lending library for the use of parishioners was to be opened in the vicarage on October 12th, for which some four hundred books had been collected. The following were the rules for borrowing from the library:

1. Subscriptions, one penny per month, school children one half-penny.
2. Subscription to be paid the first week in each month.
3. One book at a time to be taken out by subscribers.
4. No book to be kept longer that a fortnight.
5. All books to be returned clean and in a proper order.
6. Books may be changed every Monday between 3 and 4pm and between 6 and 7pm.

Subscribers breaking any of these rules will be liable to a fine not exceeding 3d.

Sonning Water Sports: 'The sports were held on August, 27th. The races were excellent, and the decorations – the old brick bridge and the horse-bridge being illuminated – looked very effective when lit up at night. Two bands, one on each side of the river, greatly added to the pleasure of the day.'

December 1903
Christmas Day: 'The Services on Christmas Day will be the same as usual. We have a Choral Celebration of the Holy Communion at 8am and a second Celebration after morning Service, we hope that this will make it possible for family Communions on the great Family Festival.'

Sonning School Inspection: The Oxford Diocesan Inspector of Schools examined the schools on October 22nd and gave an excellent report. Comments made by the Inspector included: 'The Sonning Boys' School – The boys showed a very intelligent interest in their work. The Sonning Girls' and Infants' schools – In the Girls' Department the answering in each class was bright and general, the tone and order are admirable. The Infants' said their repetition nicely, and some of them answered easy questions very fairly well.'

January 1904
The East Window (Sonning Church): 'The East Window in our Church has been very greatly improved by Mr. Bodley. The flaring drapery has been toned down and the glaring white in the figure softened. The effect is most satisfactory.'

Parish Library: 'The Library has evidently supplied a want in the Parish. The number of books taken out in four consecutive weeks came to 304, making an average of 76 per week. We hope to make fresh additions to the books from time to time if we find that the Library continues to be valued.'

Children's Entertainment: 'The piece selected for the children to act this year is "Jack and the Beanstalk". The entertainment will be given on January 20th, when we hope to give and get much pleasure. Half of the proceeds will be given to *The Society for the Prevention of Cruelty to Children*.'

February 1904

Christmas: 'It would be difficult for the Church to be more decorated than it was this year, and we must make an exception to our usual plan of mentioning no names and say how much pleasure Mr. Plumb's decoration of the East end gave. It was exactly what was wanted.'

Choir Boys Tea: 'The Vicar entertained the Choir boys of Sonning to tea on Wednesday, the 13th. The boys have worked well at their music and have gained good words from Dr. Boggiss, and we hope that they enjoyed their play as much as, we are sure, they enjoy their work!'

April 1904

Views of the Thames: 'Mr. Wing has kindly offered to provide us with entertainment in Easter Week, consisting of a Lantern Exhibition of Views of the River Thames, lasting about an hour and a half. Mr. Wing has an exceptionally good series of about 180 views of the river, tracing its course from its source to the Tower Bridge.'

Mr. J. H. Walters: 'With regret we record the death of Mr. Walters, the proprietor of the French Horn Hotel.'

May 1904

Sonning Hospital Association: 'The quarterly collection of boxes made on Monday and Tuesday, April 11th and 12th, produced the satisfactory total of £11 17s 7d. We again congratulate the box-holders on the excellent results produced and urge them not to slacken their efforts. No one who has a box can feel that he or she is "trading on charity" if in need of a Hospital ticket. Our principle of self-help makes this impossible. We remind our readers that any villager can now have a Hospital ticket, either as an In-patient or an Out-patient, on application to any member of the committee.'

June 1904

The Sonning Church Roof: 'An examination of the Nave roof proved that it is in a most unsatisfactory condition. The North Porch has already been repaired, and the estimate for putting the north side of the roof into watertight order is nearly £30. The rain is coming through the south roof too, and that must be taken in hand as soon as possible.'

William Holman Hunt: The Pre-Raphaelite artist lived in Sonning for a period of time and in this issue an article was printed which had been taken from a weekly paper [title not mentioned]. The article gave a brief account of the artist's life, from a young boy working in a Manchester auctioneers office, to sharing his first studio with Rosetti in Fitzroy Square, London where the Pre-Raphaelite Brotherhood was founded.
[*The Sonning home of William Holman Hunt (1827-1910) was The Acre, Thames Street*]

Rev. Richard Hart Hart-Davis: It was announced that the Vicar of All Saints', Dunsden, Richard Hart Hart-Davis, had resigned after a thirty-three years connection with the ecclesiastical parishes of Sonning and Dunsden. The new vicar of All Saints', Dunsden was to be a Sonning coadjutor, Rev. Herbert Wigan.
(*see: Vicars of All Saints' Church, Dunsden 1876-1945. – page 298*)

August 1904
New Working Men's Club: 'Thursday, June 30th, will be a red letter day in the life of club-land in Sonning, and will always be connected, by the working men of Sonning, with the names of the generous donors of our new Club, the Misses Dashwood. After many ups and downs, and in spite of difficulties which caused long delay and seemed at times to be almost insuperable, we have our new club, and we freely challenge any village of our size to show us a better one.'

September 1904
Punting Contests at Sonning: 'A very successful meeting was held on the Lower Sonning Reach on Wednesday, August 10th. The races, for which most of the well known punters had entered, were closely contested, and fine finishes were seen in most of the events. The course, which was a little over half a mile, proved so good that it is hoped that this meeting will become annual.'

November 1904
Parish Council: The quarterly meeting was held in the Pearson Hall on October 3rd. It was reported that during the meeting the formation of a Sonning Fire Brigade was discussed.

December 1904

Sonning Gymnastic Club: A gymnastic club had been formed and the first class had taken place on Thursday, November 10th, in the Pearson Hall. 'At the time of writing three drills have taken place, and these shew that there is plenty of talent in the village, waiting to be developed in this particular branch of sport.'

Women's Social: 'Mrs. Cuncliffe-Owen has started a working party for women. The work is for our soldiers and sailors. Tea, recitations and music, make a very pleasant afternoon.'

Sonning's Roads: 'The roads in the village are in a very rough and dangerous condition; we live in the hope of finding the steam roller at work some fine morning. May it be soon, but perhaps it is but a vain hope!'

January 1905

A Happy New Year: Ernest Holmes welcomed the new year in this issue with the following appeal: 'Let us make 1905 really a *new year* – putting away old sins, old feuds, old discords, old divisions, and let us begin the new year full of new hopes, new beginnings, new efforts, new lives. So shall we spend A Happy New Year.'

Christmas Day: 'A dark and fog-laden morning ushered in Christmas Day, although the mist lifted during the day, we cannot congratulate the Clerk of the Weather on his catering for an English Christmas 1904.'

The Fatal Cigarette. An article which had been reproduced from the *Daily Paper,* concerning the growth of cigarette smoking among boys, reported upon the death of a thirteen years old boy who had become an habitual smoker. The inquest decided that he had died from natural causes, accelerated by cigarette smoking.

Domestic Economy Course: The Berkshire County Council Education Committee announced a course of six lectures on the subject of "Sick Nursing" that would take place in the Pearson Hall on Wednesdays, beginning on January 11th. Wives and daughters of labourers and artisans were to be admitted free.

March 1905

Woodley Coal and Clothing Clubs: Both clubs continued to thrive and in this issue the 1904 accounts were printed. The coal club consisted of 102 members and the clothing club of 275 members.

Sonning and Woodley Nursing Accounts: Income amounted to £21 8s 9d and expenditure was £15 4s 2d. The balance in hand was £17 13s 4d.

April 1905

Gravestones: 'Arrangements have been made for the erection of a simple oak cross, with the name of the departed, together with the date of birth and death inscribed on it, at the grave of any parishioner buried in our Churchyard. The cost will be only ten shillings, and help will be given to any villager to put up such a cross, but who cannot afford it.'

June 1905

Heavy Scoring: 'The Sonning Cricket Club played Leighton Park on Saturday, May 20th. The visiting team batted first, and ran up a respectable total of 112 runs. Sonning, however, thanks to the brilliant batting of G. R. Joyce (68 runs) and G. Humphries (54 runs) made 113 runs without the loss of a single wicket.'

Dunsden Concert: 'On May 6th, an excellent concert which Mr. Deare had arranged for us, was given in the School on behalf of the Organ Fund. The performers included members of St. Giles' Choir, Reading.'

July 1905

A new feature that had recently been introduced into the magazine was the reporting of events, unrelated to the local area that had been reproduced from various newspapers. In this issue an account of a motoring accident in Sydney, Australia appeared, and the record catch of an eight and a quarter pound trout in a reservoir near Bristol. A reader's letter to the *Daily Telegraph*, from the editor of the *Fishing Gazette*, disputing the trout record, also appeared in this issue.

Fire Brigade: A brief mention was made of the Sonning Fire Brigade which had been established, and the election of the captain, lieutenant and committee.

Sonning Parish Library: 'The Vicar has received promises of nearly two hundred more volumes for the Library which is now becoming as good a Library as almost any village possesses.'

Woodley School: An H. M. Inspector of Schools had visited the Woodley mixed school, following which the report stated: 'The School continues to be conducted with care and regularity. The tone is very pleasing and the instruction is painstaking and generally effective, but the principles of Arithmetic need further attention.'

August 1905

This issue comprised of eight pages, of which over three pages were given over to detailed results of cricket matches played by Sonning C.C. during the three months from May to July.

Cyclists' Service: 'This Service seems to have developed into "a hardy annual". Some 300 cyclists met for service at 3.30pm on Sunday, July 2nd, and nearly 100 remained for tea at the Vicarage, and cycled back in the cool of the evening.'

Motor Warning: The increasing number of motor vehicles travelling through Sonning was now causing concern: 'Following a long correspondence between the Vicar and the Auto-Mobile Club, danger posts have been placed at the entrance to the village. A few lives may thus possibly have been saved.'

September 1905

The Chancel Walls (Sonning Church): 'The Vicar now sees his way, financially, to make the Chancel walls worthy of the roof. All the stencil work will be wiped out, and the walls will be plain vellum-white with simple figures, beautifully designed by the artist who did the roof – Mr. Botley A.R.A. The work will be commenced almost as once and will be an immense improvement.'

October 1905

Sonning Fire Brigade: 'The Sonning Fire Brigade is a reality – and more than that, it "means business". Considering that the Brigade is only two months old, the smart turn out, and brisk work of the men is extremely creditable.' There followed an account of an exercise that had been carried out, resulting in the water pressure being of such force that: 'when the hose was directed at the Vicarage trees, the water went higher than the Vicarage roof.'

November 1905
The Nelson Centenary: Commemorations in Sonning were recorded on the centenary of Lord Nelson's death and the Battle of Trafalgar on October 21st 1805. The commemorative events included a torchlight procession around the village on Saturday evening and: 'On Sunday evening a fine Service in Church with a large congregation present.'

December 1905
The Bull Hotel Hospital Box: 'We wish to congratulate Mr. Webb on the excellent amount in the "Bull" hospital box, which has just been opened. It produced £1 0s 5d, which has been paid in to the hospital account.'

Missionary Meeting: 'A Missionary Meeting, in connection with the Society for the Propagation of the Gospel in Foreign Parts, will be held in the [Dunsden] School on Thursday, December 7th. A Missionary from Corea (*sic*), is coming to tell us about the work in that interesting country, which was really the cause of the trouble and the scene of the first part of the war between Russia and Japan.'
[*The Russo-Japanese War 1904-05*]

Lecture on Sick Nursing: 'The second course will be given in the Pearson Hall, beginning Tuesday, 9th January.'

January 1906
Rifle Club: 'A Rifle Club has been started at Twyford. A range has been chosen and sanctioned by the Deputy Adjutant-General, and targets and a hut have been built on the ground. The Club will, it is confidently believed, be self-supporting. Sonning is cordially invited to join, and we hope that all who can, will do so. We heartedly commend the enterprising scheme to all our men readers, and no doubt, before very long, women will be welcomed! A shot is a shot, whether fired by a man or a woman, so that it be a straight one.'

The Unemployed: 'We are fully of sympathy with the unemployed. We must not, however, let our hearts run away with our heads. There is "another side" to the question, and the *real* unemployed, the suffering poor, are being much damaged by the noisy do-nothings who make a trade of living on other people's earnings.' The following quotes from daily newspapers were then included: 'A distribution of some tickets for goods was made to a large number of unemployed – many of the recipients were drunk, and a considerable number of police were in attendance to keep order. One man, using the most violent language, remarked that it was not much worth coming – "as all I got was this blessed ticket for 3cwt of coal".'

The General Election: This brief article advised readers "keep cool" and "keep clear" when deciding to which party they should cast their vote. [*The General Election was held between January 12th and February 8th with the Liberal Party which was led by Henry Campbell-Bannerman, gaining a decisive victory over the Conservative Party.*]

February 1906
Diocesan Guild of Church Bell-Ringers: The 25th annual meeting of the Sonning branch was held at Wokingham. 78 ringing members and six clergy attended. It was noted that Barkham tower had joined the Sonning branch, which then consisted of 10 towers, 33 honorary and 112 ringing members.

Sonning Recreation Ground: 'Due to the generosity of Mrs. Wade-Palmer, the new Recreation Ground is now in the hands of the Trustees.' Extensive details of the trust agreement were listed, which included access to be restricted from Sonning Lane only.

Woodley Church: 'A great improvement has been effected in the lighting of Woodley Church. For a long while past the lamps, which have been suspended there since the consecration of the Church in 1873, have been burning dimly. They have now been replaced with others of a more recent design and of far greater power.'

Woodley Working Men's Club: 'Thanks to the kindness of Miss Ellen Dashwood, who has very generously consented to lend one of her houses in Woodley, it has become possible to re-open a Working Men's Club. We cannot but hope that the re-opening of the club is likely to prove a great boon to many in the parish and we wish it every success.'

April 1906
Gully Passage: 'The pathway which leads from the Sonning Mortuary Chapel to the tow path has been taken in hand by the Parish Council, which is responsible for the upkeep of the pathway (a public right of way), the Vicar being responsible for the land either side of the path (glebe land). The path has been made neat and tidy, and will, we hope, be kept so by both parties responsible.'

Gas Meeting: A public meeting was held in the Pearson Hall to discuss the installation of gas into Sonning. The vicar, who chaired the meeting, explained that those present were being asked to comment upon whether gas should be made available for cooking and lighting purposes in the houses and cottages of Sonning. The meeting was not asked to comment upon street lighting which would be the subject of a formal council meeting. After questions were put to a representative from the Reading Gas Company, the general conclusion was that the installation cost and gas usage would be too expensive as compared with the current cost of coal and oil.

May 1906
The Education Bill: This Education Bill had been introduced by Augustine Birrell, and had become the subject of heated comment within several issues of the magazine. A large part of the concern revolved around the future teaching of religion as a subject in schools.
[*Augustine Birrell was President of the Board of Education and introduced the 1906 Education Bill which addressed non-conformist grievances arising from the 1902 Act. The Bill became controversial and was eventually dropped.*]

Sonning and the Civil Service: 'A Sonning boy has been a successful competitor in the Open Examination for Clerkship in the Civil Service. Ernest Hoyle has followed his brother and has won this distinction.'

June 1906
St. Luke's Home Woodley: 'On the afternoon of Saturday, May 12th, a

large number of friends assembled together at the opening and dedication of the new St. Luke's Home for Sick Children at Woodley. Canon Holmes, gave a very interesting account of the work of the Home. A Home he said, which was true to its name – a Home to cure medical and physical pain, and a fitting memorial to a little boy who was one of God's sweetest flowers, which he picked before it had time to fade.'

August 1906
Missions to Seamen: 'Sunday, August 5th, is our Sunday for the Seamen, and Mr. S. Knox is sending us an excellent "deputation" again this year. The year 1906 is the *jubilee year* of the Mission, and "all hands" must help to make our contribution a "Sonning" one.'

Resignation of the Vicar: A letter from Ernest Holmes, dated July 31st appeared in this issue. Holmes explained that he had been offered, and accepted, an appointment to be a member of the Chapter of the Royal Chapel of St. Katharine – the only appointment vested solely, since 1148, in the queens of England. He confirmed that he had tendered his resignation of his Sonning appointment to the bishop.
[*Ernest Edward Holmes (1854-1931) was appointed Chaplain to Queen Alexandra and later Archdeacon of London (1911-1930).*]

September 1906
A three column letter from Ernest Holmes, to *"My Dear Parishioners"*, was his extensive appreciation for the support that individuals, and the parish as a whole, had given to him during his ministry. Holmes conveyed his good wishes to all his parishioners and asked that they should give his successor the degree of support that he had very much enjoyed whilst in Sonning.

Woodley and Sonning Flower Show: 'The thirty-third Annual Show was held in the Recreation Field, Woodley on the afternoon of Wednesday, August 15th. The exhibition was in every way an admirable one.'

October 1906
Swimming: 'The races for both the "Rodnam Wanamaker" and "Canon Holmes" challenge cups were held during Saturday, September 15th.'

The senior race was won by H. Brown with F. W. Harries taking second place. The junior race was won by L. Russell, with the runner-up being R. Wadhams.

Woodley Penny Bank: This regular savings bank continued its attraction to local residents. It was reported that in 1905 there were 93 investors in the bank, £22 13s 0d had been paid in and a total of £25 9s 0d had been withdrawn. The depositors balance in the savings bank amounted to £18 1s 5d.

The Old Candelabra: 'The valuable old candelabra was used for the first time since the Restoration of the Sonning Church. The soft light of the 16 candles made the chancel and nave look very fine.'

November 1906
New Sonning Vicar: An appointment of a successor to Rev. E. E. Holmes had not yet been announced. As a consequence the following message was included in this issue: 'The Bishop of Oxford has sanctioned the appointment of the Rev. R. S. O. Taylor to take the duty at Sonning during the months of October and November.'

December 1906
New Sonning Vicar: It was announced that the Bishop of Oxford had offered the living of Sonning to the Rev. Arthur Smith Sturges, who for many years had been the vicar of Wheatley, and he had accepted the position. It was noted that Rev. Taylor would continue to take duty until the end of December.

The Sonning Air-Rifle Club: 'The first meeting to consider the formation of the Club was held on October 25th, and such was the enthusiasm displayed that by the end of the first week in November, the Club was formed and the first shoot had taken place.'

January 1907
This issue comprised of one leaf (two pages) and no doubt was brief due to no permanent incumbent having arrived to take up the Sonning ministry. In the past years, each resident vicar had appeared to be in personal control of the magazine's editorial matters. It is likely that a

churchwarden or other leading member of St. Andrew's Church had taken on the role of temporary editor during this interregnum period.

New Sonning Vicar: The announcement was printed in this issue that 'in consequence of illness, the Rev. Arthur Smith Sturges has withdrawn his acceptance of the living at Sonning.'

February 1907

Sonning Boys' School: 'The attendance during the month of December made 99.5 per cent, the highest of any school in Berkshire. This is a meritorious achievement when we consider the time of year and the distance of some of the homes from Sonning. Boys attend here from places as far apart as Boro' Marsh, Loddon Bridge, Colemans' Moor, Playhatch, Sandford, Charville and Land's End.'

March 1907

Appointment of a Vicar: 'The Lord Bishop of Oxford has appointed the Rev. Gibbs Payne Crawfurd to the benefice of Sonning, rendered by the resignation of Canon Holmes.' Gibbs Payne Crawfurd, the vicar of Bicester Church, had been born in 1854 and was married to the Hon. Edith Fiennes the daughter of Lord and Lady Saye and Sele.

April 1907

The New Sonning Vicar: 'On Wednesday, April 3rd, at 11.45am, the Rev. Gibbs Payne Crawfurd will be instituted at Sonning by the Lord Bishop of Reading, acting under commission for the Lord Bishop of Oxford, he will afterwards be inducted by the Ven. Archdeacon of Berks.'

Resignation of Sonning Organist: 'Dr. W. Boggiss, the organist of Sonning Church, has been appointed to the post of organist of St. Mary's, Reading. He has acted as our organist for eight years, and his organ playing has been a delight to us all. We wish him all happiness in his new sphere.'

May 1907

The Vicar's Letter: Within this issue Crawfurd included his first letter addressed to the parishioners. He announced that in future all daily services would be held at 10 a.m. and 6 p.m. in St. Andrew's. He also included the following paragraph: 'Lastly, I will say at once that the Magazine will be the way in which I hope to reach all the homes in the parish with all that the Church in the place is doing, and with everything that I have to say. I shall be grateful, therefore, if every home in the parish will take one of more copies of the Magazine each month.'

The Parish Magazine: Further comments from Rev. Crawfurd relating to the magazine's future were included in this issue: 'It has been necessary to prepare the Magazine at short notice and rather hurriedly for the printer. Another month it will be out in good time and have the local pages well filled. As it will form a regular medium of communication between the Vicar and his parishioners, and also be a record of church doings, the Vicar hopes that a copy will find its way into every home in the parish. It is too early to say much about its cost, but he hopes to make it in time one penny for everyone and self supporting. But at present the subscriptions that have been kindly given will be welcomed. Miss Dashwood is good enough to manage the distribution as hitherto. Copies will be sent regularly by post to any old friends of the parish wishing to have it, if they will send their address and 1s 6d. for the year's Magazine to Miss Dashwood.'

The appearance of the magazine changed with this May 1907 issue. A light blue cover paper was introduced as a "wrap" around four pages of printed text. The front cover was printed with the same *half tone* block of the church photograph which had previously been used. The design of the front cover was markedly different. The text had also changed appreciably, having been composed in a bolder typeface and widening of the two column layout. The content of the magazine had noticeably taken on a more informal style of writing; this had coincided with the arrival of the new Sonning vicar. The magazine now seemed more "user friendly" and likely to appeal to a wider audience.

(*see: August 1907 cover and text page – page 142*)

June 1907

The Parish Magazine: 'We want every house in the parish to take a copy every month; and the Magazine would then be nearly, as it should be altogether, self supporting. It is sure to interest the people of the parish as it will be the monthly link between them and the news of their Parish Church, and all that the Church is doing and wants to do in the parish.

SONNING PARISH MAGAZINE.

The Bishop's Visit.

We had a very successful time. First there was the parish gathering at Holme Park, for which we have to thank Mr. and Mrs. Sutton. The weather just served us kindly and everybody enjoyed the occasion. At the tea Mr. Sutton gave the Bishop a welcome in the name of the people of Sonning; the Bishop happily replied, claiming for himself a long acquaintance with Sonning; and the Vicar proposed the health of the Churchwardens, congratulating Mr. Sutton on his recovery of health and voicing a message of sympathy to Mr. Knox in his continued illness. On the Sunday the Bishop celebrated the Holy Communion at 8 a.m. and was with us at Morning Prayer, walked out to Dunsden in the afternoon, and preached an excellent and most helpful sermon at Evening Prayer from Hebrews x., 24, on "Considering one another," with closing reference to the clergy for whose assistance the Queen Victoria Clergy Fund was instituted. The offerings of the day amounted to £13 14s. 0d.

The Choir Tri

This took pla
gate with the
the parish peop
and men who
the boys went,
Vicar; Messrs.
and of the bel
Hands, and I. 1

WHAT

(1). The peo
as the priest en
to have a Pray
intelligently, an

(2). The mo
church should
that the priest
which began at
it for the Less
the Lesson is
leave the churc

(3). There are two places in the service where a hymn can come in suitably, viz., after the Lesson, before the body leaves the church, and at the close of the service at the grave. It breaks up the order of the service to introduce hymns at other places.

(4). All should walk in silence to the grave; it is an unseemly thing to talk.

(5). At the grave, let the mourners arrange themselves near it; so that they may hear the service and join in it. Their part is to say the "Christ have mercy upon us" before the Lord's Prayer, the Lord's Prayer itself, and the "Amen" of the prayers. *The undertaker and his men should not talk; the men should know what to do; and a simple look or sign from a competent undertaker should be enough.*

(6). The flowers upon the coffin should be taken

The Sonning Parish Magazine.

August, 1907.

A Monthly Record of Church Work.

The Parish Church, Sonning.

Copies may be obtained of Miss Dashwood, Sonning: or of Mr. Allnatt, Sonning: or the Verger.

Reading: Blackwell & Gutch, Printers.

Cover and text page: August 1907 (25 x 19cm.)

We hope if any are supplied with the local pages only, without the inset Magazine inside, they will forgive it; as it can be put right after a few months when the Magazine has settled itself, but, at present, we are having only the old number of full Magazines and supplying the local pages only to new customers. Miss Dashwood would be glad to send a copy monthly to anyone who wishes to have it, or to send it by post to anyone if payment of Magazine and postage is made in advance for the rest of the year.'

July 1907
The Parish Party: The Bishop of Oxford was to spend a weekend visit to Sonning and celebrate Holy Communion at St. Andrew's on Sunday, July 7th. During the Saturday evening of his visit, a welcoming parish party for the bishop was to be held in the gardens of Holme Park, to which everyone in the village, above the age of fifteen, had been invited.

Gas at the Vicarage: 'The convenience of the Vicarage house has been greatly increased by the installation of the acetylene gas. We hope that future occupants of the house will have as good reason to be grateful for this fine addition to its convenience as are the present ones. It is an economy as well as a comfort; for it saves all the care of the many lamps which a large house requires.'

Relic of Ancient Sonning: It was reported that a sculptured head of a monk had been dredged up from the river at Sonning Bridge and was given to the Reading Museum: 'It is perhaps work of the 13th, Century. Where did it come from? Was it ever in the Church? Did it come from the old Manor House of the Bishop of Sonning which stood in the present Holme Park? '

Circulation of the Magazine: ' The circulation has considerably increased, and this month we are able to get out 25 more full Magazines; and if they are needed we will have 25 more next month.'

September 1907
The Magazine: 'The size of the Magazine is larger this month than it has been, so as to include the cricket scores and the Flower Show. The Vicar has intended that it should supply the Church news only on four

pages, and had arranged this in such a way as to make the Magazine self supporting; but he has been urged to print other news also and this he has consented to do, with the hope that the extra cost of printing will not be allowed to fall on the Church funds.'

October 1907
Nursing in Sonning: 'A meeting was convened to discuss the question of nursing in the parish and to arrange plans for the future. The present arrangement *The Sonning and Woodley Nursing Association* commenced as an experiment in cottage nursing some five years ago. It was felt that there was no need for a permanent resident nurse in the village, but that there should be a fund for providing nurses or assistants as the need arose. This fund was created by subscriptions, increased by fees charged on a sliding scale according to the position of those employing the nurse. After thorough discussion, it was agreed that the work of the Association should be continued at present on the same lines.'

December 1907
The Parish Magazine: 'The price of the Magazine will be one penny to everyone. By way of advertisement, a copy of the Magazine will be left at every house in Sonning on the first of January. No payment for this first number will be required, but if given will be gratefully received. This first number will contain a pretty well-got-up coloured picture which is called "Sweet Hearts". All who pay 1/- in advance of the year's Magazine will have the chance of buying in three month's time "Sweet Hearts Still", the companion picture.'

Meeting in Reading: 'The Vicar would like to make up a party to drive in a closed carriage to Reading for the yearly Foreign Mission Meeting, to be held in the Large Town Hall, on Monday, December 9th, at 8pm. The cost of conveyance will be 1/- for each person.'

January 1908
Considerable changes to the magazine occurred with the publication of this issue. The front cover page was printed in three colours; black with a red and blue border design, and the photograph that appeared on the cover page featured a view of the River Thames at Sonning Bridge. A vast change of policy resulted in the appearance of advertisements for

the first time; four pages of the ten pages were given over to commercial advertising. The advertisers were mostly Reading based companies who offered a variety of products and services, however, five Sonning businesses were also featured: Whatley Brothers *Coal and Coke Merchants*, J. Wadhams *Cycle Maker and Repairer*, George Robinson *Builder and Contractor*, Edward Allnatt *Sonning Village Stores* and C. W. Cane *Family Butcher*. A further advertiser, Amos Brown a *Plumber and Decorator* was based in Woodley. An announcement concerning the future financial policy and content of the magazine was carried in this issue:

'The Magazine starts the New Year as a business venture on business lines; that is, it will not come on charity; it will stand or fall by the number of its customers. The news of the Church in the parish and matters of general Church interest will have the preference; but with a view to embrace the whole of life it will gladly receive the news of the Parish Council, the Cricket Club, the Football Club, the Rifle Club, and other institutions, and print them as far as the space of its two pages permits. The "insets" for one year have been kindly made a present to us by a parishioner, and will, we trust, be much appreciated by those who read them.'

(see: cover and advertising page: January 1908 issue – page 146)

February 1908

Sonning and Woodley Nursing Association: 'A meeting was held on January 15th, with Mrs. Sutton presiding, to start the new scheme for Nursing in the parishes of Sonning and Woodley. She said that they were met to hear the arrangements which were being made for a Queen's Nurse to live amongst them. The scale of fees and special charges for midwifery cases had been fixed. The expense was great and would require the co-operation of all; and the scheme would soon be in the hands of the people of Sonning to see if they meant to make it a success.'

The Magazine: Gibbs Payne Crawfurd gave the following assessment of the magazine's progress: 'I am very pleased at the results of our efforts to increase the circulation of the Magazine, last year twelve subscribers having increased to no less than 102; this will make the publication of much more use to me, and will keep you all the better informed of what is going on in our midst.'

JANUARY, 1908.

SONNING

Parish Magazine.

Vicar—REV. GIBBS PAYNE CRAWFURD, M.A.

Churchwardens—MR. H. KNOX, Sonning Grove, Sonning.
MR. MARTIN J. SUTTON, Holme Park, Sonning.

Organist and Choir Master—MR. JESSE SPYER, F.R.C.O.,
116, Basingstoke Road, Reading.

Verger—MR. SOUTH, Sonning.

COPYRIGHT DESIGN, No. 8.

*Cover page
and trade
advertising
January
1908.
(25 x 19cm)*

March 1908

The Territorial Army – Berks Association: 'In Berkshire, in addition to the existing troops, a battery of Horse Artillery will have to be raised. In the South Midland District there will be formed two Cavalry Brigades. Berkshire, Oxfordshire and Buckinghamshire will form one of these, and Warwickshire, Worcestershire and Gloucestershire will form the other. The Vicar has offered the help of the Magazine in distributing the orders or leaflets of the Association.'

The Magazine: 'At the present time there are 160 copies circulating in Sonning, 100 in Dunsden and 50 in Woodley. Look out in an early issue for advice about apprenticing. Apprenticeships are coming up'.

Burials: 'The Vicar has had to refuse two burials of non-parishioners in the last month, due to so little room being left in the Churchyard.'

April 1908

Archdeacon Alfred Pott: The news of the death of Alfred Pott, Vicar of Sonning (1882-1899) at the age of 86 years, appeared in this issue. 'The [Sonning] bell tolled out the news of his death, and was tolled again at the time of his funeral; and all through the last stages of his illness the prayers of the parish had been asked in his behalf.'

Contribution to the Archives of the Magazine: Crawfurd listed a number of past issues of *The Sonning Parish Magazine* that were missing from his collection, and asked for anyone who had any of these copies to forward them to him. He wished to have a book bound with the inclusion of each issue from January 1900 to March 1907, and have the book kept at the vicarage for future reference.

[*A volume was bound and included all issues from 1900 and from January 1902 to March 1907. It has been a valuable source of information whilst compiling this work.*]

July 1908

Insurance: 'Our careful churchwardens have largely increased the sum for which the church was insured, taking £10,000 as a probable sum for rebuilding the entire church; but liability for the chancel proper falls on the Rector. They are also placing appliances, known as "minimax" in the church for first use in extinguishing fire.'

Weather Forecasts: 'If anybody wants to know the weather for the day they will find a report shown in the window of the Post Office. Mr. Sutton has kindly arranged, for the sake of the village and its visitors, that a telegram from the Metrological Office in London should be posted there every morning between 10am and 10.30am.'

August 1908

Apprenticing: A lengthy article was published which included a number of contacts for those parents interested in encouraging their children to apply for trade apprenticeships. 'The whole subject must come to parents of the working class. The position of the unskilled is becoming more and more untenable; and every year the difficulty is made greater by the increasing number of employed persons who are practically all unskilled, while there is a shortage in nearly every trade of skilled workers.'

Dunsden Parish Fete and Jumble Sale: 'Our Parish Fete for 1908 is a thing of the past, and I think all will agree that it was a great success. The entrance gate was a record as also was the gate for the dancing.'

September 1908

Sonning Regatta: 'In delightful weather our Regatta was held during Wednesday, August 12th, and it is the general opinion of those who witnessed it that it was the most successful ever held in Sonning.' Results were included of the various races that took place.

October 1908

Dunsden Union Jack: 'A fine fifty foot flagstaff was put up in the School playground during the holiday, and a splendid Union Jack has been presented by the farmers. We hope to have a formal unfurling of the flag on Wednesday, October 7th. Mr. Hullcoop, has kindly taught the children a few patriotic songs to sing on the occasion, and we shall, of course, conclude with the National Anthem.'

Old-Age Pensions: An informative article provided helpful details of the necessary qualifications and benefits for receiving the state pension payments which were available to men and women on reaching the age of seventy. The conditions included a scale of payments, whereby to be eligible to receive any pension the individual's income must be below £31 10s 0d per year. A further condition required a claimant to have been a British subject and having lived in the United Kingdom for at least twenty years.

December 1908

Tree Cutting: 'Some of the trees in the Churchyard have had to be cut back recently, one of which threatened the Bull Inn and alarmed the Vicar and Churchwardens, who are trustees of the property for the parish. Others along the wall of the Deanery Garden are being lightened at the top for their preservation.'

The Church Army Van at Dunsden: 'The Evangelists have paid us their promised visit, we were favoured with exceptionally fine weather for the time of year, and the attendances were very good, sometimes beyond our seating capacity.'

January 1909

Thrift Clubs: 'At the beginning of the new year all are reminded of the useful help that is offered by the Clothing Club and the Coal Club. The clubs are open to all those living in any part of the parish, to those on both sides of the river, and to the cottages at Charville Farm, at East Park Farm, at the Model Farm, as to the rest.'

Insurance: 'Owners insure their cottages against fire; but such insurance covers only the building and not its contents of the building. Cottagers should know, and mark carefully, that for 2/6 a year they can make good their possessions against loss by fire up to £100. Knowing this, they have only themselves to blame if they run the risk and lose their all.'

March 1909

Sonning School: 'The Berkshire County Council has nominated Mr. Sutton to act as one of the Managers of the Sonning School. There are six managers of every denominational school, four who are called Foundation Managers representing the denomination to which the school belongs, in our case the Church of England, and two others, one representing the County Council, and one the Parish Council.'

May 1909

The Choir Boys: 'The attendance in the last quarter has been very good. Out of a possible 70, Halls made 64, Hay 56 and 14 missed by illness, Forward 65, Gutteridge 40, Cole 36, Norcott 65, Pilden 69, Jeskins 69, Martin 69, Ansell 28. Probationers may come to any practice and will be admitted, as vacancies in the Choir occur.'

June 1909

Blue Coat School, Reading: 'The names of any Sonning boys who wish to try for the vacancy in the Blue Coat School, Reading, should be sent at once to the Vicar, as Chairman of the Rich and Reade Endowment. The examination will take place on the last Saturday in June; and the boy will go into the school in September.'

July 1909

Hospital Collection: 'The Sonning Branch of the Reading Workpeople's Hospital Association have arranged for a house-to-house collection in Sonning on Sunday, July 11th. The members of the Committee will start with the boxes in Sonning Eye at 2pm.'

Woodley Churchyard: 'The paths of the Churchyard have now been re-gravelled throughout. We must all feel very grateful to the many friends who have contributed to this much needed improvement. The cost of carrying out this work was £10 4s 0d.'

September 1909

Old Sonning Bridge: 'Every subscriber's copy of the Magazine this month contains a reproduction of an old print of Sonning Bridge, which appears in Ireland's "Book of the Thames" published in the year 1792.'

October 1909

St. Andrew's Church Repairs: 'A new boiler and fittings have been fixed in the Church. The cost (£48 10s) has been defrayed by a grant from the Caroline Palmer Fund. Also, a handsome oak cupboard with wrought iron fittings and some wainscoting to match has been fitted in the Vestry for the choirmen's surplices, cassocks, and coats; and the churchyard gates, near the Bull Inn, which were very rotten and decayed in parts, have been thoroughly restored.'

November 1909

Dunsden Parish Hall: 'The Parish Hall is now finished and ready for use. It has become something far better, both for convenience and in appearance, than anything that we originally anticipated, and we are most thankful to God for the likely way in which people have been moved to help it. We shall now have the use of it for our Concerts, Lantern Lectures, School treats, Meetings etc., in place of the School room.'

December 1909

The Royal Navy and The Merchant Service: 'Any of our lads who think that they would like to get a little insight into seamanship with a view to joining the Royal Navy or the Merchant Service can be put in touch with the training brig just started at Caversham, if they will tell Mr. Harries of their wish.'

Sonning Church Monument Restoration: 'Our careful Churchwardens have been restoring some of the monumental slabs on the floor of the Church by re-cutting and re-painting the lettering. It is surely a great pity when any of these old monuments of the past become obliterated and meaningless; and a very proper thing to restore them.'

Old Alms Box: 'The old oaken box which was found in the Vicarage and is supposed to have been used for collecting the alms in Sonning Church has been placed in a wooden case and put up on the wall of the Vestry.'

January 1910

The General Election: 'Our Bishop writes to us – We are coming near to the time of an Election which seems to be marked with special difficulty and to involve matters of great importance. The questions are hard enough to task to the upmost even the ablest mind; and the welfare of Great Britain and the Empire for many years to come may be affected by what is done within the next few weeks. At such a time the Church has, at all events, one clear duty; the duty of prayer.'

[*The General Election, held between January 15th and February 10th resulted in a hung parliament The Liberal Party leader, H.H.Asquith formed a government with the support of the Irish Parliamentary Party.*]

Display of Lantern Pictures: 'A very excellent display of animated and other pictures was shown in the Woodley School Room on Tuesday evening, November 23rd, by Rev. The Hon. Grey Neville. The Room was well filled, and the pictures, both the beautiful and the humorous ones were much appreciated.'

February 1910

The Sonning Fire Brigade: 'Men of the Fire Brigade had an interesting and useful afternoon's work at the Church and Vicarage on Thursday, January 13th. The idea was to show what they would do and how their apparatus would cope with fire at these buildings. The men turned out with their manual engine, hose-cart and 950 feet of hose. A connection was immediately made with the hydrant at the gates near the Bull Inn. In the evening all dined together at the White Hart on the invitation of the Vicar.'

Thrift in Sonning: Information was provided concerning four clubs that existed for the benefit of parishioners. The coal club, clothing club, Sunday School clothing club and a savings bank, the National Deposit Friendly Society.

Woodley Working Men's Club: During the annual general meeting of the Club, the accounts: 'shewing a satisfactory balance in hand for the year of £2 15s. 2d were submitted and passed. A hearty and unanimous vote of thanks was accorded to Miss Dashwood for her great kindness in granting the use of the house to the members of the Club.'

April 1910

Red Cross Society: 'A branch is being formed for the villages of Sonning and Woodley, and a public meeting will be held in the Pearson Hall on Monday, April 4th at 8pm., when Sir James Clarke will explain the work and purpose of the Society. All in Sonning and Woodley, men and women, who care for the welfare of our soldiers in time of war or invasion, are invited to the meeting.'

Items: A news column had been introduced into the magazine headed "Items". This mainly comprised of local Sonning information, events and changes that had occurred with residents moving in and out of the village. Within this issue the column included the following: 'Mrs. Freeman of Charville Cottages, wishes it to be made known that she is always glad of work as char-woman; and Miss Freeman, her daughter, as dressmaker. References can be given in both cases from those that have employed them.'

May 1910

Woodley Football Club: 'Woodley is to be congratulated this year on the success of its football team in winning the cup of the Wargrave and District League. Twenty-three friendly matches were played, of these 17 were won, 5 were drawn and 1 was lost. 76 goals were scored by Woodley against 29 scored by their opponents.'

Apprenticeships: 'The Vicar of Sonning has for a very limited time the refusal of the following apprenticeships and he will be glad to receive suitable applications for them – mechanical dentistry, silver-smithing, cabinet making, painting and decorating, plumbing. The Rich and Reade Trustees would provide premiums for suitable cases, and the Vicar of Sonning is able to offer favourable terms for board, lodging and general care of boys in Boys' Homes in London.'

June 1910

Art Prints: A first in a series of monochrome printed art plates of Sonning worthies, accompanied by biographical notes entitled "Benefactors of Sonning", appeared in this issue. The first subject was Sir Thomas Rich (1601-1667). It was noted that the original painting was in the Town Hall, Reading, and was the property of the Reading Corporation.

Memorial Service: 'On Friday, May 20th, the day on which the Funeral of the late beloved King Edward VII took place, a Memorial Service was held in Woodley Church at 2 o'clock. The honour and sense of devotion felt for His late Majesty was borne witness to the gathering together of a large and most reverent congregation which more than filled every sitting that the Church contained.'
[*This was the only mention of the death of King Edward VII which was included as the last item in this issue. Moreover, no mention of the new sovereign, King George V, was made.*]

July 1910

Motor Speed Limit: 'The Highways and Bridges Committee of the Berks County Council does not see its way to recommend a speed limit for motors passing through the village of Sonning; but they have notified the Chief Constable of the County upon the subject.'

Widows' Land: 'The Barker Charity contains property consisting of two roods forming part of Wangel field, and produces 12s 6d yearly as its proportion of the £20 rent. It is given in small sums of money to poor widows of Sonning.'

August 1910

Pearson Hall: 'The conveyance of the Pearson Hall and of the buildings attached to it, from Holme Park Estate to the trustees representing the people of Sonning, has been recently executed.'

Art Prints: The art plate and biography featured this month was of Robert Palmer (1793-1872). *(see: page 28)*

September 1910

Churchyard Bulbs: 'The Vicar will be very glad to receive any quantity of bulbs for planting in the grass of the churchyard. The flowers looked well last spring and with a little care could easily be increased.'

Woodley and Sonning Horticultural Show: 'The 37th Annual Show was held at Woodley in the Recreation Field, on Wednesday, August 17th. The Show was an excellent one, and the number of entries amounted to nearly 600. The Sonning Brass Band played during the afternoon.'

Art Prints: The art plate and biography featured this month was of Susanna Caroline Palmer (1804-1880). *(see page 50)*

October 1910

Mr. Holman Hunt: 'It is an honour for Sonning that it should have had even the chance of competing with St. Paul's for becoming the resting place for the ashes of the great artist. Some years ago Mr. Holman Hunt expressed to Canon Holmes his desire that his body should be laid to rest in a certain spot of our churchyard, and immediately upon his death, the Vicar was asked to allow the use of this spot for that purpose, but the offer of burial in St. Paul's naturally deprived Sonning of the possibility of receiving the remains of the distinguished man who had been for some time a parishioner.'

Art Prints: The art plate and biography featured in this month's issue was of Canon Hugh Pearson (1817-1882). *(see: page 56)*

December 1910

The Palmer Estate: It was reported in this issue that: 'a great change had taken place in Sonning that affected all parishioners directly or indirectly. The whole of Sonning had passed from the Palmer family to whom it had belonged since 1772.' Heavy death duty taxation, which had been introduced during the mid 1890's, had caused many estates to be sold or greatly diminished in size. In 1897 Mrs. Ruth Fairfax Wade-Palmer had inherited the Holme Park Estate which included much of Sonning. There followed a series of disposals that culminated in 1910 with the sale, by auction, of large portions of the estate, mainly to the South Berks Syndicate Limited. Some tenants were able to buy their own homes, many other domestic properties were bought by local landlords. The degree of concern about the ending of the Palmer dynasty was clearly immense; many inhabitants had lived under the patronage of the Palmers for all of their lives, having attended a school and church, as well as being housed and employed, by the benefaction or business interests of this family. *(see: Palmer Family Tree – page 22)*

January 1911

The Magazine: 'An indirect way of helping the Magazine and the parish through it is to give the benefit of custom, or even a casual order, to the firms who advertise in it. Every Magazine costs one and a half pence to produce; therefore, it is obvious that but for the advertisements it could not be sold at one penny without a loss. We should like to make advertisers feel that they received back at least the worth of their advertisement.'

Children's Health: 'The report of the first year's medical inspection of the children in the elementary schools of England and Wales has just been published by the Board of Education. The result of the inspection show that 10 per cent of the children suffer from bad sight, 3 to 5 per cent from bad hearing, 8 per cent from adenoids, 20 to 40 per cent from bad teeth, 40 per cent from dirty heads, 1 per cent from ringworm, consumption and heart disease. The report makes matters for serious reflection.'

March 1911

The Vicar's Foreword: 'Lent is now with us, bringing with it the great opportunity of getting to know better and trust better the love of God for us in Jesus Christ. Lent is not an end in itself, it is a preparation for Easter. It is meant to lead our faith by the way of the Saviour, humbled for our sakes, and His precious death to the glory of His Resurrection and new life for Him. All through it from first to last, from the humbling of Ash Wednesday to the joy of Easter let us be "looking unto Jesus". He and only He is our confidence and hope.'

Sonning Church Furniture: 'A new bit of furniture has been made for the vestry in the shape of an oaken press, to hold the papers, cloths, and other things appertaining to the service of the Church. It was designed by Mr. Ravenscroft of Reading, and well carried out by Mr. Russell.'

Woodley Entertainment: 'A most successful Entertainment was given in the Schoolroom on Friday, February 10th. The first part of the programme was composed of songs, violin solos and readings. Mr. Gwynne Witherington brought down the house with his songs and reading. The musical play "The Sleeping Beauty" filled the second part of the programme. It was performed by nine of the children from St. Luke's Home and Nurse Pagden who had trained them. The play was extremely pretty and reflected great credit on the performers. It was enthusiastically received by the crowded audience.'

April 1911

Thrift in Sonning: 'For the sake of new settlers in the parish, it will be useful perhaps to say that there are these ways amongst other that we try to help those who will help themselves.'

1. Two sound Benefit Clubs, both take men and boys, women and girls.

2. The Nursing, into which people pay by scale according to their means, and thus having the services of a Queen's nurse at their free disposal.

3. The Robert Palmer Coal Club, into which people may pay on the first Tuesday of each month in the Pearson Hall.

4. The Sunday School Club, into which any children attending the Sunday School may pay every Monday in the Girls' School and have a gift added in November according to the child's attendance.

5. The Doctor's Club, about which people should speak to Dr. May.

May 1911
New Archdeacon of London: 'Every person in Sonning must have been deeply interested to know that the Bishop of London has chosen its late Vicar, Canon Holmes, for the Archdeaconry of London which carries with it canonry in St. Paul's; and most people in and out of Sonning will agree that the Bishop couldn't have made a better choice.'

June 1911
Endowed Charities of Sonning: Reports of eleven local charities, including income and expenditure for the year 1910, were included in this issue.

Palmer Estate Ownership: Details of the Palmer family members who had inherited the Palmer Estate were printed in this issue. The generations mentioned commenced with Thomas Palmer (1678 - 1762) to Ruth Harriet Wade-Palmer (1856 - 1935).
(see: Palmer Family Tree – page 22)

Woodley School: 'The School was visited by His Majesty's Inspector, on April 24th and 25th. The Mixed School is a very happy and most ably conducted country school. The teaching at the school is carried on with conscientious zeal, and the discipline and tone are of the best. The children work with goodwill, and are interested in their lessons. Infants are controlled by kindly tact, kept bright and happy and skilfully taught; they evidently enjoy their school.'

July 1911
Coronation Day: Far the majority of this issue was given over to various accounts of the Coronation of King George V which had taken place on June 22nd. Church services had been held and entertainment, including many sporting events, of a wide variety had been arranged throughout Sonning, Woodley, Dunsden and Eye. Streets had been

decorated and in Woodley a large bonfire celebration commenced at
9.30pm to complete a joyous day.

August 1911
Sonning Water Usage: The following report was included concerning the
Sonning water supply: 'The average minimum amount of water sent up
from the Water Works and used in Sonning daily is 40,000 gallons.
Lately the amount has gone up to 60,000, and on Thursday, July 20th, it
went up to 70,000. On subsequent days it gradually declined.'

October 1911
The Bishop of Oxford: Francis Paget, the Bishop of Oxford, had died at
the age of 60 and was succeeded by the Rev. Dr. Charles Gore (1853-
1932) A monochrome printed plate of the new bishop's portrait was
included in this issue. 'Everybody will know by this time that the
Bishop of Birmingham, Dr. Gore, is to be translated from his present
diocese to our own at Oxford, and the vast majority of Church-folk in
the diocese will welcome to their spiritual leadership the new Bishop.'

December 1911
Lantern Lectures: 'The Central Church Committee offers to give us next
February three or four lantern lectures, illustrating the place of the
Church of England in England's history; and the Vicar has accepted
their offer on behalf of the parish.'

January 1912
Atlantic Voyage: 'Our good friend, Mr. Lewty sailed from Liverpool for
Capetown, by the White Star Line *Persic* on December 14th, and should
reach his destination early in the New Year.'

Foreign Missions: 'A Missionary Meeting was held in Woodley School
Room on Tuesday evening, December 12th. There was a good
attendance and the excellent address illustrated with magic lantern
pictures was delivered by Rev. E. H. Day, a deputation from the S.P.G.
on work being carried out by the Society in Burmah.'

February 1912
Council Tax Payments: 'The latest published accounts of local taxation

shew what an immense amount of our money is being spent by County Councils, Rural District Councils and Borough Councils. It is time for us all to urge our representative on these Councils to vote for retrenchment and economy. The latest rate for Sonning was, for the year 7s 0d, for Woodley 3s 8d and for Sonning Eye 4s 8d.'

March 1912

Sonning Church Bells: It was reported that the Sonning bells had: 'not been working comfortably for some little time, and the tenor bell is most at fault. Lately, the Churchwardens decided to call in expert advice.' Following an inspection by a bell-founder it was agreed to place a new frame in the tower at a cost of £270. It was noted that the late Miss Caroline Palmer had left £5,000 for future repairs to the church and that the repairs to the bells would be paid for from this fund.

April 1912

Swimming Club: 'A well attended meeting was held at the Working Men's Club on Wednesday, February 28th, to consider the desirability of forming a Club to look after the interest of bathers in the village, and to undertake the care and maintenance of the bathing house, diving boards etc., It was unanimously agreed to form such a Club, to be called The Sonning Swimming Club. The subscription was fixed at the sum of 6d per annum for men and 3d for boys under 15 years of age.'

[*The loss of the RMS Titanic occurred on April 15th and the reaction on both sides of the Atlantic to the tragedy was great. No mention of this disaster was made within the magazine.*]

June 1912

Royal Berkshire Hospital: 'The buildings have been enlarged for out-patients and eye-patients. The children's ward has been added as the Berks Memorial of King Edward VII. The number of beds is now nearly 200. The number of In-patients last year was 2,150, the highest number ever recorded at the Hospital and 6,907 Out-patients, less by 62 than in the previous year.'

Land and Property Sale: 'The Manor House and land, Charvil Farm, Borough Marsh House and farm, East Park farm and some islands in the Thames are to be offered by auction at the White Hart, Sonning on June 12th. Among the other attractions it is mentioned that an 18-hole golf course at Sonning is in contemplation.'

July 1912

Insurance: 'This is a notable month, inasmuch the National Insurance Act comes into working on the 15th. Every employed person, male or female, between the ages of 16 and 70, who does not earn more than £160 per year must be insured under the Act. Men pay 4p a week and the employer 3d, women pay 3d a week and the employer 3d – though the employer in the first instance pays both.' There followed details of information concerning sick pay, disablement, maternity payments and medical cost benefits. Conditions were applied to the commencement date of these benefits, as a certain period of time qualification was necessary before any benefit could be claimed.

South Berks Syndicate Limited: The valuable benefaction bestowed by the Palmer family, to which Sonning and its residents had become used to over many past years, appeared to be abruptly ended with the disposal of Palmer family interests to the South Berks Syndicate. The following somewhat curt notice appeared in this issue: 'The trustees of the recreation ground are under notice to deliver it up to the Syndicate at Michaelmas.'

August 1912

Repair of the Sonning Bells: 'The principle of the repair work has been to substitute steel and iron for the old wood frame on which the bells were hung. It was a glad day with us in Sonning when on Sunday, July 14th, the bells were heard again from the tower of the Parish Church, which have been silent for four months.'

September 1912

The Boy Scouts: 'As many as thirty-one of the Sonning and Woodley Boy Scouts went under canvas in the meadow of the Red House for a week, beginning on the Friday before Bank Holiday, with Mr. Clarke as Commandant. The weather was most unkind to them, but young spirits do not seem to make much of the discomfort.'

Property Transactions: 'In a whirligig through which our farms have been recently passing, it will perhaps be news to our readers at a distance that Mr. Gard, of Charville Farm, has bought Mr. Hobbs' Farm, and will come into residence there; and that Mr. Righton, of Woodley, is becoming the tenant of East Park Farm, lately bought by Mr. Saunders, of Reading.'

October 1912

Sonning residents: 'There are more changes among the inhabitants taking place in Sonning this Michaelmas than can ever have happened previously at any one time. It will be some weeks before we settle down to know who our neighbours are; a large number of cottages are changing their occupants'.

Sonning Recreation Ground: 'The Recreation Ground, as such, has now ceased to be; but with some money raised by the late Trustees by letting the ground, Mr. Mathews has secured the ground, as before, for the use of the Football Club.'

December 1912

Sonning Football Club: 'It will be pleasant reading to those interested in football to see how successful the Club has been up to date. All the players belong exclusively to the village, and they play a very good game, as the results show. Out of the 5 matches played, Sonning have obtained 13 goals against 4, winning 4 games and 1 a draw. As the Sonning Football Team deserves every encouragement let us hope a large number of those interested in football will show their appreciation by being present at the next match played on the home ground.'

Christmas Day: 'The [Dunsden] Church decorations looked very nice, but the bad weather interfered with the attendance at the services. The Communicants numbered thirty.'

Rich and Reade Trust: 'An application for assistance in apprenticeships from those who have resided five years in Sonning, Dunsden, Woodley and (part of) Earley should be sent at once to the Trustees. The Trustees would like to hear of two openings in engineering work, for which they have applications but cannot find the work.'

January 1913

National Health Insurance: 'This is one of the greatest months in the social history of England. The benefits of the National Insurance Act begin on January 15th. Any insured person who is unfortunate enough to be ill after that date can apply for their benefit.'

Electric Lighting: 'The Reading electric light company has been actively canvassing the village with a view of ascertaining what type of reception it would have if it extended its system into Sonning.'

Sonning Golf Course: 'The laying out of golf-links on the fields lying to the right of anyone going along the London Road from Reading to Twyford, on lands which were part of the East Park Farm, has now begun.'

February 1913

Gas Installation: 'In the course of our "development" in Sonning, it seems that we are to be offered the privilege of electric light and gas. The gas is first in the field, and is racing along the London Road to Sonning, where it will be laid along the streets to which our houses are built and be in easy reach of all who want to have it on the Berks side. We believe the Gas Company is to celebrate its arrival in Sonning by a week's exhibition in the Pearson Hall of its usefulness for heating and cooking.'

April 1913

Gas in Sonning: 'The gas has now reached Sonning, and the Company is seeking customers. A notice of the Company's terms should be found in every magazine this month. We congratulate Mr. Elmore, our butcher, on being the first to show the gas in use on Saturday evening, March 15th.'

[*There is no example of the gas company's notice within the magazine archives, and it is likely that it was a loose inset placed into this April issue of the magazine.*]

May 1913

Sonning Camp: 'A large camp of Boy Scouts' from London, is to be held in Holme Park, at the time of the August Bank Holiday.'

The Pearson Hall: 'This Institution has now entered upon a new manner of government. A Committee is in future to manage its affairs. A report shows that the Hall is without endowment and derives its income entirely from charges made for its use. The expenses consist chiefly of payment to the caretaker, rates and taxes, lighting, heating and repairs. The report recommends; (1) all bodies that use the Hall should pay for its use, (2) that a discretionary power to reduce payments should be vested in the Committee, (3) that application should be made for a grant from the Caroline Palmer Fund, if there is a deficit at the end of the year. It draws up a list of changes for the use of the Hall in which distinction is made between parochial and non-parochial use.'

June 1913

Sonning Church Expenses: The Rev. Crawfurd made the following appeal in this issue: 'We have given away more than twice as much as we have kept for ourselves, and that is satisfactory. No one can say that we have been a selfish or self-centred parish. We have to face facts that actually exist and limited our aspirations. The ugly fact is that our Church Expenses account is in debt; we are in a ditch, and the churchwardens rightly expect me to put before the congregation the means of getting themselves out of it. For the purpose of the Church expenses I cannot too earnestly request all who worship in the church, seeing that the expenditure has increased and the income decreased, to raise the standard of their giving on the Church Expenses Sunday. It is not the spurts that tell, but the regular normal giving.'

July 1913

Vicar of Woodley: The death was recorded, together with an obituary, of Ernest Angel Gray (1845-1913). He came to Sonning in 1873 and later became the vicar of Woodley (1881). A monochrome printed plate bearing a portrait of Ernest Gray appeared in this issue.

August 1913

The Sonning Working Men's Club: A considerable decrease in the number of members had occurred and as a consequence the financial position had become of serious concern to the committee. The prospect of closure was being considered and a general meeting was to be called in the hope of ensuring the future of the club.

Military Camp: The following news item was reported which concerned a body of Royal Engineers, consisting of four officers and 110 men, that had recently encamped alongside the River Thames at Sonning: 'It was a great disappointment to us all when the camp of soldiers, who spent some weeks with us since June 10th, was unexpectedly broken up, as a precautionary measure for the health of the horses. Everybody must regret their departure. They afforded the village much interest and we hope they may come to us again another year.'

October 1913
Boy Scouts: 'A successful fortnight's Camp of the Sonning and Woodley Troop of Baden Powell Boy Scouts was held in the early part of August in Mr. Rose's meadow under the command of Acting Scoutmaster Bristow who was ably assisted by Mr. Leonard Russell. The weather was ideal for life under canvas and the Troop had a pleasant contrast with the conditions prevailing during the Camp last year when the weather was continually wet.'

Sonning Cricket Club: 'The season just closed will be remembered as one of the most successful of recent years, both on account of the number of matches won and the excellent weather with which we were favoured. Our record shows nine wins, six losses, one draw and four scratched matches, the latter due to various unavoidable causes. Our thanks are due to the various ladies who again kindly provided cricket teas.'

November 1913
Cost of School Attendance: Contribution to the cost of the schools was graphically explained in this article: 'Each child in the Sonning Schools last year cost £4 10s to educate.   Every child that makes a perfect attendance, never missing a morning or afternoon in the year, earns towards this from Government £2, leaving £2 10s to be paid by the rates. But each time a child is absent, it takes one and a half pence off the Government grant and puts it on the rates.'

December 1913
Canon Pearson: 'It is said that Canon Pearson is the original of Philip More in the tale of *Sunningwell*, by F. Warre Cornishe. The Vicar would be grateful to anyone who can tell him of this tradition.'

Sacred Cantata: 'After Evensong on Sunday, December 28th, the choir will give a sacred cantata called "the Babe of Bethlehem". It is a tuneful work by Frank Adlam, and consists of the Story of the Birth from Holy Scriptures, interspersed with appropriate carols.'

Aberlash House: 'Mrs. Witherington had left Aberlash, and so comes to an end as far as a connection with Sonning is concerned, a family which has had a close and honourable connection with the life of the village for over sixty years. It was in 1852 that Mr. C. H. Witherington bought the mill and house from Mr. May, pulled down the old house and built the present Aberlash.'

Sonning Almshouses: 'The Almshouses have come under the provisions of the Local Government Act, and a new scheme for their management has been proposed by the Charity Commissioners, and has been submitted by them for suggestions by the existing Trustees and to the Parish Councils of the three Liberties interested in the charity.'

SONNING PARISH MAGAZINE.

Wycombe. He is to be consecrated Bishop in Canterbury Cathedral on New Year's Day. He is to be called Bishop of Buckingham. All the diocese is glad that the choice has fallen upon him.

The Finance Committee of the Diocese is understood to be asking £5000 for diocesan needs this (1914) year.

The Oxford Diocesan Calendar, telling a churchman all he can want to know about the machinery of the diocese, is now published at 1/-, and can be obtained of all booksellers.

From the Rural Deanery.

The Rev. G. F. Coleridge, Vicar of Crowthorne, is the Rural Dean. He has just held a meeting of his clergy, at which he announced the Bishop's views on some points that had been submitted to him. One was that in the case of non-parishioners seeking burial in a churchyard that the Churchwardens should be consulted; another was that he should support a clergyman who refused to marry with the Church of England service a person who was unbaptized (and therefore not a member of the church). The rural deanery had contributed rather more to the diocesan funds than had been asked of it, viz: £235 instead of £205. A meeting was to be held in Reading early in the year of a clergyman and a layman from each parish to settle in what proportion the different parishes of the deanery should give to the sum required of it.

Missions.

All who care to see the Church of England going forward to her task of winning the world for its Saviour will rejoice to know that at the end of October the S.P.G.'s income was £23,500 more than at the same time in 1912; that the annual meeting of S.P.G. in Reading on November 27th was the finest ever held, the large Town Hall being full; and that the speech of Lord William Cecil on China was a very fine one.

We had a collection for S.P.G. on our St. Andrew's Day, which amounted to £3 10s. 9d., on the next day prayer for Missions at 8 a.m. Holy Communion, at Matins, at 3 p.m. for Mothers' Union, and at 5.30 p.m. Except at 3 p.m., when there was a nice attendance, there were very few at each of the other services; but there were some, and so Sonning did send its prayer along with all the rest, and expects its answer.

And on Tuesday, Dec. 2nd, we had a missionary meeting and a small sale of work for Missions. The Vicar of Woodley gave us an excellent address, and the sale made about £10. It could be more now if friends of the cause would buy off the work remaining, and also a very nice oil painting of Sonning Bridge, Church and Vicarage, which is offered at 10/-. The painting would be a pleasing memento of the village.

Collections.

The collections on January 18th will be given to the Society for Promoting Christian Knowledge, the oldest existing Missionary Society of the Church of England, and what has been called the Church's handy man. A leaflet in the Magazine will explain its work. The preacher will be the Rev. J. M. Douglas Thomas, Secretary of the Society.

The collections in the Church last month were—

	£	s.	d.
Dec. 7.—Church Expenses... ...	1	6	0
„ 14.—Diocesan Candidates' Ordination Fund ...	4	6	5
„ 21.—Church Expenses... ...	2	12	5
„ 25.—Sick and Poor	5	14	4
„ 28.—Church of England Waifs and Strays	5	5	4

Blue Coat School.

There will be two nominations to this School, made by the trustees of the Rich and Reade trust, in July of this year: one will be from Dunsden, and one from Woodley, or these failing, from Earley and Sonning respectively.

The boys have to be taken from the Church Schools in ancient Sonning; they must have attended their school for two years; must have passed the 4th Standard, and be over 11 years of age; and produce certificates of character from their clergyman and school-master.

Items.

We draw attention to the advertisements in our Magazine, and beg subscribers to do the advertisers a good turn when they can. The advertisements help out the Magazine, and pay the bit of each magazine which every subscriber leaves unpaid.

Amongst the advertisements will be found one of the Royal Berks Friendly Society, which is a

Text page: January 1914. (24.5 x 18cm)

CHAPTER FOUR

1914 - 1918

W ith the arrival of the year 1914 those engaged in publishing *The Sonning Parish Magazine* were about to witness and record the largest and most destructive war that had, at that time, occurred on this planet. For over four years normal life in Sonning, Woodley and other local villages had to be 'put on hold', whilst the war raged and the toll of casualties of family members and friends, fighting on foreign fields, rose to a level unparalleled in history.

The Great War, which in time became known as the First World War, brought with it massive technological development and demands for social change. The transformation from Edwardian Britain to the involvement in the Great War resulted in men and woman, from all parts of the United Kingdom, being recruited to fight or work for 'King and Country.' Before that occurrence very little communication existed between the population living in various towns and villages around Britain. However, the war ensured that men and woman from a wide range of social groups would be brought together, inevitably causing discontent with many, and in time creating demands for improvements in their standard of living. The rapid development of military weapons, equipment, vehicles, aeroplanes and communication systems brought about by the war, ensured that dramatic changes would take place once peace had been achieved. Any remaining vestige of the Edwardian era was about to be abruptly consigned into the history books.
(*see: a timeline of the First World War. – Page 168*).

During the war the page extent of the magazine had varied between twelve and sixteen pages, half of these pages were given over to trade advertising. The archival bound volume for the years 1914-1918 includes some copies of an inset supplied with the magazine. This inset

1914 - June 28	Arch-Duke Ferdinand assassinated in Sarajevo, Bosnia.
1914 - Aug. 4	Britain declares war on Germany.
1914 - Aug. 7	1st British Expeditionary Force (BEF) arrive in France
1914 - Sept. 6	1st Battle of the Marne.
1914 - Oct. 19	2st Battle of Ypres.
1915 - April 22	2nd Battle of Ypres, first use by Germans of poison gas
1915 - April 25	Dardanelles Campaign - Allies landing at Gallipoli .
1915 - May 7	Sinking of the liner *Lusitania* by German submarine.
1915 - June 30	Germans use flame throwers for the first time.
1915 - Oct. 31	Steel helmets supplied to British troops.
1916 - Jan. 8	Evacuation of Allied Forces from the Gallipoli Peninsula.
1916 - Feb. 21	Battle of Verdun commences and lasts for ten months.
1916 - June 8	Voluntary enlistment in Britain replaced by compulsion.
1916 - July 1	Somme Offensive commenced.
1916 - Sept. 26	Battle of Thiepval, Allied tanks play vital role.
1917 - March 11	Baghdad falls to Allied Forces.
1917 - March 15	Bolshevist Revolution in Russia, Russian Tsar abdicates.
1917 - April 6	USA declares war on Germany.
1917 - July 31	3rd Battle of Ypres.
1917 - Oct. 26	2nd Battle of Passchendaele.
1917 - Nov. 20	Battle of Cambrai commenced.
1917 - Dec. 11	Jerusalem liberated by British, ending Turkish rule.
1918 - March 21	2nd Battle of the Somme.
1918 - July 15	2nd Battle of the Marne.
1918 - Sept. 27	Battle of St. Quentin.
1918 - Nov. 11	Armistice signed.

A timeline of several important happenings during the First World War.

"*The Dawn of Day*" was published by The Society for Promoting Christian Knowledge and cost the parish magazine one-half penny per copy to purchase. (*see: p198*) The inset, which varied between eight and twelve pages, comprised of stories having a Christian message, an article giving gardening advice and several trade advertisements. The parish magazine issue dated January 1918 carried the following message:

'A small envelope will be found in every magazine which should be sent to the Vicar, with 1/- in it for free delivery in the parish; or 1/6 or 2/- by post, according as only the local portion or the whole Magazine is desired. The Magazine contains an inset which brings a bit of fresh reading for every month. Perhaps some would place into their envelope a larger sum than the minimum 1/-. Another way still would be if twelve people would pay the twelve amounts of 7/- a month which it costs to put an inset into the local leaves. It is thought that to many homes the inset brings with each monthly edition a bit of healthy and useful reading'.

January 1914

The following paragraph appeared in this first issue of 1914: 'How quickly the years roll by: it is difficult to realise that the time has come to ring out the old year and ring in the new. What has 1914 in store for us? We none of us know, but this we know that God is good and "His compassions fail not".'

February 1914

Property Purchases: 'Holme Park has really been bought this time and will be shortly inhabited by Mr. and Mrs. Cory Yeo. A new house, called Charfield, has been built by Mr. Capon on the side of Charville Lane and is nearly ready for habitation.'

Sonning Golf Links: 'The gentlemen's golf links and the club-house are in course of completion and are to be opened on May 1st. The ladies' course on the other side of the line in Woodley parish has been begun.'

Royal Berkshire Hospital Linen League: 'The League supplies the garments and linen required for use by the patients in hospital. Everyone is asked to make two garments or articles of house linen a year. They have to be made to pattern, and of certain materials.'

March 1914

From the Rural Deanery: 'A meeting of the Clergy and Churchwardens of the Sonning Rural Deanery was held in Reading to settle the contribution which each parish in the deanery would make to the £235 required of it for diocesan purposes. Sonning undertook £10 10s. Other parishes undertook what they could, Crowthorne £27, Earley £19, Twyford £12, Wargrave £25, Wokingham £40.'

Woodley Clothing and Coal Clubs: 'This year 242 are paying into the Clothing Club, and 104 into the Coal Club.' The accounts for 1913 were printed: the clothing club paid £109 18s 9d to tradesmen which was funded by £92 2s 0d of member's contributions and £19 1s 8d of donations and bank interest. The coal club paid £83 7s 6d to coal merchants and received £61 9s 6d from members and £21 81s 0d from donations and bank interest.

June 1914

Preservation of Gravestones: 'Anyone who knows the family of Charles and Sarah Flowers and their daughter Mary Ann to inform them that the gravestone of the daughter, who died in 1852, can now at the cost of a few shillings be saved from losing its face, whereas, if left much longer, it will have quite perished. It is a pity for us to lose these old memorials of the dead in our churchyard if a little trouble can save them.'

[*The graves of Charles and Mary Flowers, but not Mary Ann, are recorded in Record of Burials, etc – Church of St. Andrew 2012.*]

Empire Day at Woodley School: 'On May 22nd, there was a nice gathering of parents in the school play-ground at 3 p.m. to witness the children's commemoration; this consisted of the singing of patriotic songs and an exhibition of Morris dancing by the elder girls. The afternoon was brought to a close by singing the National Anthem and saluting the flag.'

July 1914

Act of Arson at Wargrave Church: 'The whole parish will wish to place on record its deep and indignant sense of the cruel wrong which has been done to our neighbours at Wargrave, in the firing of their Church, our heart-felt sympathy with them in their bereavement, and the promise of our unfailing interest in their work of rebuilding their House of God.' [*The church was destroyed by the fire and it was thought that the arson attack might have been a mistaken target of the suffragette movement.*]

Restricted Opening of Sonning Church: 'The following notice has been posted in the church porch. It has hitherto been the pleasure of Sonning people to leave their Church open to visitors; but now it is thought well to close it except during the mornings (10 a.m. to 1 p.m.) when the Verger is in the Church, and from 5 p.m. to 6 p.m.'

Photographic Record: 'A very choice souvenir of Sonning has been prepared by Mr. Bamford, in the shape of an album of photographic views of Sonning village and Church. The original is in the charge of Mr. South (Verger).'

August 1914
Telephone Directory: 'Mr. Newberry of London Road, Twyford, has lately published a Telephone Directory for Sonning, Woodley, Twyford, Wargrave, Hurst, Shiplake, and will be pleased to forward a copy to anyone who likes to ask for it.'

September 1914
An address by Sonning's Vicar, Rev. Gibbs Payne Crawfurd: 'One thought dominates our minds. It is hard to think of anything else other than the war. Last month we have endured the trial of suspense. This month it is certain to be the trial of facts. It is almost useless to write anything in forecast about the war. In the few days of printing before the Parish Magazine appears on September 1st, any forecast may be disillusioned by actual happenings. What must remain the same is the need for every man, woman and child among us at home to put their trust in God and go forward to meet the storm bravely and patiently, backing up the courage of our men on sea and land with own grim determination to do and bear our part in the country's cause.'
[*This issue was the first to include any details of The Great War in which Britain entered on August 4th. Reports on the conflict, particularly matters related directly to local parishioners, were regularly printed in this magazine until the war ended, under the headings – "Sonning and the War" and "Woodley-War News".*]

Sonning and the War:
'The Vicar at Matins on Sunday, August 2nd, bid that all the people pray for "peace with honour", and he used the Collect for 5th Trinity. In the evening he voiced a Gods-speed to all the men who had gone and commended their wives and children to the sympathy and prayer of the parish.'

There followed in this issue the dates and reports during August that related to the war. A number of these reports listed the names of local men in the armed services and territorial army who had left to join their regiment or ship. Also, men who had immediately "signed up" for military duty.

'August 5th - Sonning knew certainly that England had declared war.'

'August 12th - At 6 p.m. a meeting summoned by the Special Constables was held in the Pearson Hall. Measures were taken for the safeguarding of property. Men offering their services.'

'August 16th - At 11 a.m. and 6.30 p.m. the Form of Intercession put out by authority on behalf of both sailors and soldiers was used. The collection was for the National Relief Fund, amounting to £46 16s 2d.'

'August 18th - A meeting was held in the Pearson Hall to organise relief during time of war for Sonning and Woodley, Committees were elected.'

October 1914
Sonning and the War:
'A weekly "War" Celebration of the Holy Communion was begun in the Sonning Church; the special Collects and Scriptures were used. The alms were given to the Belgium Relief Fund.' A number of other special church services were announced in this issue which included: 'September 22nd, "War" Communion at 8 a.m.; collections throughout the week and in the alms-box for Soldiers' and Sailors' Families' Association; other services throughout the day.' The names of more local men, who had joined the armed forces during September were also printed.

'At the Harvest Thanksgiving, offerings of socks and mufflers, or of the wool for making them, were made at all services.'

Sonning and Woodley Nursing Association: 'The ladies of the Committee have thought it their duty to release their Queen's Nurse to do service in nursing the sick and wounded soldiers in a Military Hospital at Brighton. They have procured a nurse in her place, and they beg the subscribers to accept the position cheerfully for the country's sake, and to make the best of the temporary arrangement. A letter had been received from the Nurse. She is with 91 other nurses in the Eastern General Hospital.'

The Red Cross: 'The Sonning Branch of the Red Cross Society began its good work when war was declared. The sum of £33 4s 6d. was collected, and more was promised, if it should be required.'

The Committee for War Help: 'Like every town, and like many villages, we set up our organisation at the beginning of the war for helping need arising out of it. It was decided that Sonning and Woodley together should be the unit for care and for the distribution of funds.'

The War and the Charities: 'A Bill is in the House of Commons to enable trustees of Charities to divert them temporarily to the Prince of Wales' National Relief Fund. It would enable trustees of such charities as Barker, Clifford, Payne and Blagrave (known as dole charities) to hand over the proceeds to the National Relief Fund.'

November 1914
Sonning and the War:
'The bell is sounded each day at noon, asking people to remember their country's cause and all the men of Navy and Army who are serving it. Every day there is Morning and Evening Prayer, with remembrance of sailors and soldiers, and every Friday there is a "War" Communion held at 8 a.m. The collections at the Friday Communion, and the money from the alms-box have been given to the Red Cross Society for its motor ambulances. The list of those serving King and country from Sonning stands thus:' There followed a list of thirty-six men and one woman who were now on active service.

War Fatality: Confirmation in this issue that Willy Hughes, a local Sonning inhabitant, had been killed in action, was the first of such announcements that would take place whilst the war was in progress: 'The sorrow of the war which has come to most of us individually in the loss of friends has come to the parish through the death of William Hughes, Gunner in the Royal Field Artillery, at the age of 20, whose parents lately came to live in Sonning. The parish offers its deep respect in sympathy to the family for one who has served the King and country even unto death. The Church bell was tolled at noon on October 27th.'

The Coal Club: 'In this year of stress, when every shilling is important, can the members of the Club not think of some co-operative scheme among themselves by which they can get the best coal and the greatest possible amount of it at the lowest price?'

January 1915

'A Happy New Year to all our readers. Who knows what this year of grace 1915 may bring to us? We pray earnestly that to ourselves and our Allies it may bring peace, and peace with honour.'

Sonning and the War:
'Our list of Sonning men serving King and Country in the war grows in number. No doubt in the future – "may God bring the day along" – the names will be kept in some permanent memorial.'

'Mrs. Rose, one of our last summer visitors, and wife of Captain Arthur Rose of the Essex Regiment who was killed in action recently, feels the deepest gratitude to all in Sonning, who thought of her in her great trouble.'

A Sonning Record: 'Miss Arlette has nine volumes of the Sonning Parish Magazine from its commencement in 1869 onwards for eighteen years (two years in a volume). She wishes to realise their value, and as she is leaving the parish she has asked the Vicar to receive offers for them. The volumes are a valuable record of eighteen years of the palmy days of Sonning, and time will aid their value. The Vicar will be glad to receive any handsome offer for Miss Arlette's books.'

An Appeal from the Vicar of Sonning: January 3rd, 1915 had been declared a national day of Intercession for Peace. The following appeal was made by Rev. Gibbs Payne Crawfurd: 'January 3rd, makes a great appeal to the nation. We at home are asked to stand behind our gallant men at sea and on land and beside our good fellows preparing to go out for our sakes and pour into the forces of the war the untellable power of believing prayer. Will you all do it? Will those who as a rule do not use our Church come with us for this one occasion at least?' The offerings from this special national day were given to the sick and wounded, which was managed by the Order of St. John and the British Red Cross Society.

February 1915
Sonning and the War:
The report consisted mainly of a list of local men who were serving in the Royal Navy and Army.

Lt. Colonel Frederick Arthur Deare: The death of the colonel who had been appointed in command of the Royal Berks Regimental Depot, Reading, at the outbreak of the war, was recorded in this issue. He died of natural causes at the age of 53 years on January 23rd. Deare had distinguished himself during the Second Boer War, and on his return to Sonning he had been greeted with a hero's reception.
(*see: page 117*)

The Magazine: 'Everybody will be pleased to know that the Magazine has at last paid its own way. On the working of last year there is a profit of nearly £5. But of course it should be understood that the magazine sold at a penny could not possibly pay its way if it were not for the advertisements. Subscribers therefore owe a debt of gratitude to the advertisers, and they can show it in a practical way by a deal with the tradesmen who offer us their advertisements.'

The Parish Magazine in Woodley: 'Last month 94 copies of the magazine were taken; we should like to reach a circulation of 100. There are something like 185 houses in the parish, and if the magazine is not seen, often-times opportunities of joining in parochial events are missed.'

March 1915

Sonning and the War:
More local men were included on the list of those who were now serving on active service in the armed forces. Although compulsory military conscription did not commence until 1916, the public naming within this magazine of men volunteering to serve "King and Country" was a potent force to encourage any reluctant recruit to come forward and join the ranks.

Two further deaths on active service were recorded; Edward Knight, 2nd Royal Berks who had been living in Charville Cottages and Captain Frank Rushby, Royal Field Artillery.

Sonning and Woodley Nursing: The seventh annual report confirmed that 1914 had been a financially satisfactory year. The summary of the year's work noted that the nurse had paid 5,046 visits: 'It is easy to see from the report what a great blessing the nursing has been to the two villages.'
[*The visits made by the nurse represent on average almost 14 visits every day of the year.*]

Sonning Graves: 'It is very desirable that graves in the churchyard should now be made to receive three or at least two burials. It is the best way of making sure that families shall lie together. The time is coming when the churchyard will be full, and friends cannot be buried together. Even now the Vicar and Churchwardens have to be most careful that the remaining ground is kept for parishioners only.'

Shiplake and Dunsden Flower Show: 'I am asked by the Show Committee to announce that, owing to the war, the Flower Show will not be held this year.'

April 1915

Sonning and the War:
A brief report gave an account of two local men one serving in the Navy and the other in the Army. It was also reported that Edward Holmes had returned home on compassionate leave following the death of his wife, and that Robert Wadhams had been promoted to the rank of sergeant and was quartered at Malta.

Parochial Quotas: 'Sonning is asked this year to give £20 to the work of the Church in the diocese; and a further £60 to the work of the Church overseas. The request comes to the parish from the Rural Deanery, which is asked to give £235 to the diocese and £1,400 to the Church overseas.'

Woodley Men Serving the King and Country: Names were listed of three local men serving in the Navy and forty-two further local men serving in the Army.

Club Subscriptions: 'Friends of men on service should take every care that in their absence their clubs are paid up. There was a talk at one time of clubs letting off the men's payments and yet offering benefits. It can't be done. It would break any club to do it.'

May 1915
Sonning and the War:
A report consisted solely upon the whereabouts and promotion of a number of named local men who were on active service.

Belgium Visitors: 'Our Belgium guests who have been at The Acre since the middle of November, have now changed their quarters, by the kindness of Mr. John Blandy, to the French Horn Hotel, where they are comfortably housed.'
[On May 7th, a German submarine torpedoed the Cunard liner "Lusitania" off the Old Head of Kinsale, and 1,134 passengers, many of them Americans, were drowned. The decision to attack the liner was a massive error made by the Germans that ultimately contributed to the United States entering the war.]
(see: World War One Time Line – page 168)

June 1915
Sonning and the War:
The monthly news reported under this heading, had now become a means by which information upon local men, who were serving overseas, or had been wounded and returned to Britain for convalescence, could be conveyed to the parishioners. In addition, an updated list of sixty-seven local men and one local woman who were serving in the forces was also included.

The Schools and the War: 'The boys have been all through the winter bringing a great number of books and magazines for the sailors who Miss Player has kindly forwarded to the fleet for them. Now they are collecting eggs for the sick and wounded in the hospitals, they have sent off 351 since May 14th.'

Woodley School: It was reported that the school had reopened having earlier been close, due to cases of whooping cough and measles.

July 1915
Sonning and the War:
Mention was made of the need to contribute to the Joint War Committee's Fund for the Sick and Wounded. Readers were also reminded that the alms-box in St. Andrew's Church is accessible every day to receive donations to the sick and wounded.

'Our men on service everywhere, and specially those abroad, like to have the Parish Magazine. They ask for it often in their letters. The Vicar sends any spare copies he has; but they are not enough. It would be a kindness to many of them if friends after reading their own copies would post them to the men.'

War Loan Vouchers: The Government had called upon the public to contribute to a new interest bearing War Loan Voucher scheme. In this issue Gibbs Payne Crawfurd addressed the "Children of Sonning" and encouraged them to invest their existing and future savings in this scheme. Crawfurd's appeal included the following call: 'The country must have money to carry on the war. The more money it has the better our sailors and soldiers will be able to fight; the safer their lives will be; the sooner the war will be ended; and a blessed peace come to end this awful strife. But where is the money to be got? It must come from us all.'

August 1915
Sonning and the War:
The report gave details of promotions received by local men serving overseas. A current listing of serving men and one woman, Lily Woolcombe, who was with the Red Cross in France, was also included.

Postponement of the Vicar's Holiday: 'The Vicar does not care to go on holiday while so many brave fellows in the parish are facing the perils of war; but to relieve a little of the pressure of Sunday for himself, at least in the holiday, there will be no morning Sunday School; and he is inviting other clergy to occupy the pulpit during some periods in the next few weeks.'

The [Sonning] Churchyard: 'The Vicar and the Churchwardens have had under their consideration the question of the space available for burials in the Churchyard. In order to postpone as long as possible the great expense of a new burial ground, it is necessary to lay down the following regulations, which will be strictly enforced.'

1. Graves in future will be made deep enough to receive more than one body.

2. Parishioners only can be buried in the churchyard, except for burials in existing family vaults and graves where space permits.

September 1915

Sonning and the War:

Sympathy was extended to the wife and family of John Sumner. It was reported: 'it seems that he was out to take up the German dead when he was shot down himself.'

The list of those in the services who had died during the war had now risen to five.

St. John's Church, Woodley: 'We shall keep our Harvest Thanksgiving day on Sunday, September 26th, and let us keep it with renewed purpose, for we have many blessings to be thankful for in the midst of so much that saddens and humiliates us. We trust that it will not be too late for flowers for the purpose of Church decoration.'

October 1915

Sonning and the War:

A further six names were printed of new Army enlistments. Seventy-seven local men were now serving in the armed forces and one woman.

'On September 7th, we sent to the Sick and Wounded Fund £3 15s 3d which had been collected in the previous month.'

Dunsden Coal Club: 'Messrs: Talbot are supplying the coal at 31/6 per ton to the Club, and I am able to let the members have it at 26/8 per ton or one shilling and four pence per cwt, by devoting to the bonus money which would in ordinary times have been spent on excursions. The new year will start on October 5th when new members will be welcomed.'

November 1915
Sonning and the War:
'Edgar Pope, of the 8th Berks, was wounded in the great rush forward at the end of September. And in the same engagement Captain Wilfrid Oldman was killed. He had not lived of late years in Sonning; he was in South Africa at the time that the War broke out, and returned to put his services to the use of his country. Still another of our men, Lieut. Charles Romer, was wounded at the same time. He was hit in the head, but there is every hope that he will soon recover.'

'We collected £21 in the village for the Russian flag day. Will not somebody take up and organize a Serbian flag day? Our brave Allies must sadly need such help for their funds.'

Sonning and Woodley Nursing: 'Miss Andrews, Queens Nurse, has left the district, to the very great regret of the Committee. We have been fortunate enough to find another Queen's Nurse, and the Committee have therefore appointed Mrs. Morgan. She began work at once and is residing at Mrs. Perry's, Fairholme, Western Avenue, Woodley.'

December 1915
Sonning and the War:
The monthly report opened with the following announcement: 'Of course Sonning will take its place in the national act of penitence, prayer and trust that is to be made on the first Sunday of the new year.'

'A very hearty welcome and recognition of his bravery was given to Private Philip Henry Andrews, of Spring Cottage, Sonning, in the course of the short leave which he spent last month in his native village. He had received the Distinguished Conduct Medal for bravery and resource on the battle-field in France.'

The War Communion: 'Every Friday at 8 p.m., the Holy Communion is celebrated for the war. The names of our men on service are read out, and then they are specially commended to God's care; the sick and wounded are prayed for, and the offerings of the communicants taken for their cause; prayer for peace, and prayer that God will mercifully bring good out of the horrors of war, is worked into the service.'

February 1916
Sonning and the War:
'Mr. and Mrs. Young received a letter from their son in R.A.M.C. On his voyage to Salonika he wrote the letter with directions for the postage, put it in a bottle and threw it overboard. It was picked up by fishermen who gave it to a British Agent, who posted it to the parents.'

Sonning Post Office: 'Our Post Office arrangements have been a little altered. There is no "post out" at 10 a.m. or "post in" at mid-day. All these trifling inconveniences are valuable helps in bringing the sense of the war into the daily life of us at home.'

Christmas Parcels: 'The Christmas parcels sent to the men on our Roll of Honour have in almost all cases been acknowledged; only one was returned, and that has now safely reached its owner'.

Woodley Children's Christmas Carol Band: 'The sum raised by the Band was £2 14s 6d and of this amount £1 10s 0d has been given by the children to the Disabled Soldiers Fund; 12s 0d has been reserved for wool for soldier's socks, and the balance has been divided amongst themselves.'

March 1916
Sonning and the War:
'The alms-box in the Church is open at all times to receive gifts for the Red Cross. The Church is always open also; so that all anyone has to do is to open the door, enter, and place a gift in the box. What is given at the Friday Intercession goes to the same purpose.'

Sonning Church: 'The church has been insured under the Government scheme against damage by aircraft.'

Services Mail: 'A circular letter has come out from the Post Office saying that books and magazines suitable for the men on service may be handed across the counter at any Post Office. The Post Office takes charge of the books and sends them out to the men.'

Old Age Pension: 'There is no need for candidates to old age pensions to spend money on clergymen and clerks in getting certificates. The best way on feeling that the age of 70 is at hand is to ask at any post office for a pension application form, this should be filled up and sent to the local Pension Officer, who will make the necessary enquiries as to age.'

Rural Deaneries: 'A re-arrangement of the local deaneries has taken place in the diocese. The two Earley parishes and Dunsden have been taken from the Sonning rural deanery. The two Earleys have gone into the Reading deanery, and Dunsden into the Henley-on-Thames, as well as into the Archdeaconry of Oxford. The two Earleys and Dunsden leave our rural deanery; Barkham and Finchampstead come into it.'

April 1916
Sonning and the War:
The list of local men who were serving in the war had increased to eighty-two plus two woman Lily Woolcombe and Cecil Witherington who were both with the Red Cross, the former in France and the latter in Egypt. It was noted that: 'The great prayer of the parish for our men is made every Friday morning at 8 a.m.'

Woodley Alms Bags: 'It may interest our readers to know that the original Red Alms Bags which served for so many years in our Church are now being made use of elsewhere. They have been sent, in response to a request received, for use in a temporary church in an English Prisoners of War Camp in Germany.'

Our Wounded Soldiers: 'We have received a report from Miss Pantin of the Woodley Working Party. So far 531 bandages and other articles have been made, and £6 0s 11d has been collected for material. The demand for bandages is certain to be even more urgent through the spring and summer than it has been in the winter. More workers are needed to take the place of those who have been compelled to give up.'

May 1916

Sonning and the War:

'We keep on collecting for the Sick and Wounded in the war. We at home cannot possibly give too much. Last month we sent £3 14s 3d which was made up of a Sunday's collection £2 13s 5d, of Friday's Communion 9s 8d and of the Alms-box 11s 2d.'

River Travel Times: 'The Oxford and Kingston Steamers begin to run on May 25th. There are slight changes in the timetable; the morning boat will leave at 10.15a.m. and the afternoon one will leave at 3.55p.m.'

The Terrible Gale: 'On Tuesday afternoon, March 28th, the terrible gale worked devastation among the trees of Sonning. In the Holme Park alone 65 trees fell; along the main road in the space between Sonning Lane and Pound Lane fell some 25; the beautiful variegated elm tree in Grove Park was laid low, and the fine old cedar on the Vicarage lawn. No amount of lamenting will recover our loss. Far more useful and practical is it for everyone who can to plant a tree or trees which will grow and re-make Sonning for the future inhabitants.'

Miss Ellen Dashwood: The death was announced of Ellen, one of the four Dashwood sisters who had lived for many years in Sonning. She had distinguished herself as a substantial benefactress and by her interest in the wellbeing of both Sonning and Woodley.

June 1916

Sonning and the War:

'News has been received of Lieut. Phillimore. He is a prisoner at a camp in Westphalia. He writes bravely and cheerfully, and says he has no complaint to make of his treatment. It is supposed that he was struck senseless by a piece of shrapnel in the forehead, and when he came to his senses found himself in the German lines.'

Barker and Payne Trustees: 'Mr. Sumner and Mr. Goodchild have been appointed trustees of the Barker Charity on behalf of the Parish Council; and Mr. Webb of the Payne Charity. The income of the Barker Charity is derived from a field, next over the railway, near the keeper's cottage, in the occupation of Mr. Wright; and the Payne

Charity from a rent charge upon land in Sonning Eye, which is now paid by Mr. Phillimore and Mr. Crawshay.'

July 1916

Sonning and the War:

'Major Frank Woollcombe, Royal Garrison Artillery, who has been at the Front in France since the beginning of the war has now been awarded the Military Cross. Lieut. Frank Ash Yeo, in command of the armoured train, is mentioned in General Maxwell's despatches.'

'Some 120 wounded soldiers from the Reading War Hospitals made a river journey to Sonning, and were entertained to tea in the Mill House garden.'

Waste! Sonning. No Waste! Rev. Gibbs Payne Crawfurd made a forceful demand with this statement concerning water waste: 'It is no use to save and waste at the same time. It is of no use to be saving for the country and to be wasting in Sonning. And yet the notice posted in the village seems to mean that *we are wasting water*. There are probably many who don't know about our water supply on the Berks side of the parish, and don't understand that the cost of supplying it comes upon the rates. The water is pumped up from the station on the Holme Park farm into a reservoir near at hand, and flows hence to the village. The water that has been used for domestic purposes passes into the sewers, and thus to a sewerage station on Mr. Gard's farm, where it is pumped onto the land. The water therefore is twice pumped, once for the supply and once for sewerage. An engine which uses oil pumps the water at both ends, and the oil alone, to say nothing of the other incidental expenses, costs more than twice as much as it did two years ago. The more water, the more oil, therefore, take care not to waste water!'

August 1916

Sonning and the War:

'The War Savings Certificate scheme of the War Savings Committee to get the shillings and sixpences of the many lent for the war has gone forth in our parish. The children have the savings-card which takes 31 sixpenny stamps; and many of them are doing little jobs in order to

earn their sixpences.   It will be a kindness to them and a help to the
country if people will give them the jobs and then themselves affix the
sixpenny stamp; or if they will encourage the saving scheme in any way
they think well.'

Rifle Cartridges: A leaflet was enclosed with this issue of the magazine
which emphasised that a War Savings Certificate fully completed to a
value of 15/6 can purchase 124 rifle cartridges for the serving men.
The leaflet gave six reasons "why you should save", these included –
1. Because when you save you help our soldiers and sailors to win the war.
2. Because when you spend on things you do not need you help the Germans.

September 1916
Sonning and the War:
'A War Saving Association has been formed for Woodley and the
district, and a letter has been received from the Hon. Secretary saying
how willing the Association will be to receive any subscribers from
Sonning.'

'Mrs. Russell has four sons who are presently serving with the forces;
Sydney, John, Leonard and Thomas Dennis. Dennis has been made a
lance-Corporal. Mr. and Mrs. Woollcombe, of the Barn House, have
also four sons and one daughter on service.'

The death toll of local men serving in the war had risen to seven.

Declaration of War Remembrance Service: 'The second anniversary of the
war's declaration was marked by special services in Woodley church on
Sunday, August 6th.   At 6.30 p.m. the names of all Woodley men
serving were read, with their regiments etc., recent additions make up
the list to some 105 names.'

Woodley - War News: It was recorded that three Woodley men serving in
the Army had been killed.

October 1916
Sonning and the War:
The news of the war casualties was particularly grim in this issue.

Ernest Reginald Jacobs of the Charville Cottages, Frank Rackley who once lived in Sonning but had moved to Western Avenue, Woodley, Mark Lemon Richie Romer who had lived in Sonning and John Collins of Charville Cottages were each reported to have died. The "Soldier's Bell" had been tolled for them at the soldier's hour.

Edward Thumwood had his leg amputated and Philip Henry Andrews, who had recently received the D.C.M. had been wounded and had been taken to a Birmingham hospital.

It was reported that Thomas Dennis Russell had been awarded the Military Medal.

Woodley - War News: The death of John Brind was recorded and that of Frank Rackley, the latter having also been included in the *Sonning and the War* column. Three Woodley men had been wounded, one was missing, one was a prisoner of war and three had "fallen in the service of King and Country".

Letter Post: 'People who are in the habit of posting their letters at the pillar boxes in the village should know that the mid-morning post is not done away. The pillar boxes are only cleared in the early morning and in the evening, but letters posted in the box at the Post Office are sent out in the afternoon and again in the evening. The pillar box clearing about 8 a.m. only catches the afternoon clearing at the Post Office.'

December 1916
Sonning at War:
'Church people of the diocese, and especially its bell-ringers, will rejoice to know that Rev. Cyril Jenkyn, Master of the Diocese Guild of Bell-ringers, has been given the Military Cross. When one of the batteries was heavily shelled, he went at once under shell fire and assisted the medical officer with the wounded.'

'News was received in the village early in last month that George Penstone Gould, second son of Mr. and Mrs. Gould of the Telephone Office, Sonning, had been killed in action in France. We are all very sorry for the home that has lost such a good son and brother from it'.

Whist Drive: 'A whist-drive was organised lately for Christmas parcels, and was eagerly taken up by the whole village. Truly they are being spoiled, we should say if they were not our sailors and soldiers. As it is we say – What can be too good for them? What is the next thing we can do?'

Woodley Christmas Parcel Fund: 'The house-to-house collection realised the splendid total of £10 18s 0d which was further augmented by a gift of £4 from the Misses Player. The concert held on November 15th, has placed a further sum of over £12 to the credit of the Fund.'

Dunsden Roll of Honour: The names were listed of seventy-five local men serving in the forces and three further names who had "fallen in their country's service".

January 1917

The *Sonning and the War* column did not appear in this issue.

The Printing of the Magazine: 'The printing company who have printed and published our Magazine since its first publication in 1869 have closed down their works. We have now transferred ourselves to another old firm in the town, Messrs. Bradley & Son, The Forbury, Reading.'

The National Mission: 'The Message of this Mission was delivered in this Parish from December 9th to 12th by the Rev. E. E. B. Grant, Priest-in-charge of Chavey Down. As regards the Message itself, many, alas! in this the greatest crisis of our nation's history, passed it by entirely. Those who did come must, we believe, go forth stronger people in this year 1917, and may their witness in the Parish be blessed.'

February 1917

Sonning and the War:
News was given concerning the recovery of local men, who had been wounded on active service.

'A lad, Frederick Ernest Edwards, not of Sonning, but who at one time was assistant in the White Hart kitchen, has been killed in action, and at the request of his chef the bell was tolled for him.'

The Woodley Vegetable Collection: 'The following collection for wounded soldiers will go on this month: The City February 1st, Crockham Well 8th, Western Avenue 15th, Woodley Green 22nd'.'

Woodley Vicarage Supper: 'A most happy party of fourteen Choir boys sat down to supper in the Vicarage Parish Room on December 27th, and at the Men's Supper on the following evening at the Vicarage we mustered 10, and sadly missed those who had been called to active service.'

March 1917
Sonning and the War:
Four further names had been added to the list of local men now in the armed forces.

Ringing of Bells: 'We began the use of our bells for Evensong on Sunday, February 4th. For some time they have been silent under the regulations of the Defence of the Realm Act.'

St. Andrew's Church Plate and Rich Monument: 'There was sold at Christie's last month a cupping bowl by the same maker as was our original alms dish given by Sir Thomas Rich Bart., only that the bowl was made in 1648 and our alms dish in 1661. It was a pity that the old church plate was melted down and remodelled in 1852, along with the restoration of the Church, but the mistakes made at that time, under Canon Pearson, were supernaturally and almost miraculously so few that we must not judge hardly (sic). One great mistake made since that time was the removal of the Sir Thomas Rich monument to the space under the tower. Perhaps a future generation, mindful of the fact that Sonning has taken about £150 a year from him since 1666, will give the benefactor's monument a place of greater honour in the Church.'

The Magazine: The cost of printing had increased and together with a reduction in the number of copies sold in Sonning, the magazine had produced a smaller profit during 1916. However, it was noted that it was satisfactory that the venture was self supporting.

Sonning Schools: 'The winter weather tested the heating arrangements of our Schools and they were found wanting.'

April 1917
Sonning and the War:
'The Censor wishes that with a view to withholding information from the enemy our lists shall give the name of the soldier and his regiment without further addition of his battalion. Our magazine travels to the battlefield and it is just possible might communicate information to the enemy.'

'With sorrow we note the death in hospital abroad, from spotted fever, of Alexander Neville Blair, Black Watch Regiment, the husband of the lady who was in Sonning for a few months last year.'
[*On April 6*[th]*, 1917 The United States of America declared war on Germany.*]

The Magazine: 'The necessary economy with the Magazine requires that only the very fewest copies over and above those pre-paid shall be printed. Now that the Magazine has been got out of debt and made to pay it must not be allowed to fall back again into debt.'

River Timetable: 'The steamers on the river will begin to run on May 24th at the same times as last year.'

Summer Time: 'Please note that "Summer" time will begin on April 8th, Easter Day; watches and clocks should be put on one hour before going to bed on the Saturday night.'

All Saints' Church, Dunsden: 'On Sunday, March 25th, the Sermons were preached by the Rev. D. V. O'Meara, Secretary of the Irish Church Missions, and on the Monday following he gave us a Lantern Lecture in the Mission Hall which threw much light on the difficult problems in Ireland which are now confronting our Statesmen.'

May 1917
Sonning and the War:
A column length obituary of Sergeant Thomas Dennis Russell, who was killed on active service, appeared in this issue. He and his family were well known residents of Sonning. As with all those who died during the war, the Soldier's Bell was tolled at the Soldier's hour on Tuesday, April 24th.

'Last year we sent up from the Church a total of £24 6s 4d to the British Red Cross and the Order of St. John. The contents of the alms-box and the offerings at the Friday Communions are given to this object.'

Magazine Inset: 'It is with much regret that we have decided to issue our Magazine for the remaining period of the war without an inset. The great increase in the cost of producing the Magazine has rendered this step necessary. It is a temporary measure, and we intend at the first favourable opportunity to return to the old order.'

Giving in [Sonning] Church: 'This year we gave £67 10s 7d to the Church abroad, £21 16s 6d to the Church at home, £21 6s 5d to the Church in the Diocese and £91 12s 8d to benevolent objects. These latter were the Royal Berks Hospital, British Red Cross and Order of St. John, British Red Cross (local branch), Royal Agricultural Institution, the children in Belgium and the Armenian Refugees.'

Dunsden Magazine Involvement: Rev. Herbert Wigan, vicar of All Saints' Church, announced that, with considerable regret, Dunsden would no longer participate in the magazine venture as they had incurred considerable losses on it for several years.

June 1917
Sonning and the War:
'We expect to have some new names on our list this month. First among them is Dr. May who though we shall all miss him in his work in the village goes with the good wishes of us all to serve of his country in the R.A.M.C.'

The Hospital: 'The Royal Berks Hospital in Reading has just issued its annual report, and it discloses among other things the appalling fact that the Hospital of which all Berkshire is proud, and whither hundreds of Berks folk every year go for healing is £10,655 in debt! It is nothing less than appalling that the first charity in the County is in such a condition! What is to be done? It seems that every village and town in Berks should have a monthly flag-day for the hospital until the debt is wiped out.'

Woodley - War News: It was recorded that Pte. William Brind of the Royal Berks had been killed in action. Also, that Pte. Sidney Deadman, an old choir boy, had been badly wounded in the mouth and was in a Red Cross Hospital in London.

July 1917
Sonning and the War:
Where known, the whereabouts of local men engaged in the war were reported: 'Dr. May is under orders for Salonika in the R.A.M.C. Leslie Gould is one of the interchanges between the American Navy and ourselves. He has gone on an American battle-ship as signal boy.'

Potato Crop: 'A meeting was called by the Parish Council to consider the potato-spraying. Mr. Christie-Miller offered a sprayer if the Council would be responsible for its care and use. A cottage garden can be sprayed twice for about 2s. The country asks us to grow and keep every potato we can. It is only a few that each garden loses by disease; but all these "fews" put together make very many tons for the kingdom lost.'

Woodley - War News: Four further local men had been recruited into the Army. A report confirmed: 'The parents of Pte. George E. Miles, Royal Berks, have been informed that he must be regarded as having died. He had been reported missing last July.'

Vegetables for the Wounded: 'It is hoped that we should soon be able to recommend sending the hamper weekly. The Western Avenue District will start as soon as there is a sufficiency of vegetables to send.'

August 1917
Sonning and the War:
'We regret to say that Charles Quelch of the Charville Cottages is now reported as having been killed on the field of battle in France and buried there on October 7th, 1916. He was reported missing and now his parents have received the official announcement of his death.'

'It will generally be known in Sonning that a fine attempt to escape from imprisonment has been made, and for eight days was successful, only failing at the moment when liberty was in sight. We must remember now the severe penalties that the Germans inflict on recapture and let it inspire the prayer that we offer for prisoners and captives.'

War Sunday at St. Andrew's Church: 'The first Sunday in August, as we enter on the fourth year of war, will be observed with special prayers and form of Services.   There will be special Collects, Epistles and Gospel at the Holy Communion, and at the Morning and Evening Prayers a special address on the war; and special Prayers.'   A similar notice was included by Woodley's vicar, announcing services that will be held on the same day at St. John's Church.

Sonning Churchyard: 'The late keeper of the Churchyard wrote from France to ask how the Churchyard was looking this year. We were able to tell him that in June and the early part of July its roses were very pretty and we have been able to keep up the care of the yard pretty much as usual.'

September 1917
Sonning and the War:
'If our Magazine should come under the eyes of any of our men on service we should like them to feel how well they are remembered in the old Church at home. We collect money for them when they are down in hospital; morning and evening of every day we commend them in the Church to God's care; every Friday we have Communion for the war and we offer our prayer for them in that best way after their names have been read out in the Church; and when they come home how we shall fill the old Church with our thanksgivings!'

The Schools: 'The new Education Bill must interest us all. It should be remembered that its proposals are not yet law. They may be altered before they pass into law. They propose – Children should go to School at 6 years and that without exception shall all remain at School till 14. No child under twelve may be employed for payment; no child under 14 may be so employed till after School on a School day.   The new proposals will cost a great deal, and the money will have to be paid through taxes, rates, rents and prices. But they are worth the money.'
[*The Education Act 1918: see page 204 and 210*]

Woodley - War News: It was reported that two Woodley men had been killed on active service; Pte. Montague Miller of the Grenadier Guards and Pte. Christopher George Barrett of the Royal Berks. Three further local men are mentioned who had sustained serious wounding during active service.

October 1917
Sonning and the War:
'It was indeed most joyful news for the village when on September 12th we heard that Leonard Powell, who had been missing since April, was held as a prisoner of war in Germany. However, it was an equally bitter disappointment when a week later news was received of his death. It seems that the lad died of his wounds on a German ambulance and was buried at Tournai in France.'

'News has been received that Alfred Polden, R.G.A., has been wounded and is in hospital in France.'

Waste Paper Collection: 'The Berkshire Printing Company, King's Road, Reading, is very helpful to persons who will save their wastepaper to help the Country's need at this time. It will send a sack in which to collect it gradually, and receive it and pay for it when the sack is full. All sorts of paper may be saved. The Company sorts it.'

Chestnut Collection: 'The children of our schools are busily engaged in collecting the chestnuts in answer to the appeal of the Government.'
[*Horse Chestnuts "conkers" were used in the making of acetone a component of the smokeless propellant for shells and bullets.*]

Woodley - War News: Seven local men were mentioned as either being wounded or missing. One of those missing was Sergt. S. Edgington of the Royal Flying Corp, who together with his pilot was engaged in an aerial battle over the German lines on September 11th.'

The Magazine: 'The Vicars of the two Parishes are seeing if anything can be done to get back an inset for the Magazine next year. It was dropped because of the increased cost of printing which would have got the Magazine into debt if it had been continued. If it is found impossible to do it we hope that the people of the two Parishes will all subscribe their 1/- for next year. It would be a great pity to let the Magazine fall under the pressure of war when it has been going for so many years. Of course everybody can understand that it is only the advertisements that make it possible to produce it at all. Therefore, will our readers do the advertisers a good turn when they can.'

November 1917

Sonning and the War:
'Another honour for Sonning. Pte. Albert Knight, Royal Berks has won the Military Medal. And another! Lance Corporal Walter Perris, Royal Berks, who won the Military Medal last year has received a distinguished conduct notice from the Major-General Commanding his Division.'

'The great prayer for the war and all those in it goes on at the Friday Communion of each week. And any of our sailors, soldiers, airmen and women on service who come home on leave are earnestly invited to come and strengthen with their sympathy the prayer of those who are remembering them at home.'

Mothers' Union: 'We held a capital meeting of members of the Mothers' Union and a few missionary workers at the Vicarage on the second Friday afternoon of last month. Some needlework made for the mission cause was sold; but there is still some remaining which we shall be very glad to sell.'

Woodley - War News: 'Good news has now reached us of the safety of Sergt. Oakley. Though wounded in the shoulder he writes cheerfully from Germany where he is a prisoner.'

'Since our last month's issue several from this parish have been called up including Frank and Fred Saunders.'

Queen Mary Needlework Guild: 'On November 8th, the Woodley Sub-Branch of Q.M.N.G. will have completed its second year of work. During the two years, upwards of 2,500 articles have been made and despatched to headquarters and the work has been highly appreciated.'

December 1917
Sonning and the War:
'Yet other honours are falling to Sonning! Arthur Powell, elder brother of Leonard, has been awarded the Military Medal. It is very nice to know that the sorrowing father and mother have had this bit of comfort brought to them through their other son.'

The Magazine: 'The two Vicars are making a great effort to keep the Magazine going in 1918 – with an inset; and they appeal to the good-will of their people to support the endeavour which they are making for them. They feel that it would be a great pity to let the Magazine go under when it has been doing so well until the war came. It keeps everybody in touch with the local church news; and when it has an inset gives everybody a bit of fresh reading every month.'

No Waste: 'Don't waste Sonning water - It takes oil to pump it up and water and oil again to pump it out as sewerage. Don't waste paper - The Berks Printing Co., King's Road, Reading will send a sack and then buy it from you.'

Woodley - War News: 'A list of our men serving has been written up, and very effectively framed in oak and hung on the west wall of our Church. The names of those who have fallen have also been written on a special card and framed and hung on the centre of the west wall.'

January 1918
The title of the magazine was now the *Sonning and Woodley Parish Magazine* and the printing was undertaken by the Berkshire Printing Co, Limited. Whilst the page size had not been altered, some changes were made to the layout and typesetting design. The half-tone printing block, featuring a monochrome photograph of Sonning Bridge and the Thames, had been retained on the front page. The magazine had twelve pages, seven of these given over to advertising.
(*see: page 196.*)

To Win the War: 'Men who know say it is going to be won in England. How? By the saving of the people at home. Therefore look in your Magazine for a leaflet explaining the League of National Safety – read it

Cover: January 1918. (24.5 x 18cm)

carefully. Then look for two copies of the food pledge, and if you mean it, sign it and send it by post without stamp. Let Sonning, well to the front as it is in giving men, work and money to the country's cause, now rise as ever to - save the food.'

Sonning Bells: 'Two delightful peals on the bells were given by our ringers, one on the evening of November 22nd for the victory at Cambrai, and the other on December 12th for the taking of Jerusalem.'

Sonning Church Lighting: 'The candles in the aisles cannot be lighted because of the lighting restrictions. All persons are invited to take any seat they like in the nave of the church at the 6.30 p.m. Sunday service.'

Woodley Men on Service: 'We deeply regret to record the loss of another gallant man on our list, Sergeant James Sammons, Berks Yeomanry, was killed in action on November 29th.'

The Magazine: 'The circulation in Woodley last year was 110 copies. It is hoped that Parishioners will support the Magazine well this year, appearing with a new inset, "*The Dawn of Day*".'
(*see: page 198*)

February 1918
Sonning and the War:
'We collected £11 18s 0d on the War Sunday for the British Red Cross Society and the Order of St. John of Jerusalem.'

A short obituary of Arthur Henry Norcott, who had been killed on active service, appeared. He had been a Sonning choir boy, a church bell-ringer and a member of the Sonning fire brigade.

Whist Drive: 'It was very satisfactory that the whist drive organised by Mr. and Mrs. Goodchild to provide thick overcoats for the special constables of Sonning and Woodley produced £11; more than was wanted for coats; the surplus will be spent on other things for their use.'

Woodley - War News: The death was reported of Reginald Hearn who died of his wounds on December 19th whilst on active service in Jaffa.

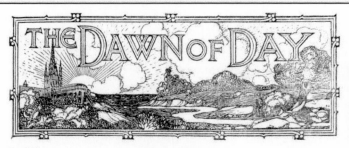

No. 484.]   **APRIL, 1918.**   [Registered as a Magazine for Transmission to Canada.

SOME CURIOUS CONTRIVANCES.

BY THE RIGHT REV. J. E. MERCER, D.D.

How the Fire-drill drilled Fire.

HOW hard it often is to find out why words mean what they do! Here is this word "drill," and it stands for two such different things as boring a hole and drilling soldiers. I do not happen to know how these two meanings are connected by word-scholars ; but I intend to connect them together in a way of my own. I am going to tell you how by boring holes man made fire obey orders.

Look at the fire in your grate. It is quite fair to call it "drilled." It burnt up just when you wanted it, and it goes out when you have done wi h it. It keeps to the place you make for it. It obediently boils your kettle, warms your hands, drys your clothes. And this is only a tiny instance of the endless ways in which man makes fire o ey him. It drives his engines, works his factories, sails his ships, smelts his ores— where shall we stop?

But there are times, as we know to our cost, when fire gets the mastery, and burns down the house or the factory. It is no good trying to drill it then ; it must be fought. When I was in Tasmania, every summer I saw "bush" fires. (Bush is the Australian name for forest.) Often miles and miles of timber and crops are destroyed ; sometimes human dwellings are caught in the sheets of flame, and human lives endangered. Special ways of fighting these fires are employed by the settlers, or the damage done would be much greater.

How was it first done?

By this roundabout way I have come to the matter I really want you to think about. How did man first tame fire and drill it for his use? Let us imagine ourselves on a picnic, and wanting to light a fire. Has anybody a match? No, there is not one to be found. (Think, by the way, how splendidly fire is tamed when we carry safety matches about in our pockets !) Perhaps a clever member of the party suggests that

Producing fire with a drill in Southern India.

flint and steel struck together will make a spark. If a flint can be found, and some dry leaves or moss collected, the situation may be saved. Alas ! there are no flints Another member of the party asks if anyone has a magnifying glass for examining insects or flowers. No, even that way of getting a fire, by focusing the sun's rays to a burning point, is not possible, for no one has such a glass. What is to be

"The Dawn of Day", published by The Society for Promoting Christian Knowledge (SPCK). This inset was first included in the January 1918 issue. (24.5 x 18cm)

Lent: 'Never before has the call to keep this holy season come in more compelling ways than this year. For the fourth time Lent finds our country in the throes of a death struggle for existence, a struggle which can only come to a right issue if, under the Good hand of God, we each strive to bear one another's burdens in the spirit of self-sacrifice.'

Years Ago: An abridged version of an extensive article, (*with comments updating to 1918*) that originally appeared in the July 1877 issue of the magazine, was now included in this February 1918 issue:

'In July 1877 Miss Caroline Palmer writes – I will go back to what I can remember of Woodley and Earley before 1818 when the enclosure of all the remaining heaths and commons there situated was begun and in less than two years so far completed as to bring all roads and fences into very much the same state as they are at the present day. Let us cross the London Road at the top at Pound Lane and proceed as far as the point of the larch plantation [*1918: green No.8 of the Sonning Golf Links*] at the junction formerly of three lanes now of two other lanes. Here was a gate across the road known by the name of "Phillis Hatch". There were many similar gates in those days and very needful they were to keep all the animals living on the commons from straying into the turn-pike roads. At this point the road to the left hand led, as now, to Sandford; the middle one passed Woodley Green on its way to the Common; the right hand turn, always called Mustard Lane and since cut off by the railway, soon came out on another part of the same common called Bulmarshe Heath [*1918: here she describes this Heath*] and the race course. [*1918: which was circular and began and ended near the Chequers public house which is not at all altered since those days*].'

March 1918
Most unusually, there was no direct mention of the war in this issue.

Woodley War Distress Committee: 'It was unanimously resolved that in view of the hard times, to open a Soup Kitchen for Woodley, in the hope of helping the larger families and elderly people in the Parish. It is hoped to provide soup on Tuesdays and Fridays, price 3d per quart.'

Summer Time: It was noted that summer time was to commence on Sunday, March 24th and continue to Sunday, September 29th.

April 1918

Sonning and the War:

'An honour has come to Sonning in the promotion of Leonard Russell, born and brought up in the place, to a Second Lieutenancy. Percy Brown, who had been held back from the Army duty through ill health has now joined up. William Phipps, who came home wounded, has now recovered and is attached to the R.A.M.C. in Ireland.'

Housing: 'The Rural District Council have announced that about 40 cottages appear to be needed in the district of which Sonning should have 15 (7 on the farms and 8 in the village); and Woodley, 6 on the farms. The Committee recommends that everything should be done to encourage farm owners and private persons to build these cottages before recourse is had to rate and tax built ones. But we ought to have the cottages by one way or the other as soon as we possibly can. They have been badly wanted for a long time.'

Almshouse Charity: 'The new scheme for the Almshouse Charity which includes Mr. Yeo's benefaction is now almost complete, and will no doubt be signed and sealed this month. But the enquiry into the Robert Palmer Poor Charity and the other charities still hangs fire owing to the Assistant Commissioner, who was to have held the enquiry, being called up for the Army.'

May 1918

Sonning and the War:

'A lad not known in Sonning but whose parents came lately to the Charville Cottages, fell in the great battle of last month. He is Edward Thomas Frewen, son of Alfred and Ellen Frewen.'

'Our War Savings Association just started by the Head Mistress in connection with the Girls' and Infants' School is doing well. It has 37 contributors, and the sum already contributed is £27 11s.'

Woodley - War News: 'We deeply grieve to record that we have lost two men in the Great Battle which began on March 21st. Pte. Harry Johnson died of wounds received in action and Pte. Sidney John Deadman also fell in action.'

The Magazine: 'It is getting more difficult to obtain enough insets to put one into every Magazine. In July we have to reduce our monthly order by fifteen per cent. This means nothing worse at present than that a few people in Sonning and a few people in Woodley will be asked to receive only the local part of the Magazine. We feel sure that our subscribers will help us readily to bear the present pressure in hope of continuing our Magazine through the time of war.'

June 1918
Sonning and the War:
The progress was recorded of three men who had been wounded during active service and were now convalescing; Major Clement Williams who was in No.1 War Hospital, Albert Knight M.M. who had been badly gassed and Second Lieut. Leonard Russell who was making some slow recovery from an accident.

'As an instance of the valuable war-work which is being done by the Sonning workroom in connection with the Queen Mary's Needlework Guild we may mention that an urgent order was lately received by telegram for 400 bandages. The work was immediately taken in hand; urgent summonses were circulated for new workers who readily came forward with assistance and the whole order was completed and despatched in a fortnight. The order has exhausted the whole supply of material, approximately 600 yards, and new funds are urgently needed to purchase more material.'

Woodley - War News: 'On May 1st a postcard arrived from Private Sidney Deadman to the joy of his parents and friends stating that he is a prisoner of war in Germany but wounded in both legs. He had been officially reported as killed on March 24th. At the time of writing a second postcard has been received from him.'

Sonning Gravestone: 'A curious thing lately happened about a monument in the Churchyard. The facing fell off a gravestone near the Palmer and Pearson graves, which bore an inscription to the memory of John William Ladd, a schoolmaster of Sonning, who died 1847. The pieces were carefully preserved and could be put together again; but enquiries failed to discover any relative who would care for the grave. During last

Whit-Monday a visitor in Sonning casually remarked that she had a grandfather who a long time ago had lived here. The grandfather turned out to be this very Ladd; and from her it was found out that a son of the schoolmaster was still living at Eton.'

July 1918
Sonning and the War:
'We sent £3 8s 7d from the collection taken in church last month to the Berkshire Prisoners of War Fund. There are now about 700 men of the Royal Berks held as prisoners of war; and the bread bill alone amounts to some £300 a month. Donations should be sent to the Treasurer, Admiral Cherry, Highfield, Brimpton, nr Reading. Three hundred new prisoners were added in May.'

'We are very sorry to hear that Lieut. Abercrombie has been badly injured. He has been with the Motor Transport in France.'

'On July 7th the Sunday nearest to the great July 4th, the American National Anthem will be sung in church in honour of our allies.'

Missionary Sale at Wellington College: 'We are able to take any quantity of vegetables (cucumbers, peas, young potatoes, lettuce, tomatoes), of fruit (cherries, currants, raspberries, etc.,), of eggs, of rabbits, chickens, and gifts of money will be very useful to meet necessary expenses or to buy things to place on the Stall.'

Woodley Recreation Ground: 'The Village has learnt with considerable regret that the Recreation Ground has been sold for building purposes. Consequently a need for a suitable field for cricket, football, etc., has again become apparent. If the Parish Council are unable to find a ground, under the powers which they possess, it is to be hoped that someone with suitable accommodation, who realises the great part which sport has taken in the making of our Navy and Army will not fail to offer another "Rec" in time for the return of our brave village lads to peaceful occupations. Might we not consider what steps should be taken in the village for the setting up of a War Memorial. Other villages have already started by the formation of a representative committee. Practical suggestions would be very welcome.'

August 1918

Sonning and the War:
'Several of our older men have been called up for medical examination and graded, but as yet have not been ordered to join the colours. Among those who have responded to the latest call and will soon be leaving us is Mr. Osman, our grocer, who is closing down his business, and Mr. Lewenden, gardener to Miss Dashwood.'

Patrick or Patter Stream?: 'In the old Tithe Map the stream, nowadays called Patrick stream, is marked as Patter stream. Which is right? Has Patter grown into Patrick, or was it Patrick and became at one time known as Patter?'

The Agricultural Wages Board: 'The Board has fixed minimum wages for male workmen in Berkshire and this came into force of July 8th. A minimum for a man of 18 years and over is 30/- for 54 hours in summer and 48 hours in winter. For Oxfordshire the minimum is 30/- for 52 hours all the year round.'

Workers for Queen Mary's Army Auxiliary Corps: 'We are asked to state that workers are urgently needed to undertake clerical work, and work as cooks and waitresses.'

Woodley War Memorial: 'After the close of the War Savings Association meeting on July 23rd an informal discussion took place on the subject of a War Memorial for the Village. There appeared to be a very strong feeling in the village that the opportunity that has been given to the Parish Council and which they were unable to accept (owing to lack of powers) for purchasing the present Recreation Ground as a village memorial for a sum which appears to be extremely low, should not be allowed to pass. It would make a splendid and lasting memorial, for use even more than for ornament, but unless some action is promptly taken the opportunity may be gone forever.'

Woodley and District War Savings Association: 'The Annual Meeting was held in the Schoolroom on Tuesday, July 23rd. The Annual Report showed that during the past year the sum of £638 18s had been subscribed, this amount purchased 823 Certificates. The total number of Certificates purchased since the inception of the Association in July 1916, being 1,300. The net membership of the Association on the 30th June 1918 was 155.'

September 1918

Sonning and the War:
Helpful information concerning the whereabouts and wellbeing of local men serving in the military continued to be printed: 'We regret to hear that Ernest Pope has been made a prisoner of war. Dr. May has received a step in the R.A.M.C. and is now a Captain.'

'Capt. The Hon. Godfrey Phillimore has for the third time attempted to escape and has again just failed to succeed. He has in consequence been removed from Germany and is imprisoned in the heart of Austria. The truly noble spirit of our gallant neighbour makes him refuse to accept exchange into Holland, or to give his word of honour that he will not escape; so that he may fight again.'

The Education Act 1918: 'The Act was passed on Thursday, August 8th, henceforth a notable day in English history. Now:-
1. No child may leave school before 14. It may be made 15.
2. After 14 and up to 16, children must have 280 hours in day continuation schools.
3. No child under twelve may be employed at all; no child between 12 and 14 for more than two hours on any day, and that not till after school hours.'

Woodley - War News: The death has been announced of Sergt. Frederick George Evans and Frederick Lamble of the A.S.C. It was confirmed that Pte. John Wallace White, Royal Berks who had been reported missing on May 27th was held as a prisoner of war. No further news had been heard of Pte. W. A. Bacon. Pte. Percival Aldridge, had been severely wounded in the back.

The Woodley Recreation Ground: 'A public meeting was held in Woodley School on Friday August 16th to consider an offer made to the Parishioners of Woodley to purchase the present Recreation Ground as a "War Memorial", the offer holding good until September 21st next. A notice of the meeting had been delivered to every house in the Parish, and considering the importance of the matter the attendance at the

Meeting was small. A Committee was formed to consider the proposal and report to a further meeting to be held on Saturday, August 31st.'

The Magazine: 'The Vicar is most grateful to the subscribers who have accepted the curtailing of the Magazine so good-naturedly. We are not allowed to have so much paper.'

October 1918
Sonning and the War:
'The fete in Holme Park which was got up to pay off the debt on the Sonning and Woodley branch of Queen Mary's Needlework Guild was successful beyond all expectation. It realised £71 19s 5d, and we are pleased to report that this sum pays off the debt and leaves a small balance to the credit of the fund.'

Sonning C. of E. Schools: 'With the new headmaster there are naturally new developments in the Boys' School. Two things especially are to be noted; (1) The introduction of an outdoor game on one afternoon a week into the routine, under the supervision of the master. This counts as a school lesson, and through it the master hopes to teach discipline and give moral training. (2) The establishment of a circulating library among the boys.'

Woodley - War News: The death occurred of L/Corporal Harry Thomas Willis, Rifle Brigade. He had received a serious bullet wound in action and died a few days later.

Woodley Recreation Ground: 'The Ground has been saved to the Parish for all time. This, in a few words, is the result of the adjourned Public Meeting held on Saturday 31st August. At the time of writing a large number of donations and promises have been received. The Committee still requires £60 to complete the purchase and to cover various items of expenditure. Woodley is to be congratulated on the acquisition of the old ground for the playing of games for all time. Future generations will refer in appreciative terms to the generosity of those who are giving the necessary funds, not for their own benefit but for the good of others.'

November 1918

Sonning and the War:

'We are asked to state that the Reading Care and Comforts Committee will hold an exhibition of wounded soldiers' work and a sale on December 4th in the Corn Exchange, Reading, to raise money for their funds.'

'We are sorry to hear that both the brothers Pope are now prisoners of war. It will give us all additional interest in the urgent prisoners-of-war question. It is also a troublous thing to know that the family of Captain the Hon. G. Phillimore have reason to be very anxious about his treatment. All this together will help to put heart into our prayers for the prisoners. It is a pleasure to receive Sergeant Sydney Franklin home from the perils of warfare. He joined the Army in May 1915, went out to France, was wounded there, and has now received his final discharge.'

Parliamentary Voters: 'The number of Parliamentary voters in Sonning Town according to the voter's list is 226. Of these 64 are soldiers. Some will need to be told that in the whole and ancient Parish of Sonning there are four parts or liberties: Sonning Town, Earley, Dunsden and Woodley. Sonning Town is practically the village of Sonning on the Berks side up to Borough Marsh Lane and including Holme Park Farm.'

Heating and Lighting of Sonning Church: 'The Churchwardens have impressed upon the Vicar the need of certain economies in the heating and the lighting of the Church. There will be no heating of the Church for week-day services. No one can dispute the wisdom of this arrangement. To decrease the cost of lighting and to economise in candles it has been decided not to light the candles at the Sunday evening service in the two blocks of seats against the tower. Everyone is requested to sit where they like in the middle seats of the Church. No sittings are reserved at this service. All may take a sitting where they like in the middle of the Church, and no one will take offence.'

Woodley - War News: 'The recent sweeping advances of the Allied Forces has not been without loss to us in Woodley. Private Henry James

Saunders, King's Royal Rifle Corps, to our very great regret was killed on the night of the 23rd September. We have also lost Pte. Alfred George Millard, Royal Berks. News was received of the sinking by the enemy of the ship in which Jeffery Walter Cooke R.N.V.R. belonged.'

December 1918

THE DAY: 'Who of us can ever forget Monday, November 11th, 1918, and the glorious news it brought to us all. It is well for those who will come after and read our pages to record something of the day.'

'It had been arranged by notice given from the pulpit on Sunday that when the news reached the village there should be, after the ringing of the bells, an impromptu service of prayer and thanksgiving in the church. The news reached the village chiefly through the hooters in Reading, about 11a.m. At once some of the ringers rushed to the belfry and set a joyous peal going. Flags were got out everywhere; on the church tower the St. George's flag and the American Stars and Stripes were soon flying; and almost every house in the village had some flag of other flying from it; people were all out in the streets and work went lightly for the time. Notice was sent about that the bells would ring again at 6.30 p.m. and that the service in church would then follow at 7p.m. There were eight men ringing the full peal this time.'

During the 7p.m. service Rev. Gibbs Payne Crawfurd gave an emotional speech to the assembled congregation and his spoken words were printed in this issue. After his address he proposed that the following telegram should be sent to the King and Queen:
"*The people of Sonning, assembled in their Parish Church beg in humble and loving loyalty to offer congratulations to the King and Queen on the glorious victory and to thank them for their share in it*".

'The sending was approved and the next day their Majesties returned by telegram their gracious answer.'
"*The King and Queen thank you and your Parishioners for your message of loyal congratulations upon the victory of the Allies*".

'Thus ended the first day of Sonning's share in the rejoicing of the Empire.'

The following contribution was from Rev. Frederick F. Penruddock, the vicar of St. John the Evangelist, Woodley on the occasion of Armistice Day:

'The news announcing the signing of the Armistice, and the cessation of hostilities reached the village through the sounding of the Reading and Wokingham hooters at 11 a.m. The church bells were at once rung, and flags were soon flying. A Service of Thanksgiving had been announced on the preceding Sunday for 8 p.m. on the evening of the day on which the news should reach us, and that hour found the Church nearly filled, in spite of the wet evening, and the fact that, alas, the influenza had got a hold on many of our people. It was a simple service of heartfelt thanksgiving which it is hoped will always be remembered by those present. On the following morning a nice number were present at a special celebration of Holy Communion, the great Thanksgiving Service at 7.30. On the Sunday following, November 17th, the services were very well attended; the special form of Thanksgiving provided being used. All felt the reality of the occasion, the breaking of the clouds of war, the dawning of a just and righteous peace. The sermon preached in the evening from Psalm cxxiv. 7, drew attention to the help found in the use of the Book of Psalms during this time of war. God grant that the tyranny of war may be past for all time.'

Records: 'We hope to publish in future numbers some records of the Great War as it concerned our parish. The next number will contain a record of the Special Constables, their names and duty. Another will deal with the War Workroom. One, of course, will record the names and services of our sailors, soldiers and airmen; and others will deal with the services and sermons in our churches during the War, and the War Charities for which we collected. The great thing is to have some record which future generations will read with interest.'

Woodley - War News: 'With deep regret we have heard of the death in France of Pte. Alfred Rackley, Royal Berks. He was killed in an attack on the morning of November 1st.'

Woodley School - Influenza Epidemic: A serious outbreak of influenza was recorded which resulted in the deaths of three local people: 'The epidemic caused our School to close for three weeks.'

CHAPTER FIVE

1919 – 1925

Whilst The Great War had ended, the often violent struggle for Irish independence, which had been a cause of great concern during the years of war, had continued into the next decade. Post war Britain was not the country "fit for heroes to live in" as predicted by the Prime Minister, David Lloyd George. Those who had fought in the war came home to mass unemployment, depressed wages, high living cost and serious industrial unrest. During the seven years period between 1919 and 1925 five governments were in control of Britain. Local village life could not have been immune to the problems that Britain was experiencing, and in many ways Sonning, Woodley and neighbouring towns and villages would have shared the same concerns that were so widespread in the country.

January 1919
The Magazine: The Sonning and Woodley vicars made a joint appeal to their parishioners: 'It is very hard to carry on the Magazine at the present price. If every copy were sold at 3d. it would not pay its way. But we are most unwilling to drop what is such a useful means of letting people know about what the Church is doing in our two parishes; and also forms a record which those who come after us will read with interest; and therefore rather than drop it we mean to try every possible means of continuing it – at any rate for the present.'

War-time in Sonning: A record of the church involvement during the war listed the regular services that had taken place. Many of those services had been a welcomed source of comfort to parishioners with close relatives and friends then serving in the military: 'Almost from the beginning of the war a church bell was rung every day at noon, meant to call for the prayers of those at home on behalf of those absent on service; and whenever one of our men fell in warfare, the same bell tolled at noon made everyone know that a soldier had gone. It came to be known as the "Soldiers' Bell".'

Housing: 'Homes for working people are badly wanted in Sonning as in most other places. What the people want are free cottages – not tied to any estate, farm or other property – in which a man can live as long as he pays his rent and can work for whom he pleases. Is there nothing that can be done? Is there no one who will lead a movement at once for the better housing of the workers in Sonning? The Local Government is most ready to help in any way. It will advance on loan 75 per cent of the cost to a public body.'

Sonning C. of E. Schools: 'We wait to hear what schemes Berks Education Authority has for our parish as regards central and continuation schools.' There followed a series of questions arising out of the new Education Act.

[*The Education Act 1918 raised the school leaving age from twelve to fourteen and provided for improvements in services such as medical inspections and special education needs. Many of the provisions were not implemented due to expenditure restrictions.*]

Milk Supply: 'Will none of our people think of setting up goats? It is recommended by the Food Controller with a view to increasing the milk supply. Two good nannies will give far more milk than a working family can afford to buy of cows' milk. All over the parish are lawns and waste bits of pasture where goats can be fed.'

February 1919
Record of War-time: 'Some of the best work at home in the country's cause during the war has been done by Special Constables. It required patriotism to take up the service at all; and it required endurance and a sense of discipline to carry out to the end as it was done.'

Woodley Recreation Ground: 'A meeting of the Committee was held on January 22nd, when a most satisfactory report was submitted by the Hon. Secretary. The donations received or promised for the purchase of the ground now amounted to over £478. Owing to the high cost of building a village hall at this time, they have decided to obtain if

possible a temporary erection, and have opened negotiations with the
Y.M.C.A. for one of their "Red Triangle" huts.'

Sonning and the War: The names of those who had now returned home,
after serving in the various branches of the military, were included in
this and further issues.

March 1919

The Magazine: Issues during this period comprised of just six pages, of
which one page only carried advertising. Whilst it had been reported
that the circulation of the magazine had increased, it was clear that it
was operating at a deficit which was unacceptable. The Sonning vicar,
Gibbs Payne Crawfurd, had emphasised his determination to continue
the publication if at all possible, but survival would require a larger
paying readership and more financial support via donations from the
parishioners.

Records of War-time: 'For patient, persevering, enthusiastic service done
by women in Sonning for the country during the war, little better was
done than in the War Work-room. Various kinds of work, all for use in
hospital, comprised surgical bandages, quilts, swabs, water-bottle covers,
operation stockings and socks which, as fast as they were done, were
sent to Queen Mary's Needle-work Guild in Chelsea.'

March 1919

Bishop's visit to Woodley: 'It was a real pleasure to welcome our Diocesan
on February 23rd. The Bishop found time to visit our Recreation
Ground and he desired to congratulate the Parish on having acquired it
for all time.'

May 1919

Motor Transport: 'The tramcars are running again from the terminus on
the London Road.' There followed a timetable for motor buses leaving
the [Sonning] Halt for Reading and the return journey to the Halt.

Sonning C. of E. School: 'The schools have begun their summer term in
which there will be a short break at Whitsuntide – with 47 boys, 32 girls
and 22 infants.'

Woodley Memorial Recreation Ground: 'The first annual meeting was held in the school room on the 11th April when the Vicar (Rev. F. F. Penruddock) presided over a good attendance of parishioners. The Hon. Treasurer submitted the accounts which showed that there was sufficient funds to purchase the ground, cover the cost of certain necessary repairs and also of administration and leave a balance on the Fund of £70 14s 9d. It was decided to arrange for the playing of Cricket, Tennis, Croquet and Bowls, and Sub-Committees were appointed for each of these sections.'

June 1919

Giving in Church: 'Those who follow Church finance at all know that, under the present business-like arrangements, every parish is asked to contribute an allotted sum every year (1) to the Church overseas – which for Sonning is this year about £65; (2) to the Church in the diocese – which for Sonning is about £20. The reason why so small an amount is collected for the Church expenses is because of the endowments which Sonning possesses for this purpose.'

Car for Hire: 'It is always a treat to help on a man who is setting up on his own and so we are glad to make it public that Mr, Edward Hawkins has set up a motor car and invites custom. The car is at the Bull Hotel, and Mr. Hawkins will be found there.'

July 1919

The Women's Institute: 'A meeting was held on May 22nd with the object of forming a Women's Institute for Woodley. After a most interesting address the feeling was unanimous that a Women's Institute should be formed for Woodley and a committee was elected.'

Car Hire and Boot Repairs: 'Mr. Hawkins is still standing in his handsome car awaiting customers and treating them with the utmost politeness when he gets them. Also, our gallant ex-soldier Mr. Whay is waiting in Mr. Atwell's premises to make new boots or mend old ones.'

September 1919

Sonning Cricket: 'A meeting will be held in early October to consider the question of re-starting the Sonning Cricket Club in 1920.'

Sonning and Woodley Nursing: 'After a year's faithful service in the two parishes Nurse Lightfoot is going north to be married. She leaves us with good wishes and the gratitude of her numerous patients. Miss Pinchback (late Queen's Nurse) comes temporarily to take Nurse Lightfoot's place.'

Motor Ambulance: 'A Motor Ambulance has been established at Messrs Vincent's Garage adjoining Reading Station, under the auspices of the Red Cross Society. The charge is 1/3d. a mile. The Reading Hospital Ambulance has generally been found available; but in case of accidents or illness not going to Hospital, it is useful to know of this conveyance.'

Church War Memorial: 'The design for the memorial of those from our parish who fell in the war, has now been handed to the Vicar and Churchwardens. The memorial is to be placed on the south wall of our [Sonning] Church, below the windows and will involve the removal of two candle brackets.'

Peace Day in Woodley: The commemorations held on July 26th were only briefly mentioned, as the proceeding had been well reported in the local press. It was noted that some souvenir mugs were still available for any children who had not already received one.

October 1919
From the Producer to the Consumer: 'A society with headquarters based in Reading has been formed to buy people's surplus garden produce. Having bought a share in the business for 2/6d anyone with garden produce, eggs, poultry, rabbits (dead), etc., can send it for sale to the office and it will be sold at the market price. Profits are divided among the shareholders.'

Church-Going: 'There is a good note on this subject in the last number of our inset "The Dawn of Day". The person who does not take part in public worship is unlikely to pray well in private.'

Woodley Church Heating Fund: 'The opening up and renewing of the pipes to the drain leading to the cellar was begun on September 15th, so that the chamber is ready for the boiler for the new heating apparatus.'

November 1919

Woodley War Savings Association: The final meeting of this association was held on 28th October. The Hon. Secretary submitted the final audited accounts up to the month ending September when the association was dissolved. Since its inception in August 1916, total subscriptions of £1551 12s 6d had been received from 180 registered members.

Transport of Goods by River: 'In connection with the distribution of food by other means than the railway, and seeing that we have our own ancient water-way, it is interesting to note that the Mill has established The Thames Transport Co., Ltd., and perhaps Sonning will see coal and goods delivered at its wharf as some old inhabitants remember in former years.'

December 1919

Thrift in Sonning: The following societies and clubs were noted:
1) Royal Berks Friendly Society and National Deposit Society.
2) The Nursing Institution, in which anyone can secure the services of a Queen's Nurse, the payment is four shillings a year.
3) The Coal Club
4) The Clothing Club

The Workmen's Club: 'The Club is going very strong and is open every night. The Committee has booked the Hall for some entertainment for every Wednesday evening till March 31st, besides Boxing Day and New Years Eve.'

The Parish Magazine for 1920: The following article was included in the Woodley section of this issue: 'The question of carrying on for next year is an extremely difficult one. During this year we have been selling the Magazine at 1d. per copy; the actual cost of production is very near to five and three quarter pence per copy. Even with the proceeds from the advertisements and voluntary subscriptions the loss is considerable. We are, therefore, reluctantly obliged to raise the price to 2d. per copy. It would be a very great pity to have to give up the Magazine; for, in a scattered Parish such as this, it is a very useful means of communication and many we know would regret its discontinuance.'

January 1920
War Memorial: 'The clergy throughout Berkshire have been asked to collect particulars of all Berkshire men in any arm of the services who fell in the late war and send their names to a Committee for inclusion on a county memorial to be erected in Reading.'

Missions: 'News of the two great Missionary Societies, the S.P.G. and the C.M.S. is sad reading at this time. Money has gone down in value abroad even more than it has with us; and consequently, unless much more is given, the income of the Societies cannot do anything like as much as it did before the war. Will givers think of this when they give to any kind of Church work? Money does less than half it used to do.'

Apprenticeships: 'Parents who wish to get assistance in apprenticing their boys should bear in mind that the best firms are raising their standard of qualification. They ask now for 6th and 7th standard boys only.'

February 1920
St. Andrew's Church: 'The church in every part, inside and outside, has been thoroughly overhauled and put in perfect order. The roof, the stonework, the paving, channels and gullies, the glass, iron and metal work, the woodwork, the plaster, have all been repaired under the supervision of the churchwardens. The work has been done by Messrs. Margetts, of Reading, and has cost the sum of £253. This sum will be defrayed from the Caroline Palmer fund which this lady, the owner of Holme Park, placed in the hands of the Vicars of Sonning.'

National Savings: 'The local branch of the National Savings Association (which is the War Savings under a Peace name) which was instituted by our Headmistress has done excellent work and is still going.'

Church of England Assembly (Powers) Act 1919: 'A very important piece of work lies before us this month. It is to compile our roll of Church voters. The Enabling Act has become law, and the business of the Church depends very much more than it did on the will of the Church-people. It is the duty and privilege of all Church-people to claim their vote. Papers will be left at every house in the parish. These papers should be put in a box to receive them in the Church. The persons who do this will have their name entered on the roll of Electors for Sonning. They will have a legal voice in the work of the Church, and not others. These persons will be called together on some day before April 17:

(1) to send a representative to the Diocesan Conference which manages the finance of the diocese.

(2) to send representatives to the Conference of the Rural-deanery which focuses opinion in the deanery.

(3) to elect a Parochial Church Council to manage the affairs of Sonning Church.'

[*This "Enabling Act" provided the church with a large degree of self-governance whilst Westminster retained an overall supervision. The newly created Church Assembly was given the power to present to Parliament measures for approval or rejection but not for parliamentary modification. The Assembly was the predecessor of the General Synod.*]

April 1920

The Magazine: With this issue the title of the magazine had reverted to *The Sonning Parish Magazine,* due to Woodley withdrawing from the co-publishing venture. 'The Magazine sounds a sad note this month. Owing to the enormous expense of printing Woodley has to fall out of the partnership which it has so long had with Sonning. How much longer Sonning can continue its Magazine has yet to be seen. Parishes everywhere are closing down. This is all that can be said at present.' The vicar of Woodley then expressed his deep disappointment that Woodley had to withdraw from its involvement in the magazine. The Rev. Penruddock explained that he personally had the responsibility for the financial loss which he could no longer accept. The Woodley share of the deficit during 1919 was stated as £24 2s 0d.

The Church Vote: 'The roll of electors is to be made up by the Vicar and Churchwardens. The roll is to be published by fixing it at the door of the Church. A meeting of all persons whose names are on the roll is to be held in the Pearson Hall on Friday, April 9th. May we express a very earnest hope that all whose names are on this roll will make it a point of conscience to attend this meeting and from the very start of the movement throw the whole weight of the best-informed and keenest interest in it. The whole movement is for the enfranchisement of the laity. The laity is now on their trial.' There followed details of the agenda for the meeting.

The Church of England: 'The National Assembly is under the Enabling Act, the Church's Parliament where the Church will discuss its own affairs and make its own regulations. The first meeting is to take place on June 30th and July 1st.'

June 1920
The Parochial Church Council: 'The first meeting of the Council was held on Tuesday, May 4th. It was called to elect a vice-chairman and secretary and to arrange procedure. Mr. Wimperis of The Acre, Sonning, was unanimously elected vice-chairman, and Mr. Exton, secretary. It was arranged that at least four ordinary meetings should be held in each year; one meeting just before and one just after the Parochial Church Meeting.'

The Magazine: No doubt due to an attempt to reduce the loss being incurred with each issue, this June issue, and most future issues during 1920, were reduced in page extent from six to four pages. The greater part of two pages were given over to commercial advertising; three advertisements appeared and fully occupied page two, and three quarters of the front page carried a further single advertisement in addition to the magazine's title.

July 1920
The Sonning War Memorial: The memorial was unveiled and solemnly dedicated by Bishop Morley on Sunday, June 13th. 'The memorial consists of tablets, one for each of the twenty men of the parish who fell in the war. Each tablet, which is composed of glass mosaic, has a border of alabaster and an outer frame of Irish green marble.'
(*see: Illustration page 297*)

Parochial Church Council: 'A meeting was held in the Pearson Hall on June 15th. Finance, church-yard, parish magazine, burial ground were fixed as subjects for the future consideration.'

An Unwelcome Dinner Guest: 'Foxes have been much in evidence of late in our poultry yards, but surely the height of intrusiveness was reached by the cub which got into Holme Park and jumped up among the guests on the Sunday dinner table.'

August 1920

The Church Schools: 'The Boys' School had a great and memorable speech-day on July 20th. The school was honoured by a visit from Sir George Parkin, who addressed the parents, friends and boys and gave away prizes.'

The Royal Berkshire Hospital: 'There will be collections in the church for the Hospital on the first Sunday in August. Notice has just reached us that in future, an adult patient in the Hospital will be charged 2/- per day and children under ten 1/-. Either payment is less than half of what a patient costs the Hospital; so that there is need of much charitable help. Now that serious sickness will cost more, it would be a wise step for women and children to be insured in a Friendly Society. The Secretaries will be glad to tell anyone who writes or calls what they would have to pay each month.'

Thames Boat: 'A new Oxford and Kingston boat is running for the rest of the season between Reading and Maidenhead. It leaves Sonning Lock, going down the river at 10 a.m. and comes up to Sonning Lock again at 6.30 p.m.'

November 1920

Sonning Schools: 'The Managers had their monthly meeting to review the business of the schools on October 4th. They considered the exclusion of pupils for uncleanliness. The Headmaster's scheme for introducing gardening into the school teaching was approved. The Headmaster deserves credit for an original idea of having a hair-cutter at his school for cutting boys' hair at a reduced rate. It would help to the smartness and healthiness of the boys, and it is to be hoped that parents will respond.'

Working Men's Club: 'The annual general meeting was held on October 7th. The beer question came up again for discussion and the arguments used against its introduction were: there were already proper places to get it; ladies could not be expected to attend the entertainments if beer was about; many men would cut the club if beer was introduced. It was carried unanimously that beer should not be had in the club during the following season.'

December 1920
The National Assembly: 'The Church's Parliament, met on November 15th at Church House, Westminster. There were 467 members present. The chief discussion took place over the powers to be given to Parochial Church Councils. A Committee presented a measure which eventually received general approval and will be further revised in February; so that probably by Easter councils will know what powers they have to exercise.'

Sonning and Woodley Nursing: 'The Committee regretted the necessity of receiving the resignation of Nurse Clifford who was called away to take charge of her sister's home. She has been replaced by Miss Weaver, Queen's Nurse, who is lodging at The Laurels, Woodley, on the Reading Road near to the Woodley forge.'

The Magazine: 'After this issue of the Parish Magazine it must be closed down, so far as the Vicar's responsibility for it is concerned. He cannot face the deficit as it is - now some £30 - and as it will be still heavier if continued. If it is to be continued, it must be in some other way which lays the responsibility for its finance upon the whole parish.'

January 1921
The Magazine: The magazine had now been continually published for over fifty years, during which time there were several threats to its existence, due to the financial losses incurred by the publication. However, on this occasion Gibbs Payne Crawfurd bearing the personal financial responsibility for the cost of the magazine, had clearly given the impression that the publication could well cease. 'With this issue the Magazine enters not only on new management, but on a new order of existence. It will no longer be the mouthpiece of the Vicar only to the parishioners; nor will he alone be responsible for its contents. The circumstances which precipitated this crisis in the history of the Magazine were told in the December issue. The matter came before the Parochial Church Council, and this body, feeling the importance of having a means through which their doings could be published to the Parish, determined to continue the Magazine for one year, at least, on its own responsibility. Mr. Wimperis, the Vice-Chairman of the Council, was nominated as co-editor with the Vicar.'

February 1921

Appeal to the Parishioners: 'There are a great many in our parish, who have somehow or other got out of touch with the Church and its Services. The Clergy doesn't appeal to them; or the Service not quite what they like; sometimes the Choir is blamed; sometimes the seating is at fault. It is nothing so serious as unbelief or complete indifference to religion; but still it is enough to keep them as onlookers instead of working partners. May I earnestly appeal to those who seldom if, ever, to use the common expression, darken the door of the Church, and say how much stronger our corporate witness for Christ would be if we had their partnership.'

Special Constables: In was recorded that a parade had been held in the Pearson Hall where medals were presented by the Chief Constable of Berkshire to a large number of parishioners who during the war had acted as special constables.

Coal Charity: 'The Robert Palmer Coal Charity has now begun for the year. The Committee met to examine the claims made from Sonning and Woodley, and passed them with few exceptions. Payments from people in Sonning will be received on the first Tuesday in the month.'

March 1921

National Assembly of the Church of England: 'On February 5th the new Parochial Church Council's (Powers) measure (giving statutory powers to the Councils) was passed by the Assembly. It now goes to the Ecclesiastical Committee. If this Committee approves it, it will come up for the Royal Assent. As it stands now, Churchwardens will be elected in future by the Vestry and the qualified electors, sitting together as one body. Another great change has been made in the office of Churchwarden. "The care, maintenance, preservation and insurance of the fabric of the Church and the goods and ornaments thereof" has been transferred from the Churchwardens to the Council, though this is modified by two provisions: that the Churchwardens remain the legal owners of the goods, and that the Vicar and Churchwardens will become the Standing Committee of the Council and have the right to act on their own responsibility in the absence of working instructions.'

June 1921

The Rural Deanery: 'New Parishes recently taken into the Rural Deanery of Sonning are Ascot Heath, South Ascot, Binfield, Easthampstead, Bracknell, Sunningdale, Sunninghill and Warfield. The Ruri-decanal Conference was held on April 24th. There were about 150 parochial delegates present. The Ruri-decanal Conference is midway between the Parochial Church Council and the Diocesan Conference; much as in civil government the rural district council stands between the parish council and the county council.'

Sonning Cricket Club: 'The Working Men's Club have cast their mantle over cricket in Sonning, which has been in abeyance in the village since the beginning of the war. Under their auspices the Village Cricket Club has been started again – to the satisfaction of all concerned.'

July 1921

Parochial Church Council: Reports from meetings of the PCC appeared in the magazine, the reports were seen as a useful means of providing parishioners with information that would be of importance to them. The major agenda item in this July issue was a report by the Finance Committee for the half-year. Among the matters discussed was *The Sonning Parish Magazine* which was: 'proving itself a somewhat costly venture. It will almost certainly require assistance to the extent of an additional £20 in order that it may continue its appearance until the end of the year.'

Sonning Boys' School: 'The recent success of the Boys' School in winning the mark of "Excellent" in the Diocesan Inspector's Examination, was believed to be the first occasion on record. Mr. Wright, however, being jealous for the reputation of his old School, has looked up the files of old Parish Magazines and discovered therein that as long ago as 1875 this same mark was earn by the School.'
(see: pages 36 and 39)

September 1921

Sonning Regatta: 'The Sonning Regatta of 1921 has left behind it nothing but a pleasant memory of a village happily enjoying itself, of classes mingling together. The fun began two or three weeks before the

Regatta when the various competitors began to practice for their entries. At last the great day came and the weather ideal for the sport. The Regatta had a character of its own; it was homely and village-like; a friendly contest of neighbours, making little appeal perhaps to strangers; not engineered to make money or to put up very expensive prizes, but enjoyed by all for whose pleasure it was promoted.'

October 1921

Sonning Brass Band: It was noted that the Sonning Brass Band which was started in 1896 had now celebrated its 25th anniversary.

Harvest Thanksgiving: 'We know, of course, that a Harvest Thanksgiving is not on the same level as the festivals of our Redemption in Jesus Christ, but for all that we made it quite a special occasion when we held our Thanksgiving on the last Sunday in August. It was unusually early to think of a harvest safely gathered in, but it was not too early in this abnormal season. The harvest was practically ended.'

Sonning Pulpit: 'There is a good and appreciative account of Sonning church in the September number of the "Sign". It makes however the usual mistake about the old pulpit of Sonning church from which Archbishop Laud preached. It is not in a daughter church but at St. George's Tilehurst. The one at Dunsden is the one which replaced the old one at the restoration in 1852, and was removed from Sonning when the present pulpit was placed in our Church as part of the Memorial to Canon Pearson.'
(see: March 1885 - page 68)

November 1921

Oxford Diocesan Conference: An address by the Bishop of Oxford was included in this issue. Among the subjects raised by the bishop was the government proposal for agricultural labour conciliation boards, upon which he expressed hope that an alternative method of creating such boards by private initiative might be undertaken. He also raised concern for the lack of discipline in the lives of the younger generation, where he considered parochial church councils might encourage more support via organisations such as the Church Lads' Brigade, Boy Scouts and Girl Guides.

The Parochial Church Council: The October meeting of the PCC agreed the following matters: A new scale of fees for the digging of graves and tolling of the bell. The total payment for digging a single-depth grave should be ten shillings and for a double-depth grave fifteen shillings. Payment the cleansing of the mortuary to be five shillings.

Pearson Hall: 'The Hall is now gloriously illuminated with gas, and of course the pleasure in using it is much increased. The old lamps and their fittings are for sale.'

Sonning Fire Brigade: 'The Brigade, ever on guard for the safety of our homes and buildings, is desirous of replacing its old horse-drawn engine by a more powerful motor machine. A great whist drive and dance is to take place in the Pearson Hall to start the fund for purchasing it.'

December 1921
Christmas Day: 'The great thing before us this month is Christmas Day, and the Christmas Communion as the climax of its worship. It falls this year on a Sunday and thus we shall be able to keep it with all the more fullness and dignity. May I then beg all those who are not debarred from Communion to help and make our Christmas Communion as general and as devout an offering of worship to God as we can make it.'

The Parochial Church Council: The November meeting again discussed the future of the magazine: 'It was agreed that the Parish Magazine should be continued in 1922; but that the Council should not be responsible with regard to it for a sum exceeding £20. It was agreed that the advertisements in the 1922 Magazine issues should all be of one price – 60s 0d for a whole page, 30s 0d for a half page and 15s 0d for a quarter page.'

January 1922
The Parochial Church Council: At the December meeting Gibbs Payne Crawfurd made a personal statement: 'He said that he regretted taking steps to dispose by sale of the kitchen-garden, the yard and some outbuildings attached to the Vicarage without previously ascertaining the opinion of the parishioners on the matter; and that his proposal

had met with local opposition.' Crawfurd explained that approval had been received from the bishop and the ecclesiastical commissioners for the sale. His reason for disposal was to reduce the expenses of the present house; alternative options were to sell the present vicarage and build another one, or let the vicarage and hire another house. It was decided to appoint a sub-committee to consider the matter further.

The Sonning Church Schools: 'The Headmaster hopes to start a rough carpentry class in the New Year in conjunction with the gardening. Several parents have intimated to him the pleasure they have in expecting this new development in School routine. The Headmaster hopes in this way to give a rural basis to the teaching.'

February 1922
Proposed Sale of Vicarage Land and Building: The vicar used this issue to explain further to the parishioners his reasons for selling portions of the vicarage gardens and certain buildings. He announced that the PCC committee had reported their disapproval of his scheme and had suggested another plan: 'That the ground in question should be let to a tenant, who should assume liability for the maintenance and repair of the fencing and outbuildings.' Gibbs Payne Crawfurd concluded with the following: 'There as I write the matter stands. There is a difference of opinion between us, but I believe the aim and object of us all is to find the best possible solution of the difficulty.'

March 1922
Sonning and Woodley Nursing Association: A well attended meeting was held in the Pearson Hall on February 27th to consider the future of this service. An extensive report was printed in this issue recording comments and suggestions made from a number of those present. Six persons were appointed to serve on the committee which was to draw up the scheme for the future of the association. The annual general meeting was to be held in April, when the new constitution and other new plans were to be considered.

April 1922
Mary Ann May: The death was recorded of Mrs. Mary May at the age of one hundred years. [*see: Record of Burials etc., - St. Andrew's Church 2012.*]

Annual Report of the Parochial Church Council: 'In accordance with the regulations of the Enabling Act the Parochial Church Council of the Ecclesiastical Parish of Sonning presents herewith the Annual Report on its proceedings and on the financial affairs of the Parish.' There followed a detailed report of matters discussed and agreed by the PCC for the year 1921-22.

[*A great deal more formality was now evident in the affairs of the parish, and this was reflected in the content of the magazine where meetings of the PCC were reported in some detail. In earlier years of this magazine it was rare for the parishioners' approval or opinion to be asked for on any matter of importance. However, no doubt due to the new legislation, the actual or tacit support of parishioners was now sought for many decisions made within the parish.*]

May 1922

The National Assembly: 'It should be noted the Ecclesiastical Committee of Parliament, which on behalf of the nation, reviews the acts of the National Assembly, has referred back to the Assembly the Parochial Church Council (Further Powers) Measure. It contains the clause, so obnoxious to the Clergy, that a Parochial Church Council might object to the appointment of a Clergyman without having to defend its objections in the open if so desired.'

Sonning Schools: 'The Boys' School is full. The Managers are hoping very shortly to appoint an Assistant Master and to divide the School into three instead of the present two divisions. The Boys' and Girls' Schools did very well in the Diocesan examination.'

August 1922

Sonning Schools: The following is the text of the appeal circulated by the school managers: 'The Managers are faced with a very difficult position. There are now 68 boys in the Boys' School and since new houses have been built in Sonning and Woodley, this number is likely to be increased. It is a physical impossibility for three teachers to teach 68 boys in seven standards in the existing school-room, even if it could be suitably divided. If the School is to be maintained as a Church School and if its efficiency is to be developed, it is essential that further accommodation should be provided.' An estimated cost of £350 was given for the provision of the further accommodation.

September 1922

Sonning and Woodley Horticultural Society: 'The Forty-eighth Show of this useful and flourishing annual institution was held on August 2nd in Holme Park by the kindness of Mr. Cory Yeo and Mr. Shorney. In spite of the prevalence of storms all over the country the occasion passed off almost without interference, and was pronounced to be at all points the most successful show of recent years.'

Choir and Bell Ringers Outing: 'On Saturday, August 12th the men and boys of the Choir, the Organ Blowers and the Bell Ringers had a long and happy day at Brighton.'

October 1922

Royal Berkshire Hospital: 'The house-to-house and street collection for the Hospital on August 13th produced the sum of £22 6s 0d which has been forwarded to the Reading Workpeople's Fund for the Hospital.'

Sonning Population: 'There are 209 houses in the ecclesiastical Parish of Sonning which, on the ordinary average of persons allotted to a house, ought to yield more than the population of 650 traditionally attributed to Sonning. The fact is that it is difficult to get the exact population of a district, ecclesiastically divided in one way and civilly in another. Those who take the census cannot be expected to know the limits of the ecclesiastical parish.'

Dashwood Family: Since the eighteen-sixties there had been members of the Dashwood Family associated with Sonning. The family, due mainly to female members, were active supporters of the village and generous benefactors. It was reported in this issue that the Dashwood family had now sold their Sonning house and left to live elsewhere.

December 1922

Christmas: Rev. Gibbs Payne Crawfurd made an appeal: 'In this month Christmas is everywhere. We are all looking forward to it; we shall enjoy it. But I do entreat all who care the least for what I say to put the sacredness of the day in the forefront of its keeping. We are a village of Christians. Let our Christmas Communion be the greeting of the village to its Saviour on His Birthday. In his dear name I invite you all.'

Local Charities: Trustee meetings of three old established charities were reported upon in this issue, together with details of fund distribution to various causes:

The Barker Charity: The trustees had met to distribute £11 7s 2d. After payment made to the vicar and churchwardens of an annual amount of £1 17s 6d and 12s 6d paid to widows, they divided the remainder between the liberties of Sonning, Woodley and Dunsden.

The Clifford Charity: An amount of £5 would be distributed to the liberty of Sonning on St, Thomas's Day.

The Robert Palmer (Poor) Charity: The trustees had held a meeting on November 22nd and agreed to issue a bonus to needy Sonning and Woodley members of the coal clubs.

January 1923

The Parochial Church Council: 'Two meetings of the Council have been held since the last report of its doings appeared in the Magazine. There is not much to be said which would be of general interest to our readers, but on both occasions careful attention was given to matters of business and of finance. Mr. Wimperis (vice-chairman) spoke of the attempt that was being made in the diocese to collect £50,000 in ten years to increase the incomes of the smaller livings in the diocese to £250 a year. The Council approved the scheme.'

February 1923

Bus Service: 'Messrs: Povey and Smith, of the Sonning and Woodley bus, wish to thank the village generally for the support it gave them in the recent competition between themselves and the Thames Valley small bus, which resulted in the withdrawal of the Thames Valley bus, and they trust that they have served their customers well enough in the past to count on their loyalty if the competition is renewed.'

Christian Schools: Almost four pages of this issue were given over to informed comments upon the controversial changes being considered by government for elementary schools: 'There are two kinds of elementary schools (a) those held by Christian bodies such as the Church of England, Roman Catholic and the Wesleyans, sometimes called non-provided schools (b) those provided by the State, called Council or provided schools. The Church of England has 10,000 schools. The difference between them is religion. In those held by

Christian bodies religion is full, free and fundamental; the Church can teach its own truth. However, in the Council schools it is optional and controlled; certain things must not be taught. It is thought by many that this divided system should cease, and all go in under the same national system. The crucial question is – does it secure to the Church of England full liberty to carry on its own religious teaching in its own schools in its own unhindered way?'

March 1923
Patrick Stream: The Thames Conservancy were to clear the stream and make it more passable for boats. The existing growth of weeds and fallen timber would otherwise cause the stream to be closed for boating. (*see: August 1918. page 203*)

April 1923
Sonning C. of E. School: 'The Managers have had to take their part in the business of reckoning with the teachers over the salaries offered to them by the Berks Education authority. Some of the teachers declined to accept the offer and to them the Managers were instructed to give notice to terminate their engagements. They gave the notices which were subsequently withdrawn under fresh instructions; but at the same time they expressed to the Local Education authority their entire dissent from the policy which the County Council had seen fit to adopt.' There followed confirmation that Mr. Weight, who had been appointed assistant master last year, had now resigned his position.

Charville Residential Development: 'An ominous notice that the delightful residential estate of Charville in our parish, has plots of ground to be sold for up-to-date bungalows, suggests an increase in population in that remote part of the parish; and in the future a possible rearrangement of parish boundaries. The people there will be nearer to Twyford than Sonning church; and nearer still to Wargrave if the idea of a bridge over the Loddon matures.'

June 1923
Golden Jubilee of Woodley Church: An extensive article in this issue commemorated the fiftieth anniversary of the consecration of the Church of St. John the Evangelist. Various commemoration services

took place during the week commencing on the Sunday after Ascension Day, May 13th.

Sonning C. of E. Schools: 'Mr. Chapman has been appointed to the post of Assistant Master in the Boys' School. He is really a certified teacher, but in the dearth of school appointments, Mr. Chapman prefers to take the post and salary of an uncertified teacher, rather than remain unemployed.'

The Sonning Bus: 'The Magazine has always taken the line of supporting the cause of the "little brown Sonning Bus" not on the motive of pity, nor even on the motive of patriotism but on the ground of justice. When two young men with their life before them to make, start a venture in business and put their savings into it, is it right for a company with a lot of capital behind them to come on to the same ground and try to drive our young busmen off the road? We say it is unjust, and it is for Sonning folk to stand loyally by our busmen in the competition that is proceeding.'

July 1923

Sonning C. of E. School: 'The managers have received the resignation of Miss Connelly, the head-mistress, to take effect at the end of August. Miss Connelly who was appointed to the head-ship of the Girls and Infants Schools in 1908 is leaving to get married.'

Nursing Association for Sonning and Woodley: 'The Association ended the year with a debit balance of £11 19s 6d, however, a note adds that the overdraft is chiefly due to the need of purchasing a new bicycle for the nurse, Mrs. McMillan. The nurse has paid 1320 visits during the year.'

Sonning Cricket Club: 'We have two XI's this year, with Col. Anderson as captain of the first, and Mr. Wimperis, captain of the second.'

Electricity in Sonning: 'It is good news to hear that a supply of electricity is likely to be available in Sonning next year. The Thames Valley Electric Supply Company has lodged an application in Parliament for the needful statutory powers and Sonning has been scheduled in the compulsory supply area.'

September 1923

Sonning C. of E. School: 'The managers have appointed Miss Lindo to the post of head-mistress of the Girls' and Infants' School vacated by Miss Connelly.'

Electoral Roll: 'We remind the people of our parish again that it is of increasing importance that if eligible they should place themselves on the roll of electors for the parish.   In 1924 the number of representatives of any diocese in the National Assembly will depend upon the number of those in the diocese who have enrolled themselves as parochial electors.'

Japan Earthquake: A massive earthquake occurred in Japan during 1923 accounting for over one hundred thousand deaths.   The news was recorded in this issue with the announcement that 'a Sunday's collection will be given over to the cause.'

October 1923

Sonning Houses: 'The cry is that the houses in Sonning still come. A Parishioner told us lately that lots of our young people would get married if there were houses for them.   Perhaps it is just as well that there should be something to stay the too hasty fulfilment of this alluring prospect.'

River Steamers: 'The steamers cease to run of September 27th and the river seems now closed until the next year.'

November 1923

Rich and Reade Trust: 'The trustees have nominated Thomas Brown of Bulmershe to fill the vacancy in the Blue Coat School'. An application for assistance in apprenticeship was received in the trade of painter and decorator, a further application was received in the trade of carpenter and joiner. Grants were made in each case.

Churchyard Memorials: 'People are cleaning up some of the old family memorials in the church-yard. We don't want to see an old church set round with everything quite new and fresh in the church-yard, but it is nice to keep the old inscriptions legible as long as we can.'

Working Men's Club: 'At a special general meeting of the Club held on October 25th the resolution was carried that the Club would no longer be responsible for running the Cricket Club. It was further resolved that, as from the end of the present financial year, the Club would not continue to run the Football Section.'

December 1923

Apprenticeships: 'One of the proposals that the Farmers Union have made to the government touches education in farming work. A beginning in this has been made in the Boys' School at Sonning where besides the regular instruction given in gardening, the boys have been taught to survey farms in the parish and to set up on a map the rotation of crops on these farms. The Rich and Reade and Payne Trustees have apprenticed our boys in all sorts of town trades, but not one, in spite of all their efforts, to farming or gardening. But it is the most difficult thing in the world to bring our country boys into touch with farming.'

Social Evening: 'The ex-servicemen of Sonning gave a most enjoyable social evening to the residents at the Pearson Hall on November 12th. The Sonning band provided a very efficient dance orchestra and several local songsters enlivened the evening whilst the band and dancers were resting. About 150 people were present and severely taxed the resources of the refreshment committee who had catered for about half that number.'

January 1924

Sonning Cricket Club: 'A public meeting was held in the Pearson Hall on November 5th, to consider the resuscitating of the Sonning Cricket Club as a separate organisation. Following a full discussion on the subject it was unanimously agreed to revive the Sonning Cricket Club with its pre-war constitution.'

General Election: ' The dissolution of Parliament does not affect the laity who represent the Church in the National Assembly. It has affected the representation of the clergy and they have to elect new representatives, because of the convocations are dissolved along with Parliament.'
[*The December 1923 election resulted in a hung parliament with Ramsay MacDonald's Labour party forming the government with Liberal support.*]

March 1924

Contributory Hospital Scheme: 'The scheme has done excellent work in the parish. It came into being in the third week of February 1923 and ended up its year at the end of last December. The total collected for the year was £86 6s 2d. The membership entitles persons to free treatment at the Hospital. Members between 16 and 21 years of age pay 1d per week, over 21 years 2d a week; man, wife and family 4d a week.'

April 1924

The Parochial Church Council: 'It was reported that the work of lopping and pruning trees in the churchyard had been done and that the gate for Bone Orchard was in hand.'

Sonning and Woodley Coal Clubs: 'Applications for the membership of the Sonning Branch of the Coal Club in connection with the Robert Palmer Poor Charity will be accepted for persons whose total income is forty shillings per week or under. Exceptions to this limit may be made where there are more than three children of school age in the family.'

July 1924

Sonning Bridge Accident: 'Two steam launches, the new *Windsor Castle* and the *Duchess* were involved in an accident at our bridge last month. Although, happily there were no injuries, in both cases there was considerable damage done to the launches. However, we may console ourselves with feeling that it was not the fault of our bridge.'

Rich and Reade Trust: 'A meeting of the trustees will be held on July 16th, when an election to a vacancy in the Reading Blue Coat School will be made by the trustees. By the will of Sir Thomas Rich, Sonning, which is of course the Sonning at the time of his death, has the right to have three boys maintained in the school without payment; and every July an election is made.'

September 1924

A vast change in the presentation of the magazine had taken place with this issue. The page extent had greatly increased to twenty-two pages; fifteen full pages and part of two further pages were devoted to advertisements, the content of articles and reports were confined to less than four pages. The magazine continued with this mix of content at least until December 1925.

[*It was clearly a risk to expect parishioners to purchase the magazine in a form that carried such a large number of advertisements compared with text pages, although it is possible that an inset magazine might still have been supplied with each copy. This September issue carried forty-three advertisements; to encourage that number of local businesses to take paid advertising in a magazine with such a very restricted circulation was impressive. Income from such a large number of advertisers clearly should have transformed the viability of the magazine.*]

The Vicar of Woodley: 'It will be with great and sad regret that Sonning will have heard of the impending resignation of the Vicar of Woodley. The Rev. F. F. Penruddock means to retire from the active ministry and reside in Bath.'

Sonning C. of E. Schools: 'The Managers have appointed Mr. Frederick Weeks to the post of Head-master of our Boys' school. He was trained at University College, Reading and has seen eighteen months war service.'

October 1924

Harvest Thanksgiving: 'The day of our Harvest Thanks-giving was a notable one in our Church life. The Church looked so beautiful in its autumn decoration. Many, boys and girls, men and women helped to bring this about, some by sending flowers or fruit or vegetables or corn, and others by placing them tastefully about the Church that it is quite impossible to acknowledge them individually; but after all, the gifts were made for God's honour and glory and our thanks were not expected.'

St. Andrew's Memorial Window: 'There was dedicated on September 1st a window in the south transept to the memory of John Seymour Ingleby.' [*John Seymour Ingleby (1899-1919) served in the army during the Great War. The two figures, St. George and St. Michael, were chosen with reference to this young soldier.*]

[*The Labour minority government lost a vote of no confidence which resulted in a general election held during October 1924 in which the Conservatives led by Stanley Baldwin gained a decisive victory.*]

November 1924

Sonning C. of E. Schools: 'First from the Girls' School, the Head-mistress after consultation with her staff and with the parents has decided to adopt a uniform for the school. It is to consist of dark brown tunics and caps and it is hoped in time to add blouses. At present the blouses will not be all the same. A school badge will be worn on the cap which Mrs. Arthur Rose has kindly given. It consists of a shield on which is worked St. Andrew's cross and S.S. for Sonning School.'

The Vicar of Woodley: 'It seems a joy to all concerned that the Revd. Philip Gray is taking charge of Woodley. His people, that are to be, in Woodley are only waiting to give him a welcome. All of us in Sonning, whether we knew him personally or not, feel the romance of his return to the place of his birth and the church of his baptism.'

December 1924

Armistice Sunday: 'All in the Church and State of Sonning helped to catch the national spirit of Armistice day and to honour the day. For the 11 o'clock service no less than eighty ex-service officers and men of the parish paraded under the command of General Phipps-Hornby V.C. and assembling at the Bull green marched together to church, the bells and flag on the tower proclaiming the importance of the day. The General in the name of the ex-servicemen placed a wreath over the memorial of their fallen comrades who gave their lives during the Great War.'

Church Lighting: 'A person coming out from our dimly-lighted church recently remarked "I notice that the saints here do not dwell in light." When will someone be moved to make a gift of the electric light to our church and show up its beauty at night.'

January 1925

The Church Clock: 'The re-gilding of the clock on the church tower is the Christmas gift of some young people in the parish who have a little free-will offering scheme among themselves. There is an electoral roll on which any of our young folk between the ages of ten and eighteen years are invited to place their name – just as the older people have their electoral roll.'

Sonning Women's Institute: 'The members of the Junior branch of the Institute are arranging a masked Carnival dance at the Pearson Hall on February 4th in aid of St. Dunstan's.'

February 1925

The Parochial Church Council: 'The Council held a special meeting on January 6th to consider the provision of further burial ground. The Council resolved that no immediate action was necessary, as there appeared to be space available for burials during the next six years.'

Apprenticeships: 'Wouldn't it be a good policy on the part of parents to look to the building trade for apprenticing their boys? The engineering and motoring is full to overflowing; all the boys seem to go this way; but everybody is hoping that the building trade in which workers are wanted may be soon reviving.'

April 1925

The Parochial Church Council: 'The Council authorised the Vicar to receive a gift for the church of a processional cross. The proposed design was submitted to the Council. The Vicar explained that the idea was to receive the cross at first without the enrichments of silver mountings or jewels shown in the design; and that they may be added at any time by anyone.'

Recreation Ground: 'A good and generous service has been done to the parish by Mr. Fryer of Holme Park. He has lent to the parish for thirty years at a rent of one shilling per year five acres of land for use as a recreation ground on condition that Sonning will fence it and place a pavilion on it. It is necessary to borrow £400 from the Ministry of Health which it is thought will be repaid in the thirty years by a one penny rate laid upon the parish.'

New Vicarage at Earley: 'It will interest the people of Sonning to know that a new Vicarage house for Earley St. Peter's Church was opened and blessed on March 20th. The Vicar of St. Peter's and his people are to be heartily congratulated on the unanimity with which they have brought to a happy issue their endeavour to make a convenient and suitable home for the parish priest.'

May 1925

Reverend Gibbs Payne Crawfurd: 'I am asking the Bishop to let me resign under the Incumbents Resignation Acts during the coming autumn, I shall then be in my 72nd year; With the natural decline of even such powers as I ever had I cannot expect to serve you much longer with the zeal I should wish to do. And so I have come to the determination that it is time for me to resign.'

June 1925

Churchyard Memorials: 'Persons who are considering memorials in the churchyard would do well to consult the Potters Art at Compton, near Guildford. The material used is terra-cotta, red or brown. The advantage of it is the ease with which any design can be easily reproduced in the material. They are pleasing and artistic; and the cost is well less than of ordinary stone or granite or marble memorials.'

September 1925

Thames Challenge Cup: 'Our warmest congratulations to Mr. Light our lock-keeper. Again for the fifth time he has won the Cup for the best-flowered lock; and also the Conservators 1st prize for the district. The garden at the lock has been a truly beautiful sight and none who have seen it can doubt that Mr. Light fairly won his honours.'

November 1925

The Vicar's Last Word: 'Good-bye to Sonning. Good-bye to the place that God has blessed with such beauty, to the river with its happy associations, to the home dearly loved by our children, to the parish in which I have spent the last stage of my earthly ministry, to the honour which the holding of my office in Sonning has conferred on me, our beautiful house, the glorious church in which I have been allowed for more than eighteen years to offer the daily sacrifice of prayer and peace; to the diocese that I have served for forty-three years under six bishops; Good-bye to all who wish us well and keep us in kindly remembrance.'

The Parish Magazine: 'The Magazine has passed through times of storm and loss; but it is now well recognised and solvent. At one time the Sonning Magazine stood for the use of the whole ancient parish and was published for Dunsden and Woodley, as well as for Sonning; but from a financial point of view it was not good business, and the funds of the Sonning Magazine are none the worse for the dissolution of the partnership.   It was financed by a few persons who gave yearly subscriptions, was taken by some 30 or 40 persons and contained no advertisements. It is now issued at a flat price of 2/6d. yearly to any in the parish, is sent by post to a good many others and is taken in all by more than 100 persons. It is printed and published by the Berkshire Printing Co., Kings Road, Reading on what the Vicar and the firm know as the "Sonning Use" which guarantees its solvency and even hands back a bonus at the end of the year. The Magazine serves as a useful distributor of Church news from headquarters, and as a good link between the present people of the parish and well-wishes that have given from it: among the people of Sonning themselves; and now that the parish is expanding and a new unit of population forming up on the Sonning Land Estate, what we have known as Charville Farm, it will be more than ever useful in keeping each part of the parish in touch with the rest and all in touch with one another.'

[*The reference to the printer also being the publisher appears to imply that the printer was responsible for obtaining the advertising and the overall viability of the magazine.*]

Sonning Almshouses: 'These dwellings of our aged neighbours have been improved in some respects during recent years. A report preserved among the documents of the Almshouses reveals their insanitary condition as it was at one time when the Vicar and Mr. Mathews, the then trustees, applied themselves to amend it and connected the houses with the water supply of the village and with its system of drainage. Erected as the Almshouses were originally by the charity of Robert Palmer as farm homes for the old age of his work-people and administered at first by the Palmer family as their private property, they have gradually become a charity of the ancient parish (except Earley) and are now administered by a body of trustees under an order of the Charity Commissioners made in 1913, a law-suit having previously decided that the appointment of alms-persons should be in the hands of the trustees.'

December 1925
To the People of Sonning: The new Sonning Vicar, Archdeacon Richard Wickham Legg made the following announcement in this issue: 'Your

Vicar has most kindly invited me to say a few words in this number of your magazine. All I ask for is your prayers at this time, when, of course, I shall be remembering you. General Gordon used to pray for the people he did not know, but hoped to know, and he found it a wonderful link when he came to meet them. So may it be in our case.'

The Magazine: 'The small envelope placed this month in each magazine is meant to receive the annual subscription to the Magazine in 1926. The Magazine is delivered free of further charge to any house in the parish for 2/6d. yearly subscription. Those who wish the full Magazine sent to them by post should place 3/6d. in the envelope. Those who wish to have the local leaves only should place three shillings in the envelope. The Magazine will be sent in January to all subscribers; but after that issue only to those from whom subscriptions have been received.'

CHAPTER SIX

1926 -1935

P ast issues of this magazine, which have been published since it first appeared in January 1869, are retained as a collection of bound volumes held within the archives of Sonning Church. Unfortunately, despite extensive searches and enquiries, issues after December 1925 and until January 1936 (with the exception of a few single copies from 1933, 1934 and 1935) have alas not been located. It is quite possible that over past years a single volume containing issues from these missing years has been mislaid, or copies from that period were not retained for archival purposes.

It is most disappointing that the continuity of this magazine's rich and fascinating history is severed for some ten years. However, it has been of some consolation to establish, but not totally beyond doubt, that the magazine continued uninterrupted during the intervening "missing years". Evidence of this belief is offered as follows:

1. The final entry in the December 1925 issue (*which is included on page 238*) infers that the magazine will continue to be published into 1926.

2. Parochial Church Council Minutes of Tuesday 15 March 1927:
Parish Magazine: The Vicar asked if the CL would accept the financial responsibility of the parish magazine as he felt that it could be run by the CL at a profit. It was agreed that it was desirable that the CL should take it over at the end of the present year and the secretary was authorised to interview various printers and obtain estimates for cost of production.

3. Parochial Church Council Minutes of Tuesday 15 November 1927:
Parish Magazine: The Vicar reported that Mr. Harman had been able to place the PM on a satisfactory business basis for next year.

4. Parochial Church Council Minutes of Tuesday 17 January 1928:
Electoral Roll: It was suggested that a notice should be placed in the PM calling attention to the ER.

5. The volume of past issues held in the church archives which commence from January 1936 until November 1956 also includes six issues relating to the years 1933, 1934 and 1935.

The following entries (until September 1933) are not taken from past issues of the magazine. They are included to highlight a number of local, national and international happenings which were likely to have had an impact upon Sonning inhabitants, and those of neighbouring villages, during the years of the magazine's "missing issues".

The year 1926 opened with the arrival of a new Sonning incumbent, Archdeacon Richard Wickham Legg, who assumed the ministry during challenging times. The social and economic problems which faced Britain following the ending of The Great War only intensified during the mid twenties. Rapid changes which were occurring within Britain, and throughout the developed world, were now to have a profound impact upon local village life.

January 1926
A demonstration of moving pictures transmitted by wireless, invented by John Logie Baird, takes place at the Royal Institute in London. It was reported that: 'The pictures were crude and flickering, their quality far below that of the moving pictures to be seen in any cinema.'

April 1926
A national coal stoppage begins. The employers' final offer is a return to their 1921 minimum wage structure, which is equivalent to a 13% wage cut.

May 1926
The first general strike in British history commences on May 4th. The Trades Union Congress ("TUC") votes to back the miners who were already on strike. A large number of volunteers come forward to undertake essential work during the strike, including driving of goods

lorries, buses and even trains. The Commissioner of Police calls for capable citizens under the age of 45 to come forward and be sworn in as special constables during the crisis.

The TUC eventually decides to call off the general strike on May 12.

November 1926
Miner's leaders and the Government reach agreement to end the six months old miners' strike on November 12th.

February 1927
The British Broadcasting Corporation announces that the BBC news programmes must be accurate with information. There is thought to be some three million British homes that have access to wireless sets.

November 1927
In the calendar year 1926 motor vehicle licences issued within Britain number approximately 1,729,000 and during the same period 127,250 horse drawn vehicle licences are issued.

January 1928
British people over the age of 65 years receive their first state pension of ten shillings per week.

May 1928
Parliament agrees to give an unopposed third reading to the Equal Franchise Bill, giving the vote to all women aged twenty-one years of age.

June 1929
No party receives a clear majority following the general election. Ramsay MacDonald forms a minority Labour Government with Liberal support.

October 1929
Panic selling of shares on the New York Stock Exchange causes the "Wall Street Crash" on October 24th.

March 1930

World economies slump and unemployment in Britain rises to one and a half million, some 500,000 increase since the Labour Government came to power nine months earlier. By August the unemployed figure rises to over two million, doubling the number of unemployed during a fourteen month period.

October 1930

Adolf Hitler's National Socialist Party increase their representation in the German Reichstag and become the second largest party after the Social Democratic Party. The Nazi vote increases within two years from 800,000 to six and a half million.

April 1931

The Government announces increases in tax on a gallon of petrol by two pence resulting in the pump price rising to one and four pence halfpenny.

July 1931

Unemployment in Britain rises to an unprecedented level of 2.71 million.

August 1931

The Labour Government falls amidst the nation suffering its worst financial crisis. An all party "Government of Co-operation" is formed in an attempt to confront the emergency.

September 1931

Britain devalues the pound and is forced off the gold standard. Serious clashes occur between police and demonstrators in London and other major cities following widespread protests against the Government's austerity programme.

October 1931

The general election called for October 27 results in a massive political landslide that reduces National Labour representation in the Commons to just 13 seats. However, Ramsay MacDonald remains as a titular Prime Minister of the National Government.

July 1932

Adolf Hitler's National Socialists gain the largest number of seats in the German Reichstag but fall short of a majority.

October 1932

Protests and hunger marches increase throughout Britain against the Government's draconian measures to achieve an economic recovery.

December 1932

In the United States, Democratic candidate Franklin Delano Roosevelt is elected and becomes the thirty- second US President.

January 1933

Adolf Hitler leader of the National Socialist Party (Nazi party) becomes Chancellor of Germany.

April 1933

Jewish businesses in Germany are boycotted by orders of the new Nazi Government. Violence perpetrated against the Jewish community is being widely reported.

During the period following December 1925 until September 1933, the years of "missing issues", the magazine had clearly undergone considerable change. By September 1933 the illustrated front cover had given way to a much simplified heading with a listing of church services and "The Vicar's Letter". The whole magazine comprised of just four pages with no advertisements.

September 1933

The Vicar's Letter: The Venerable Richard Wickham Legg introduced this issue with comments about his recent holiday, and matters relating to forthcoming church services and parish events. He also referred to the cost of improvements to the Pearson Hall: 'No doubt you have all carefully studied your August magazine and noticed the two paragraphs about the Pearson Hall. This is just to remind you that the special collection to help the Hall Improvement Fund is to be held on Sunday, September 24th at all services. It is hardly necessary to point out the absolutely invaluable services that the Pearson Hall has rendered and does render to the life of the village as a whole.'

Sonning Swimming Gala: 'The Swimming Club held their fourth Annual Gala under ideal conditions in the river Thames on Wednesday, July 26th. There were many attractions including a display by Mr. E. H. Temme, the Channel swimmer, and also Mr. and Mrs. Burne, who were the Olympic Games representatives of Great Britain at the Amsterdam event in 1928.'

Women's Institute: 'The next meeting will be held on September 12th, when we welcome our county visitor, the Hon. Mrs, Glynn also Miss Williams, who will demonstrate fancy cardboard box making; the judging of the potato competition too.'

[*The "Great Depression", a crisis which afflicted much of the world in the late twenties and thirties, had eased somewhat in Britain during 1933. This would have been a great relief to the people of this parish, they would no doubt have felt the impact of unemployment and the harsh economic problems that were endured during those turbulent years.*]

October 1933
Sonning Fire Brigade: 'The Brigade held their Annual Collection for the Royal Berkshire Hospital on Sunday, August 13th when the sum of £17 9s 3d was collected and handed to the Royal Berkshire Hospital. The Sonning Fire Brigade took part in the Goring Fire Brigade Competition on July 10th in Motor Turn-out Drill and Escape Drill, and won the British Legion Cup for the two Drills – they have our best wishes and congratulations.'

Choir and Belfry Outing: 'On August 26th by the generosity of friends, the members of the Choir and Belfry spent a very happy day at Brighton. At 6.30a.m. char-a-bancs drew up at the bottom of Sonning Lane, and by 6.45a.m. were filled with choristers, ringers and their friends, the party reaching the grand total of 100.'

Missionary Guild: 'Our special Missionary effort – the support of the Holy Cross Hospital, Pondoland, is in great need of funds. We hope to arrange an American tea sometime in November in aid of the Hospital. At an American tea everyone brings something and everyone buys something.'

January 1934

The Vicar's Letter: 'A very happy New Year to you all. Let me suggest as a motto the words of the Communion Service; "Lift up your hearts". We have certainly more cause for thanksgiving than we had at the beginning of last year, for as a nation we seem largely to have weathered the storm. So let thanksgiving and gratitude to God be the keynote of our lives during the coming year.'

Sonning Village Players: 'Our friends of the Drama League are to be complimented on their performance of "A murder has been arranged", on December 14th, 15th and 16th. The house was not as full as it should have been on the first night, but we who were there were thrilled from beginning to end. It is conceivable that all do not appreciate so much "thrill" of this particular variety, but to produce the play in such conditions and in such a short time is no mean feat.'

July 1934

The Vicar's Letter: 'No doubt our readers noticed in the last number of the Magazine a charming letter from a boy living in one of the distressed areas, and his grateful thanks for what had been done for him largely through the efforts of our Sonning Boys' School Carol singing at Christmas. It is only fair to add that our girls have also been doing their bit by making garments etc., for those in similar areas that are sorely in need.'

'This is perhaps looking rather far ahead, but a great event is coming off next year, and that is the 25th Anniversary of our King's Accession to the throne. No doubt, as loyal subjects, we shall honour the day with real thanksgiving and renewed loyalty.'

Mothers' Union Sonning Deanery Festival: 'On June 15th, approximately 500 members of the M.U. met in the Deanery at Sonning to hold their festival. The procession headed by the Silver Band, started from the Pearson Hall about 2.45p.m. and marched to the Church. When all were in their places Evensong was sung, and an address given by the Rev. G. F. C Bond, Vicar of Bracknell. A choir, composed of Sonning members and two members from Earley led the singing; well known hymns were chosen, in order that all might join in and so take a real part in the Thanksgiving service.'

November 1935

The Vicar's Letter: 'Our Harvest Festival this year was kept on October 6th. There was a great dearth of fruit amongst our offerings this season, but plenty of flowers and vegetables. We are very grateful to all who sent gifts of one kind or another, and most particularly grateful to our zealous decorators, not forgetting the children, who made their Chapel a real place of richness and beauty.'

The Churchyard Extension Fund: 'I feel sure that the appeal issued to all residents in the Parish will be meeting with a glad and generous response. I gather that not only we grown-ups, but also the children are taking a great interest in helping forward the scheme.'

December 1935

Remembrance Day Service: 'This Service was held in the Parish Church at 11a.m. on November 10th, and was remarkably well attended. The British Legion (alas! In very reduced numbers) paraded on the cricket field, whence, with the Sonning Fire Brigade and the Boy Scouts they marched through the village headed by the Sonning Silver Band. At the Bull Hotel the Girl Guides joined in at the rear of the column. Everyone was very glad to see them on this parade for the first time. A new feature of the occasion was "The Garden of Remembrance", on the turf outside of the vestry door, where a cross had been marked out. Poppies and crosses were sold, and those who wished to do so, could buy them and place them within the limits of the cross. The effect of the Scarlet Cross in the green surroundings was very striking. It is hoped that in future years all those who pass by will contribute at least one poppy to the Garden of Remembrance.'

Churchyard Extension Fund: 'The appeal to donations to this fund has met with very satisfactory response. A sum of £74 10s 4d has so far been received and in addition Col. and Mrs. Moss have very generously undertaken to bear the whole cost of fencing-in the piece of land which has now been acquired in Holme Park. The proposal that parishioners should contribute the cost of individual trees in order to establish an evergreen hedge has met with a very willing response, and no less than 60 trees have so far been given.'

CHAPTER SEVEN

1936 -1939

During this period a consistent format of the magazine was maintained; four pages with a measurement of 24cm x 18cm, printed by the letterpress process in black ink. No illustrations or advertisements were included. It is uncertain whether an inset was now supplied with the magazine.
(*see: front page January 1936 – page 248*)

In 1936 The Venerable Richard Wickham Legg had celebrated the tenth year of his Sonning ministry, during which time Britain had been faced with great challenges, both at home and overseas. The four years now about to unfold commenced with Britain continuing to recover from the greatest economic recession ever recorded. For the United Kingdom and its Empire the year 1936 was to be the "year of the three kings" – The death of George V, was followed by the succession and abdication within a few months of Edward VIII and the succession of George VI.

By 1936 the rise of the German Nazi party, headed by Adolf Hitler, was causing serious concern. Hitler had become German Chancellor and his National Socialist Party had already signalled their expansionist intentions. Their plan included the "Final Solution", to remove the Jewish people from within Germany "The Fatherland" and occupied Europe. Germany's actions would eventually result in the outbreak of a further world war, which would surpass in its extent and destruction even The Great War – thought by many at that time to have been "the war to end all wars". With the outbreak of World War II many austerity measures were introduced into Britain that impacted upon every family. Military conscription was imposed and a number of local residents were killed on active service during the conflict.

SONNING PARISH MAGAZINE.

JANUARY 1936.

Clergy—The VENERABLE R. WICKHAM LEGG, M.A., *Oxon* : (*Archdeacon of Berkshire*)
The REV. C. A. M. ROBERTS, M.A., *Oxon*, "Taberna," Woodley.

Churchwardens—Mr. S. PADDICK, Pound Lane.
Mr. L. C. ROBINSON, The Centuries.

Parochial Church Council—*Chairman*—The VICAR.
Vice-Chairman—Mr. CLEMENT WILLIAMS, Shelvingstone.
Secretary—Mr. C. E. C. WATTS, School House.

Organist and Choir Trainer—Mr. E. G. YOUNGS, 16, South View Avenue, Caversham.
District Visitor—Miss A. DAVIS, Playhatch.
District Nurse—Miss ROSTRON, 16, Pound Lane.
Missionary Guild and Mothers' Union—Miss WICKHAM LEGG, The Vicarage.
Verger—Mr. ADNAMS, Mill Farm, Sonning Eye.

SERVICES AT THE PARISH CHURCH, SONNING.

Sundays.—Holy Communion 8 a.m. Also on First Sunday at 7 a.m. and on Second Sunday at 12 noon. Sung Eucharist and short address on last Sunday, 9.45 a.m. Mattins and Sermon at 11 a.m. (with Litany on 3rd Sunday). Children's Catechism 2.45 p.m. Evensong and Sermon 6.30 p.m. Holy Communion.—*Holy Days and Saints' Days* 8 a.m.

Tuesdays and *Thursdays* 7.30 a.m., (except when falling on Holy Days or Saints' Days).

MATTINS usually at 8 a.m.; EVENSONG on Wednesdays and Fridays at 4.15 p.m.

Churchings—Before or after any Week-day Service, after notice to the Verger.

Holy Baptism—On Sundays at 3.30; otherwise by arrangement. Notices of Baptisms, Marriages, Banns and Burials should be given in the first instance to the Verger Mr. Adnams.

THE VICAR'S LETTER.

My dear Sonning People,

A happy New Year to you all, and may it bring the restoration of a righteous peace to an anxious world.

The St. Andrew's Eve Festival Evensong in which the choirs of Woodley, Earley and Sonning took part, was well attended, though not so many were present as last year, possibly owing to the Swimming Club Dance being fixed for the same evening. It is, however, only fair to say that a large number of our keenest swimmers were at Church first. We are most grateful to the Rev. G. Kenworthy, Rector of Wokingham, for the sermon he gave us, and to our organist and choir for their reverent rendering of the service, more particularly for the joyous singing of the anthem, our only regret was the absence of Mr. Probert

Jones, the organist of Earley, who was laid up with influenza, from which he soon recovered. On St. Andrew's Day itself, Saturday, Nov. 30th, there was a celebration of the Holy Communion at 8 and 9.30, with Procession and hymns, the choir being supplemented by some ladies, mostly members of the Mothers' Union. They were in every way a great help and support. Considering that Saturday is not a school day there was an encouraging number of our boys and girls present as well as some of the Girl Guides, who by the way made their first appearance in Church at the Sung Eucharist on Sunday, Nov. 24th.

There will be a Confirmation at one of the Reading Churches towards the end of March, and the clergy would be glad to have the names of intending candidates as soon as possible. The next Confirmation at Sonning itself will probably be in 1937.

Congratulations to Mrs. Davis of the Alms-

Front page: January 1936. (24 x 18cm)

January 1936

The Vicar's Letter: 'A happy New Year to you all, and may it bring the restoration of a righteous peace to an anxious world. Let me suggest a useful motto for 1936 "be strong and of good courage".'

'The St. Andrew's Eve Festival Evensong in which choirs of Woodley, Earley and Sonning took part, was well attended, though not so many were present as last year, possibly owing to the Swimming Club Dance being fixed for the same evening. It is, however, only fair to say that a large number of our keenest swimmers were at church first.'

'Mrs. Evans, of the Bull Hotel is kindly supplying the Almshouses with their two daily newspapers! This is a generous gift that will be greatly appreciated.'

League of Nations Union: 'A meeting of the Sonning branch of the Union was held in the Pearson Hall on Friday, December 6th, the speaker was Commander Lewis R.N. There was a good attendance of members and others who heard Commander Lewis give an excellent address on the origin, history and ideals of the League of Nations with particular reference to the Italo-Abyssinian dispute. Following a vote of thanks, a play in three short acts entitled "Invasion" was given by the Reading Pax Players. This was staged simply but excellently acted, and was much enjoyed by those present.'

February 1936

The Vicar's Letter: 'On Sexagesima Sunday, February 16th, there will be the usual collections on behalf of the Church Schools in the Diocese. There seems to be a real prospect of the Government being willing to help us, both in the re-construction of older schools and the building of new ones. So our hopes for the future of Church Schools seem fairly bright just at present, and that should encourage us to give generously on Sexagesima Sunday.'

R. I. P: 'His most gracious Majesty King George, to the deep sorrow of all his people. God bless our new King.'

The New Churchyard: 'The extension to the Churchyard in Holme Park has now been fenced-in and is ready for inspection by the subscribers and parishioners generally. The evergreen hedge will be planted in the spring.'

March 1936
Parochial Church Council: The Report for 1935 included the following items:

'During the year the extension of the Churchyard by the inclusion of a portion of the garden of the Bull Hotel has been completed, and the negotiations for the purchase of a portion of Holme Park, adjoining the Churchyard, have been carried out to a successful conclusion.

An event which should be mentioned as bringing a considerable number of new parishioners in our midst is the transfer of Farnborough School to Holme Park, which took place in September, and we shall welcome the boys and the staff from time to time in our Parish Church.

The Silver Jubilee of His Late Majesty King George V, was celebrated in the village with every sign of loyalty and rejoicing, and the Service held in the Parish Church on May 6th to commence the day's proceedings was very largely attended.'

April 1936
Jumble Sale: 'A sale in aid of the debt on the Pearson Hall is to be held in the Hall on Wednesday, May 6th. Full details will be given later.'

Parish Magazines: This extensive article concerning parish magazines appeared in this issue:

'Parish Magazines sometimes come in for criticism of varying kinds *e.g.*
(1) They are dull and uninteresting. Well, so far as our own Magazine is concerned, that is a matter for our readers to decide.
(2) They only mention the happy side of parish life, and ignore the other side, the little rubs, the storms in teacups, and other much more disagreeable things. Well, we don't want to live in a Fool's Paradise, but do we want to dwell on such things? A Parish Magazine is meant to remind us of the good steady work that is being carried out in our village to the honour and glory of God, and in the service of others.
(3) There is too much scolding in some Magazines. Well, perhaps we all occasionally want a gentle rap over the knuckles, especially if we are getting slack in our religious and other duties. Generally speaking, the writers in a Parish Magazine aim not to scold, but to encourage.

(4) Parish Magazines only deal with purely local and petty affairs and leave on one side the wider questions that concern the Church at home and abroad, the Empire, the world in general, and the special needs of those less fortunate than ourselves. Well, we do have these bigger issues brought before us from time to time in our Parish Magazine, and quite rightly, but after all a Parish Magazine is meant primarily as a record of matters and events that naturally interest and concern our common neighbourly parochial life.'

June 1936

Pearson Hall: 'A quite successful Jumble Sale was held in the Pearson Hall on the afternoon of Wednesday, May 6th, towards paying off the overdraft at the bank. The amount raised at this sale was £26 11s 9d and as the overdraft was £149 the debt on the Pearson Hall is still about £123. During the summer months the demand for the use of the Hall is small and as "the takings" for the first three months of this year only came to £18, and the expenses of the Hall for the same period are about £17, it is clear that unless more jumble sales are held, or some kind benefactor steps forward, it will take a long time to clear off the debt.'

Waifs and Strays Society: 'A Stuart Masque and Fayre is to be held in Reading during the summer in aid of the Society's Local Home, St. Andrew's, and its work for Crippled Children at Pyrford, Surrey (over 1,200 children have been taken into the Home from the Diocese). For this interesting event Sir Felix and Lady Pole have generously consented to lend the grounds of Calcot Place, the dates are July 17th and the 18th. A "Village of Shoppes" of the Stuart period will lend a charm to the Fayre, which will include the usual entertainments and sideshows.'

July 1936

The Vicar's Letter: 'Our Bishop is coming to consecrate the two new portions of our Churchyard on Sunday, July 19th, at 3.30 p.m. The main service will be held in the Holme Park Churchyard, and the Bishop will give an address to, I hope, a large congregation. A short Consecration Service of the "Bull" portion will then be held.'

British Red Cross: 'The Flag Day for the British Red Cross will be held in Sonning and Woodley on Friday, July 10th. Will all friends of our

Nursing Association kindly note the date, as the Society makes a good grant to our Nursing Fund.'

R.M.S. Queen Mary: 'Our people's Warden, Sidney Paddick, was one of the passengers on the first trip of the *Queen Mary.* He took a "busman's holiday" for he acted as Churchwarden on board!'

August 1936
School Inspection: 'The Head Diocese Inspector visited our Schools on Friday, July 10th. He was with us all morning from 9a.m. till 1p.m. George May and Irene Whay were awarded the Bishop's prize.'

Women's Institute: 'The monthly meeting was held on Tuesday, June 16th. Mrs. Gowring presided. Mrs. Long gave a report of the Annual Meeting held in the Albert Hall, which she attended as delegate. On June 24th we were favoured with perfect weather for our summer outing to Bournemouth, and an enjoyable day was spent by 32 members and friends.'

October 1936
Boxing and Physical Training Club: 'A meeting of the proposed Club to be formed at Sonning was held on August 5th at the Manor House, Sonning. It is hoped to commence training at the beginning of September, and the Club is open to anyone living in the Parishes of Sonning, Dunsden and Woodley.'

1st. Sonning Girl Guides: 'It is now a year since the Rummage Sale which gave the Company such a generous start. Our meetings during the winter took place in the French Horn Garden room, lent most kindly by Mr. and Mrs. Wellburn. Only during the coldest spells did we find our oil stoves, aided by strenuous games, insufficient to keep us warm, then we removed ourselves to the warmth and comfort of the Pearson Hall.'

November 1936
The Vicar's Letter: 'We had a lovely day on October 4th for our Harvest Festival, and there were the usual large congregations, especially at Evensong, though there were a few less at the early Eucharist. We were

glad to welcome the Girl Guides in the morning, and the Church Lads'
Brigade in the evening. Our best thanks are due to the decorators and
the organist and choir, more particularly the soloists.'

The Bishop's Palace Site: 'Mr. Clement Williams has bought a part of the
Holme Park property including this site. This is welcomed news to us,
as Mr. Williams hopes to ensure that in any development which may
take place on this land in the future, the site of the Bishop's Palace and
the amenities of the towing path will be preserved.'

Sonning Recreation Ground: 'In connection with the appeal now being
made for the King George Memorial Fund, the Sonning Parish Council
have decided that they will make their Recreation Ground in Pound
Lane, Sonning, which they are now purchasing, as their tribute. They
therefore invite all inhabitants who are sending direct to the Lord
Mayor at Mansion House, or to the County Fund, to earmark their
donation for the playing field at Sonning. It is felt by your Council that
no more fitting memorial could be made than to purchase and lay out a
Local Recreation Ground in this way.'

December 1936
The Vicar's Letter: 'At a Managers meeting held on November 18th, Mr.
S. Aubrey was appointed Headmaster of the Sonning Boys' School in
place of Mr. Watts, to whom we now offer a very real and regretful
farewell.'

Armistice Sunday: 'The special 11 a.m. service held on Armistice Sunday
November 8th was better attended than ever. Members of the British
Legion, the Fire Brigade, the Church Lads' Brigade, the Girl Guides
and the Boy Scouts were all there in force. The Boys of Farnborough
School formed the Choir at the short 11 o'clock service. The striking
tune to Kipling's "Recessional" was composed by their organist, Mr.
Borgnis.'

January 1937
The Vicar's Letter: 'A very happy New Year to you all. Let me suggest a
motto: "Abound in hope. Hope maketh not ashamed". And let us
remember in our thoughts and prayers our new King and Queen.

The Booklet giving a short guide to the Church is now on sale, price 3d at the Post Office, Miss South's and Mr. Allnatt's.'

February 1937

The Vicar's Letter: 'We had a very happy Christmas Festival. Carols were sung at the 8 o'clock Eucharist on Christmas Day, and at the Sung Eucharist and Evensong on the Sunday following. We had the pleasure of listening to the Boys' School Choir on some days before Christmas. The boys were most hospitably treated at the houses they visited.'

The Royal Berkshire Hospital: '1937 marks the centenary of the laying of the foundation stone of the Hospital. We understand that the occasion is considered a fitting one to commence the overdue Extension Scheme which has been under discussion over the past year. Final details have not yet been reached but no time is lost in creating the machinery necessary for the purpose of raising the considerable sum required. This year is Coronation Year and many organisations will be planning celebration activities. It is suggested that no greater pleasure could be given to His Majesty the King, than to know that the numerous happy gatherings and functions were productive of assistance in providing for the welfare of the sick and injured.'

April 1937

The Vicar's Letter: 'None who attended the wonderful Confirmation Service on February 28th are ever likely to forget it, nor, I hope, will they ever forget the motto given by the Bishop of Buckingham in his stirring address "Be Loyal". The whole service was most inspiring from the beginning to the end. Sonning contributed 38 candidates, 16 men and boys, 22 women and girls.'

The Industrial Christian Fellowship: 'I am asked to remind our readers of the hope expressed in an earlier Magazine that Sonning would this year raise £10 towards the support of the Unemployed Welfare Centre in Jarrow, run by the I.C.F.'

May 1937

The Vicar's Letter: 'Our prayers for the King must be much on our lips and in the hearts of us all at this Coronation time. There are many lessons that the Coronation naturally suggests to us; perhaps the most important is that, as the King dedicates himself to God at that solemn service, so should we do the same both in faithful worship, and also in carrying out loyally our duties in daily life and work. On the Saturday before the Coronation we are looking forward to an event which means much to us all, and that is the opening of our extended Recreation Ground.'

June 1937
The Vicar's Letter: The Coronation of King George VI: 'The King's Coronation must take first place in my letter this month. The day began here with the Holy Eucharist at 8 a.m., when there was a most encouraging number present, mostly young people, including twelve of our lads. The Choir, Church Lads' Brigade, Girl Guides and Brownies came to the 11 o'clock service, which was preceded by a merry peal of bells. After which all moved to the Recreation Ground, where sports of various kinds were held, some really humorous. At 4 p.m. Mrs. Arthur Rose planted a beech tree close to the Pavilion. At 4.30 p.m. the Children's Tea followed in the Pearson Hall. Then came more sports, distribution of prizes, the King's Speech, and finally a Dance in the Pearson Hall.'

July 1937
The Vicar's Letter: 'On July 7th, there will be a fete held at the Vicarage to support the Sonning and Woodley Nursing Association. Everybody in Sonning recognises the devoted work of our Parish Nurse, Miss Rostron. It is time that she had a new car, as the old one is worn out through constant use.'

Royal Counties' Show: Reports upon two visits to the Royal Counties' Agricultural Show, held at Prospect Park, Reading, were included in this issue. Both reports gave detailed accounts of the exhibits and displays.

August 1937
British Legion: 'The beautiful grounds of The Cottage, Sonning, were thrown open to the members of the Sonning Branch of the British Legion and their friends on the afternoon of Tuesday, June 29th, for the

holding of their Annual Fete. A large number of people assembled during the afternoon. The selling at the various stalls was quite brisk, and the side-shows, as usual, proved very popular. The weather, unfortunately, was not too kind. Nevertheless, the whole programme was very satisfactorily carried out and proved a great success, the total of the takings being just over £57.'

September 1937
Our New Bishop: 'Dr. Kenneth Kirk, Canon of Christ Church, has been appointed to succeed Dr. Strong as Bishop of Oxford. Dr. Kirk is not only a great scholar and a distinguished theologian, especially on moral questions, but he has the great gift of being able to express himself simply and clearly to those of us who are not "high-brows". We offer him our respectful congratulations.'

The Fire Brigade: 'It is not perhaps known to all of our readers that the Fire Brigade are in need of a new engine. In consequence of this they are under the necessity of making a special appeal for money; and we have great pleasure in announcing that Mrs. Arthur Rose has just made the handsome donation of £100 towards this object. I am informed that thanks to this generosity the Brigade are within sight of the six or seven hundred pounds necessary to make their purchase.'

November 1937
Sonning Boys' School: 'The Pearson Hall was full to capacity on Thursday, 14th October, when a representative gathering supported the Wireless Fund of the Boys' School. There were 34 tables, and the Drive was very ably conducted by our M.C., for whose hard work much thanks is due. "Thank you" from the Boys' School to all who helped in any way. We shall be able to install an electric supply and electric radio-gramophone, with extra loud speaker in the separate class-room.'

December 1937
The Vicar's Letter: 'Let me give you all my best Christmas greetings in the words of the old Carol: "God rest you merry." Mrs. Arthur Rose has added to her many kindnesses by presenting a wireless set to our Girls' School. Both managers, teachers and the girls themselves are warmly grateful for this generous gift.'

Armistice Sunday: 'Once again Armistice Sunday has come and gone, and we in Sonning have every good reason to feel satisfied with the commemoration of that special day. In the Church there was a larger congregation than ever, which shows that the interest in, and the reverence for, this anniversary is as great as ever. A wreath was placed by the President of the British Legion on the War Memorial in the Church, and as the name of each of those names are inscribed on it were read, a young descendent placed a bunch of flowers below the tablet. In this way it is hoped that the younger generation may realise that the war means something to them, although they can never know what their country went through in those awful years 1914 - 1918.'

January 1938

Church Senior School at Wargrave: 'In view of the fact that, when it is built, this new Senior School will be the place where all our boys and girls over eleven years of age will be educated, some facts about it should be of interest to our readers. The first point of importance is that this School will be one of many to be erected in all parts of the country in accordance with the Board of Education's scheme for the improvement of Elementary Education. The main purpose of this scheme is the proper grading of all children over eleven, which is impossible in the smaller schools. Another point of importance is that these new schools may be either Church Schools or Council Schools. We should naturally desire that the greatest number of these may be Church Schools. In order that this desirable end may be achieved, the Church, that is to say Churchpeople, have to provide at least 25% of the cost of site and building, in the case of each school.'

Jubilee of the Cricket Club: 'It will no doubt be a fact of some interest to many of our readers that the Sonning Cricket Club this year celebrates the fiftieth anniversary of its founding. It is also an item in parish history, and as such should have some record in our Magazine.'

February 1938

The Vicar's Letter: 'Let me offer you my very best greetings and blessings as I enter upon my twelfth year of my work amongst you; as you all know, February 2nd Candlemas Day, is in a sense my Parochial birthday.'

The Church Lads' Brigade: 'Early in November it was decided to run the Sonning Section of the Dunsden and Sonning Company in Sonning providing enough lads joined. Several meetings were held in the Pearson Hall and by the middle of December the section was 23 lads strong. The Dunsden and Sonning Company is now split into two.'

April 1938
Sonning Parochial Church Council Report for 1937: The council met on five occasions during 1937. The report printed in this issue included the following items:

Churchyard – 'A certain amount of expense has been incurred in the repair of the wall next to the main gate. The question of putting a water tap into the Churchyard was considered, as the cost appeared to be more than was at present justified, a water tub has been placed close to the Church Tower.'

Gifts and Donations – 'The Council is very grateful to the many Parishioners for their gifts and donations, alms bags, flag for the Church Tower, trees, plants, bulbs and the help in pruning and the removal of trees.'

July 1938
The Vicar's Letter: 'How fortunate we were this year with the weather for our Rogation Procession! And we were honoured as usual by being immortalised in the local paper, some of the photographs being exceedingly good. On the same Sunday at Matins two new boys were admitted to the choir. Thanks to Mr. Youngs, admission to our choir is much sought after, that I wonder sometimes whether we shall have room enough to accommodate all the boys.'

Levelling of Graves: 'The Parochial Church Council has asked me to put a note in the Magazine with regard to the proposal to level some of the graves in the lower part of the Churchyard. These graves are all old, but the Council are anxious to consider the feeling of any who may possibly raise objections. The levelling will of course make it much easier to mow the grass on the graves and keep them in good order.'

August 1938
The Vicar's Letter: 'St. Anne's School provided us with a delightful little entertainment in the Pearson Hall on June 24th, in commemoration of the School's fifth birthday.'

'The Great Fete held on behalf of the Hospital at Englefield on June 25th was an unqualified success, largely owing to the gracious presence of H.R.H. The Duchess of Kent.'

Sonning Fire Brigade: 'Having been shewn the new Fire Engine recently, it occurs to me that others might be interested to know what a very up-to-date machine our Brigade now possesses. The Engine is of the enclosed type, the body has been made of steel, so as to be splinter proof, and gas–proof in the event of air-raids. Equipment includes spare wheel carried below the pump, flashing lamp on the front, and flexible steel section tubes. Accommodation is provided for ten or twelve men, and sleeping arrangements can be made if the engine is away from the station for considerable lengths of time.'

September 1938

The International Friendship League: 'This is no rival to the League of Nations; it is rather a Society which sets out to achieve one of the objects of the League of Nations in its own way. The object is the prevention of war; and the method is that of assisting young people of all nations to meet one another, chiefly by means of holiday centres. The Society is voluntary, non-commercial, non-political; it was started in 1931 by a small group of people in the South of England.'

Missions to Seamen: 'We are asked to state that it is hoped to knit articles for the Mission during the winter months. If any of our readers could undertake to help would they please communicate with Mrs. Clement Williams at Shelvingstone. Wool will be provided.'

October 1938

The Vicar's Letter: 'Only just a short message this month, We are passing through an anxious time. May God give us steadfast faith and courage. Above all let us pray for the preservation of peace.'

Our Fire Brigade: 'Members of the Brigade held their annual collection for the Royal Berkshire Hospital on Sunday, August 14th in the Parish of Sonning; also members were stationed at Sonning Lock and Sonning Bridge throughout the day. A sum of £19 6s 0d was collected and sent to the Hospital. Well done, Fire Brigade!'

November 1938

The Vicar's Letter: 'I wonder if any of us have ever been through a more astounding experience than that which we went through on the change from the anxiety of September 28th to the great relief of September 30th. We have indeed the cause to thank God, for it was His hand that surely was at work; as a consequence we are able to throw ourselves heart and soul into our Harvest Thanksgiving services with which were combined Thanksgivings for a deliverance.'

[*This reference was to the signing of the "Munich Agreement", signed on 30 September but dated 29 September 1938, with which the British Prime Minister, Neville Chamberlain, returned to Britain from Munich and declared "peace for our time". Regrettably, peace was not to last and ended with the outbreak of World War II.*]

December 1938

The Vicar's Letter: 'A really happy Christmas, please God, to you all in spite of the problems and difficulties we face in these times. The Remembrance Sunday services were better attended this year than ever, and I was glad to see the Field of Remembrance well filled with crosses. The day, as the years go by, loses nothing of its deep meaning and significance, and its lessons were brought home to us with special solemnity this year. On Armistice Day itself Farnborough School, represented by both the masters and the boys, formed the choir at the 11 o'clock service.'

A Munificent Gift: 'An Archdeacon will often open his daily budget of letters with some trepidation, for even in well ordered parishes like those of Berkshire, there are sometimes problems to be faced and difficulties to be solved; but a few weeks ago as I opened one letter, there tumbled out a cheque for £500 from an anonymous donor for the reconditioning of our Boys' School; needless to say not only the Managers but the whole parish would like to say "Thank you" for such a splendidly generous gift.'

January 1939

The Vicar's Letter: 'The best of good wishes and blessings to you all for the New Year. In this restless and ever-changing world, all who are trying to be real Christians can lean upon One who is unchanging, "Jesus Christ, the same yesterday, and to-day, and for ever". Please note that the collections on Sunday, January 22nd are to be given towards the refugees, who are coming in such large numbers into our country at this present time, and would warmly welcome any help and sympathy we can offer them in their distress.'

Missions to Seamen: 'A parcel was sent early in December to the Mission, containing two pairs of gloves, nine pairs of socks, two scarves, one pair of sea boots the fruits of a band of energetic workers who have been busy knitting for this cause for several months. These workers wish to continue and others wish to join them, but there is a scarcity of wool – perhaps some readers would like to help by supplying some wool.'

[*Although the outbreak of war was several months hence when all able bodied people would be expected to contribute to the "war effort", it was apparent that during peace time many local residents were willing to give time and expertise to help good causes.*]

Air Raid Precautions: 'It is proposed to hold a course of six First Aid Classes at the Pearson Hall early in the New Year; if a class of thirty is guaranteed a doctor (to give the instructions) will be provided by A.R.P., who will defray the cost of the room. Subsequently arrangements may be made for a gas course. Will those wishing to attend the First Aid Classes kindly send in their names to Captain Somerville, Spinney Side, Sonning.'

[*It had been predicted that any future war in which Britain might be engaged could well result in devastating aerial bombing of targets in Britain. As a precaution, recruitment into a volunteer Air Raid Warden Service had been commenced during 1937.*]

March 1939
Sonning Parochial Church Council Report for 1938: The council had held meetings in February, May, October 1938 and January 1939:

The Finance Committee – 'The Diocesan Quota (£94) has been paid in full. New hassocks, hymn books and prayer books have been obtained. The insurance policy now covers damage by non-hostile aircraft.'

The Churchyard Committee – 'The drainage of the path has been improved, and the levelling of the triangular portion of the Churchyard is being put in hand.'

Churchyard Extension – 'The annual expenditure on the upkeep of the new Churchyard will probably amount to £10 to £15.'

Appeal – 'The appeal issued on behalf of the Parochial Funds resulted in the sum of £106 15s. We offer our warmest thanks to our many generous subscribers.'

National Service Guide: 'A copy of the National Service Guide has been delivered to every household throughout the country. Anyone needing further particulars or advice as to how they can help is urged to communicate with the Secretary to the National Service Committee (County of Berkshire) Employment Exchange, Reading.'

April 1939

The Vicar's Letter: 'Let me wish you all a quiet Holy Week, a well kept Good Friday and a very happy Easter. I want to put in a plea for the better observance of Holy Week. It would be a very encouraging sign if more Communicants could take advantage of the opportunities offered them of making their Communion on the first four week days.'

The Pearson Hall: 'The Pearson Hall is in debt. At the end of 1938 the debt was £58 7s 10d. In order to wipe off this debt it is proposed to hold a Jumble Sale in the Hall on Wednesday, May 3rd.'

June 1939

Choir Festival at Windsor: 'On Saturday, May 6th six choir boys and five of our gentlemen of the choir, besides the organist, with several friends, went to St. George's Chapel to take part in a festival Evensong, in which a large number of choirs were singing.'

July 1939

The Schools: 'According to the Title Deeds of our Schools, Foundation Managers have to be elected by the subscribers. Now, unfortunately, we have no subscribers. Are there any parishioners who would care to contribute, say, half-a-crown, in order to qualify as electors of a new Foundation Manager?'

August 1939

The Vicar's Letter: 'The Chief Diocesan Inspector of Schools, the Rev. T. P. Backhouse, visited our Schools on July 11th, and gave us a very encouraging report.'

Vicarage Dilapidations Fund. 'I expect that a good many people will be puzzled when they hear announced on Sunday, August 13th, that the collections are to be given to the Vicarage Dilapidations Fund, and this' at the special request of the Parochial Church Council. Every year a sum of about £40 has to be deducted from the stipend of the Vicar of this Parish for the purpose of keeping the house in good order and repair. Many Parochial Church Councils in this Diocese have most generously helped their clergy by being responsible in part at least, for the payment of dilapidation expenses, and our own Parochial Church Council is making the same gesture, for which I am most grateful.'

September 1939
The Vicar's Letter: 'Congratulations to all those who won prizes at the Swimming Gala in July. Congratulations also to Ian Campbell, from our Boys' School who has been elected to the Blue Coat School in Reading. Also to John Brett, who has won a scholarship at the County School, Maidenhead, and Kenneth Harvey, who has won a place in Sutton's School, Reading.'

October 1939
The Vicar's Letter: 'So the great tragedy has come upon us, and we are at War. A list of those from this Parish who are serving in His Majesty's Forces will be found in another page. Let us all remember them in our prayers, it is just the support they deeply value and appreciate.'

'It is a great pleasure to us all to welcome the London children and their mothers and teachers who are now living amongst us. They have found a happy home at Sonning, and their presence is a great joy and happiness to us, Sonning folk. We are very sorry that Farnborough School has been closed down owing to the war; we shall sadly miss both the staff and the boys.'

'War, or no war, we are in duty bound to thank God for the gifts of the Harvest; our Festival is to be held on October 1st.'

Men serving in Navy, Army and Air Force: 'We wish to have a complete list of those serving in His Majesty's Forces and the names we already know of will be found posted in the North Porch of the Church. If anyone has a relative serving, belonging to Sonning, whose name is not on the list, kindly inform one of the clergy.' There followed a list of twenty men and two women who were already serving in the military.

November 1939

The Vicar's Letter: 'In spite of the war, we had a very happy Harvest Festival on October 1ˢᵗ, and the gifts of flowers and vegetables were larger than expected. The Church was beautifully decorated, perhaps even more effectively than ever. By the sanction of the Bishop we kept our War Intercession Day on Sunday, October 8ᵗʰ instead of on the 1ˢᵗ.

In another part of the Magazine will be found fresh names added to our Roll of Service. May God bless and keep them all. The clergy would be very grateful if they could be told as soon as possible about those actually serving at the Front, or overseas.'

The Sunday School: 'We hope to restart the Sunday School on November 5ᵗʰ at 2.15p.m. instead of 2.45p.m. The Children's Service at 10a.m., which has been attended chiefly by the visiting children, will not be held after October 29ᵗʰ, and we ask all foster parents, as well as parents, to encourage their children to come at 2.15p.m. The regular teachers have already agreed to come at the earlier time.'

December 1939

The Vicar's Letter: 'In spite of the anxious times in which we live, let me wish you all and our London guests a blessed Christmas festival; never did we need more the great Christmas message of Peace and Good-will. Armistice Day was duly kept on November 11ᵗʰ. We missed the Farnborough School Choir that used to help our service so much on that day year by year. But there was a good little gathering of people anxious to keep the two minute silence in Church.'

'As the days get shorter it has been found necessary to consider the question of darkening the Church. Mr. Somerville, our Chief Air Raid Warden, came down on November 10ᵗʰ to give his valuable advice.'

Waste Paper: 'The saving of waste paper is important for the national economy in war-time. Accordingly we are asking all Sonning people to save all old newspapers, magazines, cardboard, circulars and envelopes. Mr. Vinter of the Manor, has kindly offered accommodation for all such until enough has been accumulated for the official collectors to fetch away.'

CHAPTER EIGHT

1940 -1945

D
ue to war-time paper supply restrictions, the pages within the magazine, which had been contained to four for several years, were soon to be further reduced to a mere quarto size single leaf of two pages. The letterpress printing process continued to be used to produce the issues, in which no advertisements appeared. There is no reference as to whether a charge was made for copies of the magazine in its reduced form. Separate inset magazines had not been mentioned for some time, it would appear to have been unlikely that such additions would have been available during these difficult times.

The content of the war-time issues carried very little information about the conflict. Such omissions were no doubt due partly to parishioners being far more able to keep themselves informed through improved news communication, particularly via their wireless set. However, strict censorship of sensitive information that may have aided the enemy was in force, these restrictions would have clearly impacted upon the reporting of events. A specific example was the bombing raid by a lone German aircraft upon Reading during 1943. The location of the raid was reported in national newspapers as having taken place on a "Home Counties town". Further noticeable omissions from the magazine during WWII were reports upon many local social and sporting events. However, with as many as one hundred and fifty local men and women engaged in the armed forces, many such activities in Sonning and neighbouring parishes were understandably suspended.

Both of the Sonning incumbents, who served as vicars during the hostilities, used the limited space which was available in the magazine to encourage parishioners to strengthen their faith during the testing times through which they were passing.

1939 - Sept. 3	Britain and France declare war on Germany
1940 - Jan 7	Rationing of basic food in Britain
1940 - May 9	Conscription in Britain extended to age of 36
1940 - May 10	Winston Churchill becomes British Prime Minister
1940 - May 14	Local Defence Force (The Home Guard) commences
1940 - May 25	British troops retreat to Dunkirk prior to evacuation
1940 - July 10	Germany launches air attacks - "The Battle of Britain"
1940 - Sept 22	Germany, Italy and Japan sign Tripartite Pact
1941 - Jun 22	Germany invades Soviet Union
1941 - Dec 7	Japanese attack USA Navy in Pearl Harbor
1941 - Dec 8	USA declares war on Japan
1942 - Feb 15	Singapore surrenders to Japanese
1942 - May 20	Burma falls to Japanese
1942 - Sept 3	Battle of Stalingrad commences
1943 - May 13	German Afrika Korps in North Africa surrender to Allies
1943 - May 16	Dambuster Raids on Mohne and Eder dams
1943 - Sept 3	Allies invade Italy and Italy sign armistice
1944 - June 5/6	Operation "Overload". D-Day landings commence
1944 - June 13	Germany launch VI flying-bombs on England
1944 - Aug 25	Paris liberated
1944 - Sept 9	First V2 rockets land on London
1944 - Dec 3	British Home Guard stood down
1945 - May 8	Germany surrender - VE Day (Victory Europe)
1945 - Aug 6	USA drop first atomic bomb on Hiroshima, Japan
1945 - Aug 15	Japan surrender - VJ Day (Victory Japan)

A timeline of several important happenings during the Second World War.

January 1940

The Vicar's Letter:

'It is proposed to have a short service on New Year's Day in the Pearson Hall before the dance begins. In these difficult days, we not only need to have our lives brightened by happy social gatherings, but also to have our wills strengthened by the grace of God for all that may be in front of us during the coming year, which we hope and pray may be a year that brings with it true and lasting peace.'

Missions to Seamen: 'A number of clothing articles have been knitted by parishioners and have been gratefully acknowledged by the Mission; 17 pairs socks, 2 pairs steering gloves, 2 pairs cuffs, 1 scarf, 1 pair sea boot stockings.'

February 1940

The Vicar's Letter:

'I hope it may be possible especially if summer-time comes in earlier, to resume the Sunday Evensong at 6.30 p.m. In spite of the black-out I believe the change will be welcome to most of our Sunday evening worshippers.'

'The Girls' Day School has been reinforced by the appointment of a Supply Teacher, Mrs. Rose, who is in charge of the Infant Department. This means that all our children and also the London children have now full-time school hours.'

'We have pleasure in welcoming to the village the members of the Royal Veterinary College, with its headquarters at Holme Park.'

Roll of Service: The names of ten further local men have been added to the list as recruits to the military.

Children's Christmas Party: 'This event, somewhat enlarged for this year owing to our visitors from London, was held in the Pearson Hall, on January 2nd. A Tea, which equalled in quality, and exceeded in quantity, its predecessors, was followed by a display of conjuring and ventriloquism, and both, we understand, were thoroughly enjoyed.'

March 1940

The Vicar's Letter:

'Rather naturally, owing to the bitter weather, we had a smaller attendance than usual at our Vestry and Annual Parochial Church Meetings. But it was a pleasant and friendly gathering, and the Balance Sheet showed an encouraging surplus.'

'Confirmation classes are in full swing, we hope to have a good number of candidates to present to the Bishop of Dorchester on May 5th.'

Soldiers', Sailors', Airmen's Families' Association: 'Mrs. Clement Williams, of Shelvingstone, has most kindly agreed to undertake to act as the Correspondent for the parish of Sonning, and wives of serving men requiring information, advice or assistance, should in the first instance apply to her.'

Appeal: 'On the initiative of Toc H a house has been rented at 160 Friar Street, Reading where men of the Services, and others transferred to Reading as a result of the war, can find a welcome and the hand of friendship. Talbot House as it will be named, will be open all day and every evening, being staffed by a rota, of volunteer workers. Money and furniture is urgently required. Donations, or promises of regular financial support will be gratefully acknowledged.'

Sonning Parochial Church Council – Report for 1939.
The report included the following comments:

'The war, which has been forced upon us, has, of course, affected us as well as the rest of the Nation. We are proud of the long list of men and women who from this village are serving their King and Country.

It is hoped that the new Church Senior School at Wargrave will be opened during the year and in that case, if war circumstances permit, our Boys' School will have to be entirely reconstructed as a Junior Mixed and Infants' School.'

May 1940

The Vicar's Letter:

'The war has now entered on a more serious and searching phase. All the more reason surely for our prayers and intercession both at home and in Church to be deeper and more intense.'

Gas Helmets for Infants: 'Capt. Somerville, our Head Air Raid Warden, wishes it to be known that all mothers who have babies up to two years old and who have not yet received an anti-gas helmet for them, can do so by applying to Mr. H. Morton, Grove End. A further supply of "Mickey Mouse" respirators for children between two and three years old will be available shortly.'

Sonning and Woodley Nursing Association: 'A Rummage Sale in aid of the above will be held in the Pearson Hall on Wednesday, May 8th at 3 p.m.'

June 1940
The Vicar's Letter:
'The war waxes fast and furious, and many more nations and people are being involved. It is encouraging to know that the National Prayers Sunday was inaugurated at the request of His Majesty the King - God help us to keep our minds steady and trustful.'

'What a glorious day we had for our Confirmation, and what a glorious service it was! The Church was packed and all present, not only the Candidates, were much stirred by the stimulating address of the Bishop of Dorchester. Our candidates numbered 45 in all - 17 boys and 28 girls.'

'I take this opportunity to remind Parishioners that all the designs for monuments in the Churchyard should be submitted to me before any discussion with a monumental mason takes place. The Vicar of the Parish is responsible for monuments being suitable for the Churchyard, and they should be, if possible, of British make.'

Women's Institute: 'The Sonning W. I. monthly meeting was held in the Pearson Hall during Tuesday, April 9th. The annual egg collection was made and 157 eggs were sent to the Berkshire Hospital.'

July 1940
The Vicar's Letter:
'The war comes every day closer and closer to us; God grant we meet any trials we have to face with courage and faith.'
'Largely through the efforts of many good friends and particularly our

Treasurer, Gen. Phipps-Hornby, the electric light has been installed in the Pearson Hall. The larger part of the cost has practically been met.'
'I am only sending a short message this month, as the contents of our Magazine through shortage of paper must be considered reduced.'
[*The magazine now comprised of one leaf (two pages).*]

Red Cross House to House Collection: 'A cheque for £28 9s 6d has been forwarded to the Red Cross Fund. Very grateful thanks are due to the collectors who so kindly gave their time and trouble to this essential work, also to all who subscribed so generously.'

August 1940
The Vicars Letter:
'War-time inevitably brings many troubles and anxieties, but it also leads us to our knees in prayer. I am very grateful to the Mothers' Union for suggesting a weekly War Intercession Service on Thursdays at 3p.m. This will help to keep us all faithful and steadfast to the end.'

Roll of Service: The names of twenty-three further local men were listed as recruits to the military.

War Defence:
'The Village of Sonning, like a large number of other villages in England, Scotland and Wales has been put in a state of defence. Pill boxes and sandbag fortments (*sic*) have been placed at certain points. Some people take it as a joke that Sonning should ever be attacked, but this is far from being the case. I am far from being a pessimist. I am confident, in the end, we shall win, but only if everyone of us take a hand in defeating the Germans. To do that it is the duty of every man who calls himself a man, to take his place in the defence of his village and his home. I appeal to every man in Sonning between the ages of 17 and 65 to join the L.D.V.'s at once. We want every man we can get.'
E .J. Phipps-Hornby,
Brig. Genl. Commanding Sonning Platoon L.D.V.

Scrap Iron Collection in Sonning: 'Sonning Residents will be glad to know that the recent collection of scrap iron met with a most satisfactory response and nearly eight large lorry loads were collected for the war

effort. The A.R.P. Wardens kindly undertook the canvas of the village
and our grateful thanks are due to them and to all those who
contributed so willingly.'

L.D.V. (Local Defence Volunteers): 'Knitted pullovers, scarves and mittens
(half-fingers) are wanted *at once* for the above men, who cannot afford
to get their own. The nights are getting colder and the men have to be
in exposed positions. All who can help, either by donations or knitting
the woollies for the men of Sonning and Woodley please apply to: Mrs.
Phipps-Hornby or Mrs. Parmiter. Wool can be supplied at five shillings
per lb.'

September 1940
The Vicars Letter:
'It is unfortunate that the Death Watch beetle should have made its
unpleasant appearance once more in our Church, especially at this
critical time, when the Church is needed more than ever for quiet and
intercession.   But the beetle's ravages have been promptly and
efficiently countered, and there has been no disturbance with our
Sunday Services.'

Berkshire L.D.V.:
'There are still a few men in and around Sonning Village who have not
as yet joined the L.D.V. Perhaps they think it unnecessary to do so.
They may think there is no chance of an attack on this village. That
may be so. On the other hand a sure way to prevent any attack, that
may be made, from being successful is to be prepared for it. No man
can help in the defences unless he has been trained, knows his place,
how to get to it and what to do when he gets there. No man would be
allowed at the last moment to join in the defences who had not received
previous training. He would be a greater danger to his own side than to
the enemy. In speaking of the defence of Sonning we are not so much
thinking of the bricks and mortar as of the honour of our women and
children.
Surely no man, when he realises what is at stake, will hold back for one
minute. We ask every man to join us NOW.'
E J. Phipps-Hornby,
Commanding Sonning Co., L.D.V.

October 1940

The Vicar's Letter:

'We duly kept our Day of National Prayer on September 8th, and there were good congregations though some had to be absent on necessary duties. What a blessing it is for a nation like ours that His Majesty the King should care so much for the spiritual welfare of his subjects. May God ever preserve him and keep him from all danger.'

'During this month there are to be many School changes. Our Boys' School becomes a School for Junior mixed and infants, the elder children going to Wargrave or Woodley Senior Schools, the Girls' School being closed.'

Sonning Fire Brigade: 'As Saturday, September 7th, 1940, was the first occasion on which the Sonning Fire Brigade has officially operated outside its own recognised boundaries, it would seem well worth while not only for the benefit of the present readers of the Parish Magazine, but also as a record for future reference, to place in print a brief record of their activities on that memorable occasion. The call to report at a Station on the west outskirts of London was received at 9.30p.m., and on arriving at their Station, they were joined by a large number of other Brigades, many of whom were drawn from this County. After a short halt, the journey through the City and the East End of London to the Dock area was continued, and during the latter part of this journey, and while at work in the Docks, they were subjected to bombing from German aircraft, but fortunately sustained no casualties. After completing seven hours continuous pumping, they were relieved and returned again to Sonning, arriving home at 4.30p.m. on Sunday, September 8th.'

November 1940

The Vicar's Letter:

'The new Senior Church School at Wargrave was opened on September 17th by the Lord Lieutenant and dedicated by the Bishop of the Diocese. There was a large gathering present, many of whom took the opportunity of inspecting the various classrooms, etc. It is a School of which the Church may well be proud, and serves eight parishes.'

[*The Piggott School, Wargrave was named after the philanthropist Robert Piggott.*]

The Parish Magazine: 'We appeal to readers of this Magazine to make its existence known to the many newcomers in Sonning. An increase in circulation would be welcome; and a postcard to Miss Davis, Playhatch, will ensure its regular delivery every month.'

December 1940

The Vicar's Letter:

'I can hardly in present circumstances wish you a "merry" Christmas, but I do send my best blessings for the great Festival, which always reminds us of the Christian ideal "peace and goodwill". Owing to the morning black-out it will not be possible to have more than one early celebration on Christmas Day, and that will be at 8.30a.m. The same applies to all the early celebrations during December.'

'The canteen for the troops stationed here was opened on October 28th. The Pearson Hall was crowded. We are sorry to have lost the men commanded by Major Wicks; they were a kindly lot, and deeply grateful and appreciative of all that was done for them in the village. They were regular in their attendance at the 11 a.m. service on Sunday mornings.'

'Our Fire Brigade have again been distinguishing themselves by being summoned to Birmingham to cope with fires there. We wish them all "good luck in the name of the Lord".'

January 1941

The Vicar's Letter:

'Please accept my best wishes and blessings for the New Year. Let us pray that 1941 will bring us victory and a just and lasting peace.'

'Owing to the black-out difficulties, it has been decided that the annual Vestry and Parochial Church Meetings shall be held in the Pearson Hall on Sunday, January 26th, at 12.15p.m. immediately after the 11 o'clock service in Church.'

March 1941

The Vicar's Letter:

'R.I.P. – Bernard Abbott (R.A.F.) late of the Charvil Post Office, is the first on our Roll of Honour to lay down his life for his country. He was buried here on February 11th, with the Union Jack covering his coffin, and four airmen acting as bearers.'

[*The interment is recorded in – Record of Burials etc., - St. Andrew's Church 2012.*]

'Our hearty congratulations to our late Parishioner, Capt. Palliser, R.N., Commanding H.M.S. Malaya, on his share in the recent great attack on Genoa.'

May 1941
The Vicar's Letter:
'The Day of National Prayer and Thanksgiving was duly observed here on March 23rd. It was an encouraging sign that so many young people came to make their Communion both at 7 and 8 o'clock on that day. May the prayers and thanksgivings there offered help us true and steadfast in the grim struggle which is in front of us and of our brave allies.'

The Wargrave Senior School: 'Parents of Sonning children over 11 are strongly urged to send their children to this School: the distance is not really very great especially for the young and active, and the children will have the advantage not only of carrying on the Church teaching of their old School, but will also have the privilege of joining one of the finest and up-to-date Senior Schools in the neighbourhood. Please, parents, go and pay it a visit.'

June 1941
The Vicar's Letter:
'The annual collections and sermons for the Church Missionary Society will be given on Trinity Sunday, June 8th. I am sorry but owing to war conditions we shall not have the privilege of listening to a real live Missionary.'

Women's Institute: 'The monthly meeting took place on Tuesday, April 8th. The Government scheme for the making of surplus fruit into jam was discussed, and a small collection of eggs was made for the Royal Berkshire Hospital. The speaker at the meeting held on Tuesday, May 13th, was Miss Doris Hole who gave a talk on "How to manage a small garden".'

August 1941

Air Training Corps: 'An A.T.C. Flight has been formed at the Senior School and instruction is being given on both Tuesday and Thursday Evenings from 7.15 - 9.15p.m. Any youths between 15 and 18 years are eligible to join and will be welcomed. Instructions will be given in the following subjects; Mathematics, Physical Training, Signalling, Air Craft construction, Engines, and all subjects relative to R.A.F. training.'

September 1941

The Vicar's Letter:
'His Majesty the King has asked that Sunday, September 7th, shall be observed as a special Day of Prayer and Thanksgiving in connection with the war. Needless to say we shall all loyally and faithfully carry out his wishes, as we have tried to do on other such solemn occasions.'

'As consequence of the war-time difficulties of our Diocesan Inspectors, Mr. Roberts and I have been conducting the religious inspection of our Village School. The result, on the whole, has been quite satisfactory and encouraging.'

November 1941

The Vicar's Letter:
'On Sunday, September 21st we offered up our Thanksgivings for the victory of the R.A.F. in the "Battle of Britain" last year. On Sunday, September 28th the Civil Defence Workers came in force to Church at 11 o'clock, and we were all glad to welcome them. We hope soon to have a parade of the Home Guard. Then on Sunday, October 5th we kept our Harvest Festival.'

Women's Institute: 'The monthly meeting of the W.I. was held on Tuesday, October 14th. As a result of the Institute Potato competition 74-lbs. were sent to the Royal Berkshire Hospital.'

December 1941

The Vicar's Letter:
'Let me wish you all every blessing for Christmas; this great Festival with its message of peace and goodwill comes home to us more than ever in the stern days through which we are passing.'

'There seemed to be an even larger congregation at the special service held on Remembrance Sunday, November 9th. This is indeed a good sign, as it shews we have not forgotten the brave men who died for us in the last war, while still remembering those who have fallen in battle or been killed in air raids during the present war. The collection for Earl Haigh's Fund amounted to just over £10. At the end of the service the Russian Christian National Anthem was sung.'

Appeal for Books: 'Miss Peel of the Red Cross Hospital Libraries would be grateful for books, which are needed for forces and civilian hospital patients. Books may be sent to Miss Armine Williams at Shelvingstone.

January 1942
The Vicar's Letter:
'May 1942, under God's good hand, bring us and our allies victory and a lasting peace.'

'Please forgive me if at this stage I say very little about my proposed departure at Eastertide. You will all understand what a grievous wrench it will be to my sister and to myself to leave Sonning, where everybody has been so extraordinarily kind, and where we have been privileged to make hosts of friends. But "Anno Domini" is a serious fact, and has to be faced sooner or later.'

March 1942
The Vicar's Letter:
'I need not say how much we all wish Godspeed to the Rev. Roberts on his appointment as Rector of Woughton-on-the-Green a small parish near Bletchley in the northern part of Buckinghamshire, where there is a nice parsonage and a beautiful Church. It is hard to part with him after his twelve years of service to Sonning, but it is only right that he should have by this time an independent sphere of his own. I am thankful to be able to say that he will be staying with us until after Easter Day. Our prayers go out to him and Mrs. Roberts, that they may be richly blessed in their new life and home.'

'In our war prayers just now let us specially remember our fighting forces, and those of our allies, in the Far East.'

Sonning Women's Institute: 'The monthly meeting was held on January 13th, when a Cookery Demonstration was given by Mrs. Cummings, and many valuable hints, chiefly on the cooking of vegetables, were given to members.'

April 1942
The Vicar's Letter:
'I am afraid it will not be possible in the circumstances to pay you all a visit before I leave, but I am sure you will take the will for the deed. Some of you may be able to come to Church on April 12th when I shall be officiating for the last time as Vicar of the Parish. This will give me an opportunity of saying "Farewell" to many of you. Meanwhile God's blessing be upon you all.'

A Message from Rev. C. A. M. Roberts: 'I cannot lay down the task of editing the Parish Magazine for so long without saying a big word of gratitude, and a smaller one of farewell, to its readers and to the parishioners of Sonning. Your kindness to my wife and myself during our stay here makes our departure a mixture of regret and happy memories.
I ask all those, and I fear they will be many, whom I do not manage to see before I leave, to accept this "goodbye" in its proper sense of "God be with you".'
[*Roberts was clearly the magazine's editor for a long period. Although Wickham Legg was no doubt the author of "The Vicar's Letter", it would appear that unlike most or perhaps all of his predecessors, Wickham Legg appeared not to have taken overall charge of editorial matters.*]

The New Vicar: 'Your prayers are desired for Sydney John Selby Groves, who has been appointed Vicar of this Parish. He has been the devoted Vicar of Sunningdale since 1932, and he can be assured of a warm welcome from us all.'

Warship Week: 'Sonning is to be congratulated on the result of Warship Week. It is splendid that a village of our size should have contributed over £88,000.'
[*Warship Week was a National Savings campaign for the adoption of a Royal Navy warship by a civilian community.*]

June 1942
The Vicar's Letter:

The new Vicar, Sidney John Selby Groves, introduced himself to the Sonning parishioners in this issue: 'Mr. Hartley has kindly invited me to write a few words for your Parish Magazine. As you know, the Lord Bishop has appointed me to succeed the well-beloved Archdeacon as your Vicar. I am deeply conscious of the honour conferred upon me, and fully realise how difficult it will be to live up to the high standard of pastoral work maintained by him and my old friend, Mr. Roberts.

I hope most earnestly that you will all be able to attend my institution at the hands of the Bishop of Reading, fixed for seven o'clock in the evening of Friday July 12th.'

July 1942
The Vicar's Letter:

'I know that all those who attended the service of my institution and induction last Friday must have been deeply impressed by its solemnity and by the dignity and beauty with which the Bishop of Reading conducted it. I was greatly cheered to find such a large gathering both of my brother clergy and of the parishioners assembled to take part in the solemn rite.'

'I wish to thank you for giving me such a kindly welcome here, and to the Archdeacon for providing me with so much assistance, information and encouragement. I hope by degrees to visit every home in the parish and to know you all personally - needless to say, this will take some time. In the larger world outside the parish, the clouds of war do not show much sign of passing away. We Christians have the particular contribution of constant intercession to make to our cause, and the passage of time must not damp our enthusiasm or slacken our exertions in prayer.'

August 1942
The Vicar's Letter:

'We were glad to welcome you to the Dance on the Vicarage lawn on July 8th, when the sum of £19 10s. was raised for the Red Cross. A similar party is being arranged for Bank Holiday, when the proceeds will go to the Royal Berkshire Hospital.

In this issue you will see the list of men and women serving with the Forces divided up into sections, one of which is allotted to each day of the month. The list is too long to be read out in its entirety, but the names for each day will be read out on that day at the Church services, and you are asked to remember them on that particular day also in your private prayers. Thus all those serving will be remembered by name once a month. I think you will find this is a good and helpful plan; you should inform your relations in the Forces of the day on which they will be remembered, so that they may know that they have the prayers and thoughts of Sonning folk with them.'

[*The list comprised of 137 men and women serving in the Army, Navy, Air Force, A.T.S, W.A.A.F and W.R.N.S.*]

October 1942

The Vicar's Letter:

'It was a great encouragement to see the Church so full for the evening service on the National Day of Prayer. The experiment of holding it on a week-day was amply justified, for from all parts of the country comes the news that the day was better observed than similar occasions in the last three years. We may enter on the fourth winter of the war with renewed faith and sober trust; for the sake, particularly, of the oppressed peoples on the continent, let us pray that it may be the last winter before victory is ours.'

Wargrave Piggott C.E. Senior School: A listing of income and expenditure relating to a number of past years was printed under the heading of "Proposers' Final Accounts": 'In addition to voluntary contributions received in cash, the Proposers gratefully record the gift of the site, the electric clocks on the clock turret and in every room, the principal gates, the motto over the principal door, the orchard fruit trees, the garden shrubs, the roses, the rock plants, the greenhouse and the potting shed; the Bible and the Reading Desk for the Assembly Hall.'

December 1942

The Vicar's Letter:

'Every available seat was occupied for the Armistice commemoration, when tribute was paid to the gallant dead in a service which, I am glad to know, was universally felt to be memorable and inspiring. Sunday,

November 15th was again a memorable occasion when our beautiful peal of bells broke their long silence and summoned us to an act of thanksgiving for the victory of our arms in North Africa. The church was again filled, and a spirit of joy and hope was evident.'

'Our thoughts will later be of Christmas; we shall be meeting all our absent friends – those away on active service and those in Paradise – as we worship the Babe of Bethlehem on His Altar-Throne.'

January 1943
The Vicar's Letter:
'May I take this opportunity of wishing you every blessing in the New Year; may 1943 bring peace to our tortured world and bring all men nearer to the heavenly Father.'

'The Annual Church Meeting will be convened in the Schools on the evening of Wednesday, January 27th, at 7.45p.m. This is a meeting to which all whose names are included on the electoral roll should attend. Parishioners who have not enrolled should obtain a form from the Verger, fill it up and return it no later than January 13th.'

February 1943
The Vicar's Letter:
'I feel sure that our Christmas services were a source of great joy to all who took part in them. The church was beautifully decorated; the new arrangement of the Crib and the Children's Corner was, as far as I can gather, universally approved.'

'I am most grateful to all those who helped to make our Children's Party the success it appears to have been. Our particular thanks are due to the Principal and Staff of the Veterinary College who placed Holme Park at our disposal, and to Mrs. Grigg and her helpers who supplied such a plentiful and sumptuous tea.'

Red Cross: 'On behalf of the choristers concerned I would like to thank everybody who gave so generously to the Choir Carol Party. A sum of £25 0s 5d was collected and handed to the Red Cross Prisoners of War Parcel Fund.'

March 1943

Sonning Parochial Church Council – Report for 1942:

'Special Services were held in Lent, and in connection with various events of national importance; Days of Prayer on March 29 and September 3, the Harvest Festival on September 27, Remembrance Sunday on November 8, the Libyan Victory on November 15. On the latter occasion, as well as on Christmas Day, our peal of bells broke their war-time silence.

The Venerable R. Wickham Legg resigned the charge of the Parish at Easter, and the Lord Bishop appointed as his successor the Rev. S. J. S. Groves, Vicar of Sunningdale. The Rev. C. A. M. Roberts, who had been Assistant Curate of Sonning since 1930, also left the Parish at Easter.

The Mothers' Union holds regular meetings each month either in Church or the Vicarage, and Miss Wickham Legg has been succeeded by Mrs. Groves as Enrolling Member. The Sunday School also meets regularly every Sunday afternoon, the average attendance is 60.

The social activities of the Parish are still severely handicapped as a result of the requisitioning of the Pearson Hall for use as a Rest Centre during the war.

The Church Day Schools, although reduced in numbers, continue to flourish.

The Church Accounts show a considerably decreased balance in hand, due partly to the large reduction in the subscriptions received. This may be attributable to the ever present calls for help for objects connected to the War Effort, also the very generous response to the presentations to the outgoing Clergy.

Consideration of the use of part of the Church as a Side-Chapel for daily service and for plans for the furnishing thereof has been unanimously agreed by the Council.'

War Fatalities: It was recorded that Christopher Ronald Young and Sidney John Dean, both of the R.A.F. had been killed on active service.

April 1943

Pearson Hall: 'A Committee Meeting was convened at the Vicarage on March 3rd. The Vicar reported that he had written an urgent letter to the Public Assistance Department, asking for the release of the Hall for use by the parish, but that his request had been courteously, but quite definitely, refused. This has been the consistent attitude of the department. The Committee, therefore, feel that it is useless to make any further efforts to secure its release.'

War Fatalities: Captain Ronald Leese had been killed on active service.

May 1943

Wings for Victory Week, May 15–22: 'A programme of church services and entertainment events were listed for war fund raising. The events included a Flying Demonstration and Exhibition on the Recreation Ground, "tank-ambush" by the local Home Guard, a Whist-Drive, an Open Air Dance and Horse Show in Holme Park.'

Blood Transfusion: 'Donors of blood are urgently needed for supplies to the troops at home and those abroad, for civilian hospitals and R.A.F. Stations. The operation is quite harmless and painless. 300 pints were used in an air-raid on a well known town in February.'

[*This is the only reference, albeit obscure, to a German air-craft raid on Reading during the afternoon of Wednesday, February 10th, when 41 were killed and over 100 injured.*]

June 1943

The Vicar's Letter:

'I am deeply grateful to all of you who contributed to the very generous Easter offering, which amounted to £61 8s 5d and one and a quarter pounds of tobacco! It was most good of you to treat a newcomer with such open handed largesse.'

'Since Easter, the news of the complete victory of the Allied Forces in Tunisia has come to increase our hope and joy, and to stimulate our giving and lending to our country in "Wings for Victory" Week.'

Victory Produce Show: 'The Show in aid of the Red Cross is to be held on the Recreation Ground on Saturday, August 14th.'

Wings for Victory Week: 'We congratulate all those who were responsible for arranging and carrying out the very excellent programme of events to stimulate our enthusiasm for this important local effort to increase War Savings, and we hope that a very substantial sum has been raised to assist the Allied campaign.'

Reading and Berkshire Nursery Council: 'Will you please give your scrap materials, ribbons, cotton reels, buttons, to make toys for the children in the War-time Day Nurseries of Reading and Berkshire.'

July 1943

The Vicar's Letter:

'The year that has passed since I was instituted as your vicar has slipped by very quickly; although I have been to every house in the parish there are many of you whom I have not yet succeeded in meeting.'

'There are signs that the Chapel may soon be ready for dedication and use. The Altar, the Cross and Candlesticks, and the Credence Table have already been given or promised, while the Jacobean Benches from the Vestry will form the Communion Rails. We shall need, however, at least two fair linen cloths for the altar, and a carpet for the sanctuary to blend with the blue curtain in the screen behind.'

Missing on Active Service: 'We greatly regret to learn that Norman Collins and Frederick Pym, both of the R.A.F., have been reported "missing".'

August 1943

The Vicar's Letter:

'We all rejoice at the initial success of the Sicilian expedition, and are following our men and our leaders with our prayers that this beginning of the invasion of Europe may speedily lead to the complete destruction of the enemy's power.'

'The White Paper containing the Government's post-war educational proposals, has appeared this morning. At a first glance, these proposals appear moderately progressive and fair to all concerned. The dual system incorporating the church schools, remains, and provision for religious instruction in all schools is made. The raising of the school age to fifteen (ultimately to sixteen), and the opening of secondary education to all at the age of eleven are reforms that we must all approve.'

On Active Service: 'We are delighted to congratulate Group Captain Grindell, R.A.F., on winning the D.F.C. also Cecil Todd on being mentioned in despatches.'

Victory Produce Show: 'Please remember the Red Cross Victory Show to be held on the Recreation Ground on Saturday, August 4.'

September 1943

The Vicar's Letter:

'The victorious completion of our campaign in Sicily, the successes in the Royal Navy against the U-boats, the progress of the Allies in Russia will all add a note of special thanksgiving to the religious observance of the fourth anniversary of the opening of hostilities, which we shall be observing on September 3rd. The divine guidance and help to us during these four years of war has been constant and manifest, and calls for our constant and public recognition.'

October 1943

The Vicar's Letter:

'September has been a month of much thanksgiving; a bountiful harvest has been gathered in, and the allied forces continue to advance on all fronts. In spite of this, we are all warned that there must be no slackening of the war effort nor any undue optimism.'

'We shall have the "black-out" again with us this winter, which means that from the middle of October Evensong on Sundays must be at 3.45p.m. I hope and trust that the evening congregations will make a greater effort this winter to adapt themselves to the change.'

The Chapel: 'All, we feel confident, will agree that the furnishing of the South Chancel Aisle as a Chapel has added dignity and beauty to our ancient church. Those who use it will, we hope, love it more and more as time goes on.'

November 1943

The Vicar's Letter:

'I naturally share the universal pleasure felt at the possibility of using the Pearson Hall once more for parochial activities, and I feel sure that we shall have many delightful gatherings in its walls during the winter, though we shall miss the presence of the boys and girls who are away on service with the Forces. May this be the last war-winter!'

December 1943

The Vicar's Letter:

'The Sunday evening services seem to be meeting an important need and providing a real sense of fellowship, bringing us closer together (spiritually, I hope, as well as physically) and improving the quality and increasing the volume of the singing.'

Social Club: 'A successful gathering, attended by about eighty "young people" of all ages, was held at the Pearson Hall on November 23rd. After a most interesting and informative speech by Miss McConnell, of the Berkshire Education Authority, on the activities of social clubs in the County and the possibility ahead of them, a resolution to proceed with the formation of such a club in Sonning was carried unanimously. We shall be grateful for any gifts of games suitable for playing in the hall – e.g., Chess, Draughts, Cards, Ping-pong, bats and balls, Bagatelle.'

January 1944
The Vicar's Letter:
'We can look forward to the New Year with every confidence that it will bring peace to Europe, and freedom and food to the populations lying under the cruel rule of the German aggressor. Nevertheless, as we have been warned, it will probably be a year of stern fighting and heavy sacrifices. We must continue to sustain our fighting forces not only with the material munitions of war, but also with the spiritual weapon of constant intercession.'

Missing on Active Service: 'We regret to learn that John Harris has been reported missing; we express are heart-felt sympathy with his parents and hope that they will soon hear good news of him.'

Social Club: 'The open Social on December 8th was a real success and was greatly enjoyed by the hundred or more who attended. To date we have a membership of seventy and the Club evenings have gone well.'

March 1944
The Vicar's Letter:
'The warfare against evil is a "global" struggle, and must be waged against every form of evil. The physical warfare against Nazism is only part of the age-long struggle of God and Good against the devil and all his myrmidons. We must wage war on all fronts, as Christ our Saviour did. "By the finger of God I cast out devils," and only so can we.'

Sonning Parochial Church Council – Report for 1943:

The report to the annual general meeting held on 25th January 1944 included the following:

'During the year twenty-nine infants received Holy Baptism; six candidates were presented for Confirmation; the Easter communicants numbered 202.

Special services were held in connection with various important events; Wings for Victory Week on May 16, Blessing of the Crops on May 30, The National Day of Prayer on September 3, Thanksgiving for the surrender of Italy on September 12, the Harvest Festival on September 19 and Remembrance Sunday on November 7.

The furnishing of the South Chancel Aisle as a Chapel has been completed to the design of the Warham Guild and adds, we believe, to the beauty of our ancient church. The Chapel was dedicated and the Altar consecrated by the Bishop of Reading.

The ban on the ringing of the church bells was removed at Easter, and peals have been rung as often as the exigencies of war-work have permitted.

The Church Day Schools continue their excellent work and have received most favourable reports from His Majesty's Inspector and from the Diocesan Inspector.

The advantage has been taken of the partial release of the Pearson Hall for parochial purposes to start a social club, open to all parishioners over school-age.'

May 1944

The Vicar's Letter:

'I must express my warmest thanks to you all for the magnificent Easter offering which has been handed over to me this year. The total reached £70, which is even larger than last year's amount. I most deeply appreciate this, your renewed and increased generosity, and thank you, one and all, for your gifts.'

'We are bracing ourselves now for the final assault on Hitler's fortress, and shall be dedicating ourselves anew to the cause next Sunday, the Feast of our Patron Saint George. We shall do so with the renewed confidence that comes from Easter, and shall be constantly accompanying with our prayers the allied forces, as they go forward to the liberation of enslaved and tortured Europe.'

Roll of Service: A revised list of the men and women who had entered into the armed forces was printed in this issue. It was noted that within the list six had been killed in action, four were missing and three were confirmed as prisoners of war.

June 1944

The Vicar's Letter:

'We live in the midst of great events and on the eve, we are assured, of greater events in the drama of world history. The feasts of the Christian year, which are kept at this season, are not remote from this historic pageant, but each has its message pertinent to the occasion.'

'It has been my privilege to take part in the centenary celebrations of St. Peter's Church, Earley, and to take to our daughter church the good wishes and congratulations of the mother parish on her 100th birthday.'

July 1944

The Vicar's Letter:

'Our hopes of a speedy victory and the liberation of the enslaved peoples of Europe are higher than they have ever been during the war; we are now trying to "salute the soldier" as he battles on to Berlin. The freedom of Rome and the launching of the invasion was marked by a special service in Church on June 6th. I feel sure that we shall all do our best to assist our cause, both by saving and investing our money and also by a sustained effort of prayer, both in private and public.'

Salute the Soldier Week: The Government's national fund raising scheme included an invitation to the public to invest in a range of state savings bonds and savings certificates. Sonning's contribution resulted in a massive £100,000, doubling the target of £50,000.

September 1944

The Vicar's Letter:

'History is being made so quickly as I write that any comments I make may possibly be completely out-of-date by the time that you read them. This summer is witnessing the reversal of events of 1940 in the West, and those of 1939 and 1941 in the East. Every heart is filled with gratitude for our recent successes on all our numerous fronts and with hope for a complete victory at no distant date. We shall therefore keep the fifth anniversary of the outbreak of the war, which is to be observed as a National Day of prayer and dedication, with ready spontaneity. As September 3rd falls this year on a Sunday, all of us should use the opportunity of joining in at least one of the services on the day.'

War Fatalities: 'It is with regret that we have to record the death in action of Joseph Snowball, of Charville House Road, while Lester Guy, of Pound Lane, has been reported missing.'

Sonning Women's Institute: 'The August meeting was held in the garden of The Pippin. A Whist Drive and Dance to help the St. Barnardo's Homes was arranged for September 15th, and names were taken of those members volunteering to knit post-war garments for children in occupied countries. Books bound and gloves made by members were on view and greatly admired.'

October 1944
The Vicar's Letter:
'Our feelings of gratitude and hope were expressed to our Heavenly Father by the large congregations which met together in church on the fifth anniversary of our entry into the war. The path to victory may yet be steep and lengthy, but the end is now sure, thanks to God's help and the indomitable will and courage of our fighting forces.
It was fitting that on the following Sunday we should remember the priceless contribution to victory made by our seamen, who have borne so bravely and tenaciously the perils and discomforts of the war.'

'On September 17th we praised God for the help given by farmers and gardeners towards the winning of the campaign, as we thanked Him for the supply of our bodily needs at our Harvest Festival. We also remembered the heroism of the men of the Royal Air Force who won for us the Battle of Britain four years ago.'

'Change from "black-out" to "dim-out" means that we may now have Evensong in Church at the usual hour; if an "alert" is sounded, we shall have to continue in the dark!'

War Fatalities: 'We deeply regret to learn of the death whilst in action of Roderick Dale Harris, Lieutenant, Q.O. Hussars, of Brook House.'

Sonning Women's Institute: 'The Whist Drive and Dance which was held in aid of the St. Barnardo's Homes on Friday September 15th proved to be very successful, with an amount of £13 2s being sent to the fund.'

November 1944

The Vicar's Letter:

'I must this month solicit your interest and co-operation in our Church Savings Week to be held at St. Andrew's-tide, our Patronal Festival. The explanation of the fund and full particulars of the week will be seen enclosed. Envelopes, together with a short leaflet, will be left at every house during the month and will be called for later. I need hardly point out that this is a matter of great importance and has the support of the Lord Bishop and the Diocesan Board of Finance.'

'Our ancient church is a great treasure; even more so is the Christian Gospel of which we are the trustees for our own and future generations. Please read carefully the statement and the leaflet, contribute as largely as you can, and support the various events which will take place during Church Savings Week.' The appeal leaflet headed "Post-War Needs Fund" sought to raise some £300 per year from local residents. The funds were to be directed to three causes:

1. The Parish of Sonning: Specific needs included cleaning and renovating the church, installing a modern system of blowing for the organ, costs in connection with burial ground extension, costs relating to the Sonning School. Mention was also made of the parishioners "at the Twyford end" including Milestone Avenue: 'We must make better provision for these parishioners of ours, either by the erection of a Church Hall or the purchase of some conveyance to bring them to the Church and Hall.'

2. An allotted share of the Diocese costs including: Better stipends for poorly paid clergy, salaries for assistant curates, pensions for clergy and their widows, training candidates for Holy Orders, building repairs.

3. Christian aid work in foreign countries.

December 1944

The Vicar's Letter:

'Our sixth war-time Christmas is upon us, and there will be once more vacant chairs in many homes. In all our Christmas rejoicing we shall be remembering those who are fighting our battles for us, praying that this may be the last Christmas of strife and separation.'

'We have already received a generous response to the Post War Needs Appeal. Thank you to those who have distributed the envelopes and leaflets and hope that contributions will be received from every home.'

January 1945

The Vicar's Letter:

'May I first express my personal thanks to you all for your generosity and co-operation in our Church Savings Week. It was a notable effort which brings me much encouragement and also inspiration for the future.

May God bless the New Year to us all and grant us victory and peace!'

[*Donations to the Church Savings Week totalled £505 0s 6d.*]

February 1945

Sonning Women's Institute: The Annual Report for 1944 was included in this issue. It was noted that the membership now totalled 83, which included 10 new members having been welcomed during the year.

March 1945

The Vicar's Letter:

'Once again we approach the most solemn season of the year as Holy Week comes round again. I commend it to your observance with the utmost urgency. Thus only can we enter into the fullest experience of the joy of Easter.'

'The choir is short of treble and alto voices and we should be glad if some ladies and more boys would volunteer.'

Air Raid Precautions: 'Will all A.R.P. Firewatchers, who have not already done so, please hand in their helmets and eyeshades to the heads of their fireguard parties or their nearest warden, or leave them at the Post at Shelvinstone. Armlets may be retained.'

Lewisham: 'Under the auspices of the W.V.S. various counties are being asked to adopt some of the more badly blitzed places in the London and surrounding areas. Under this scheme Berkshire has adopted part of Lewisham, one of the most stricken districts, where over 70,000 homes are in ruins. We, in Sonning have been asked to make whatever contributions we can towards the re-furnishing of such houses as can be made habitable. Our gifts of ornaments, pictures, crockery, toys, furniture, kitchen equipment, odds and ends of all useful sorts, will help.'

April 1945

The Vicar's Letter:

'I hope that you may receive this number of the magazine in time to accept with it my best wishes for a truly happy Easter. The good news which is continually reaching us from all the various fronts will be in tune with the Festival that creates light out of darkness and life out of death, and proclaims the triumph of good over evil.'

The Chapel: 'The furnishing of the Chapel has now been completed, with the gift of an oak Credence Table, presented by Mr. F. J. Hoyle in memory of his parents. For this, as well as for all of the other previous gifts, we are most thankful.'

May 1945

The Vicar's Letter:

'The beauty of the Easter festival has been richly enhanced this year by the splendid news from the battle fronts and also by the glorious spring weather which has brought out the full glory of Sonning. We can have no doubt that victory will soon crown all the efforts and trials of the past five and a half years.'

'The passing of President Roosevelt on the eve of victory in Europe is deeply mourned almost universally, not least by English people, to whom he has shewn himself such a sympathetic and generous friend. I paid my short meed of tribute to his memory on your behalf from the pulpit on the Sunday of his funeral, and the Dead March of Saul was solemnly played in his honour. President Truman's firm insistence on the Christian values in his opening speech will be of the greatest encouragement, and we shall think especially of him in all his great responsibilities, as we pray for "all Christian kings, princes and governors".'

June 1945

The Vicar's Letter:

'**Victory in Europe at last!** The five years and eight months of Europe's agony are past, and the threat to ourselves of enemy invasion, domination, and even assault, is over – this time, we hope, for ever.'

'The first fruits of victory have come to us in the return to us of our prisoners, released from their long captivity; to them Sonning offers an affectionate and respectful welcome.'

'VE day was celebrated not only by a fine display of bunting, bonfires, rockets and the pealing of the Church bells but also by a short but heartfelt Service of Praise at 8 a.m. when the church was nearly filled by a congregation which sang the glad hymns with real fervour.'

'May final victory in the East come speedily, so that all the energies of all men of goodwill everywhere may be devoted to the constructive task of re-building our civilisation on a true and Christian basis.'

'We have started making our plans and raising our funds for welcoming home our parishioners who have served and fought to win us this great victory. We cannot pay them in full the infinite debt we owe them, we can but offer to each one of them a small token of our gratitude and affection.'

Blood Transfusion: 'Large numbers of casualties are still being sent to the Berkshire Battle Hospitals. Blood transfusion is still very necessary. The Army B.T. Service cannot come to Sonning, but, as blood is so urgently required, it would be a great help and service to the wounded, if volunteers would make an appointment with the Blood Transfusion Secretary at the Berkshire Hospital for any Tuesday or Friday afternoon.'

July 1945
The Vicar's Letter:
'Within two months of victory in Europe we are faced with a General Election, when all adult citizens have to exercise the solemn responsibility of choosing Members of the House of Commons. To a Christian the vote is a privilege to be used with the greatest care as a trust committed to him by God, from Whom he will seek guidance as to its disposal. We can happily recognise that all parties are honest in their desires and endeavours to serve their country and to lay the foundations of a just, lasting and universal peace.'

Church School: 'The staff is now complete, and we trust that no further changes will be necessary for a very long time. An extra week's holiday has been granted by the Berkshire Education Committee this year; schools will close following afternoon school on Thursday, August 2nd and resume on Tuesday September 11th.'

Sonning Women's Institute: 'This month's meeting was a garden party held in the delightful grounds of Old Tudor Place. Interesting descriptions of life in a German prison camp were given by Lieut. Ian Macaskie and Sergt. Russell Hoyle, both of whom have just been repatriated after a long spell of internment; both emphasised their appreciation of the Red Cross, for not only did the parcels keep them from practically starving, but the packing, string etc., provided them with materials for handicrafts.'

August 1945
The Vicar's Letter:
'By the time the magazine appears in print, the result of the General Election, with the exception of one or two contests, will be known. Of whatever political complexion the new government may be, we must not fail to pray for it that it may be given wisdom and courage to tackle the tremendous tasks that lie ahead.'
[*The Labour party led by Clement Attlee achieved a landslide victory in the July election, defeating the Conservative party led by Winston Churchill who had served as prime minister during the greater part of World War II.*]

Organist: 'The Vicar and Church Council have now, after six months trial on both sides, made definite the appointment of Mr. F. C. Griffin as organist'. Mr. Griffin has gladly accepted the appointment. His playing has been a delight to us all, and we look forward to an increase in the membership of the choir, so that he may have a better opportunity of making the music of our worship more worthy.'

St. John's Church, Woodley: 'We greatly regret the departure of the Rev. W. H. Trebble after four years service as Vicar of Woodley. I ask your prayers on behalf of the Rev. K. F. Way whom I have appointed to succeed him.'

September 1945

The Vicar's Letter:

'At the time of writing the surrender of Japan appears imminent, so that the whole world may soon be at peace. The invention of the "atomic bomb" opens up terrifying possibilities of destructive power; we must be devoutly thankful that its secret was not discovered by the aggressor powers before their defeat. As it is, we may trust that this mighty gift of God of atomic energy may be used for the betterment and not the destruction of mankind.'

Robert Palmer Charity: 'The Trustees for the Robert Palmer for the Poor Charity are trying to arrange for the earlier distribution of the coal this winter, and to that end are inviting applications in the immediate future, so that the necessary order may be given in good time. Forms should be returned to Miss Kemp, The Estate Office, Sonning, by Saturday, September 15th.'

October 1945

The Vicar's Letter:

'It seems difficult to believe that the burden and menace of the last six years has really disappeared, and our hearts should be full of gratitude to our Father for all His many mercies, as well as to our fighting men who under His hand have brought us victory and peace. It will be a joy to us all to greet the men on their return and to see them comfortably settled in civilian activities. It is to be feared that it may be some time before there are sufficient houses for them all.'

Victory over Japan Day: 'V. J. Day, Wednesday, August 15th must long be remembered as the day on which the six years' war reached its triumphant finale. The Church was well filled for the special service that evening, and for the thanksgiving on the following Sunday.'

Children's Victory Party: 'In spite of a damp morning on September 8th, the weather cleared sufficiently to enable the sports organised for this event to be held according to plan. About 180 children were present, and the large majority won prizes. Parents and friends assisted in a very happy afternoon. The ladies had been busy in the Pearson Hall laying out a sumptuous tea, the tables decorated with flowers and flags.'

The Pearson Hall: 'It is with great regret that we have learned that the Public Assistance Authorities require the exclusive use of the Pearson Hall from October 1st for an unknown period, in order to collect there the equipment distributed to the villages of East Berkshire, and to sort it, so that it may be removed by the Ministry of Works for despatch to the needy people of Holland for the winter.'

November 1945
The Vicar's Letter:
'All efforts to find alternative accommodation for the Rest Home Centre equipment having failed, the Pearson Hall remains closed to us for the present. Some of our activities are finding a temporary home in the Recreation Hut. Our Armistice celebrations this year will have a special note of triumph; we shall, of course, include the Fallen of this world war in our commemoration.'

Blood Transfusion: 'Mrs, Vinter has received a letter from the Army Blood Transfusion Service at Bristol thanking all those who have given their blood for the needs of the fighting services, and asked us to pass on this message to blood donors in Sonning. Although the Army's needs are no longer with us, it should be remembered that a no less important need still exists in the civilian hospitals. Donors who are willing to continue their help should get in touch with the Pathological Department of the Royal Berkshire Hospital in Reading.'

Armistice Day: 'November 11th this year falls on a Sunday, and by order of His Majesty the Two Minute Silence is to be universally observed from 11.00 to 11.02a.m. This means that the service must start at 10.45a.m. and its order be altered.'

December 1945
The Vicar's Letter:
'Our first peace-time Christmas for many years will be in tune with the song of the Angels of Bethlehem, and will bring you all, I trust, with thankful hearts to the worship of the Infant Saviour.
My best wishes to you all for a very happy Christmas; many of our serving men and women will, we hope, be able to keep the Feast in their own homes.'

Children's Union of the Waifs' and Strays' Society: 'It is with great pleasure that we are able to report that the delightful concert given last month, under the direction of Mrs. Symons of Earley, realised the splendid sum of £7 5s. All who were present will join with the Society in expressing their appreciation to Mrs. Symons and the children who performed.'

Armistice Day: 'November 11th was once again observed with all its pre-war ceremony, in which the notes of joy and solemnity are inevitably combined. In Sonning the Church was fuller than ever for the Remembrance Service at 10.45a.m., when the Roll of Honour of the two wars was proclaimed, and the two minute silence observed. The names of the Gallant Dead of 1914-1918 are well known and inscribed on the wall of the Church.'

'It may be convenient to print a list of those who have made the great sacrifice of life during the recent conflict of 1939-1945.'

'Bernard Abbott, Frank Ashcroft, Ronald Bosworth
Norman Collins, Roderick Dale Harris, Sidney Dean,
John Fass, Henry Lester Guy, John Harris,
Ronald Leese, Gordon Parkin, Frederick Pym,
Joseph Snowball, Christopher Young.'

―――――――――――――――

There are fourteen names on the memorial panels in St. Andrew's Church of those who fell during World War II. The name of Ronald Leese is not included. The name of E.S. Napthine is included on the panels, but is not listed above.

Memorials to those who died on active service during the two world wars are also to be seen at St. John the Evangelist Church, Woodley; All Saints' Church, Dunsden and Earley St. Peter's Church.

Thirty four memorial wall tablets, honouring the local men who fell in the service to their country during the two world wars. (see: page 217)
(South wall, St. Andrew's Church, Sonning)

Vicars of St. Andrew's Church, Sonning 1869-1945
HUGH PEARSON 1842 - 1882
ALFRED POTT 1882 - 1899
HENRY BARTER 1899 - 1901
ERNEST EDWARD HOLMES 1901 - 1906
GIBBS PAYNE CRAWFURD 1907 - 1925
RICHARD WICKHAM LEGG 1926 - 1942
SIDNEY JOHN SELBY GROVES 1942 - 1965

Vicars of St. John the Evangelist Church, Woodley 1881-1945
ERNEST ANGEL GRAY 1881 - 1913
FREDERICK PENRUDDOCK 1913 - 1925
PHILIP GRAY 1925 - 1930
CYRIL DONNE 1930 - 1940
W. H. TREBBLE 1940 - 1945
K. F. WAY 1945 - 1948

Vicars of All Saints' Church, Dunsden 1870-1945
HENRY EDWARD HULTON (Curate in Charge) 1870 - 1876
RICHARD HART HART-DAVIS 1876 - 1904
HERBERT WIGAN 1904 - 1947

Vicars of Earley St. Peter's Church 1869-1945
JOHN HORNE 1856 - 1870
HAVILLAND DURAND M 1872 - 1884
HARRY BINGHAM McNAIR 1884 - 1889
CHARLES HENRY FIRMSTONE 1889 - 1897
CHARLES EDWARD ADAMS 1897 - 1904
WILLIAM WEEKES FOWLER 1904 - 1923
GEORGE LEONARD HUNTON HARVEY 1924 - 1931
HAROLD HEWITSON NASH 1931 - 1943
STANLEY CHARLES ROBINSON 1943 - 1970

British Sovereigns 1869-1945

QUEEN VICTORIA 1837 – 1901
KING EDWARD VII 1901 – 1910
KING GEORGE V 1910 – 1936
KING EDWARD VIII 1936 – 1936
KING GEORGE VI 1936 – 1952

British Prime Ministers 1869-1945

WILLIAM EWART GLADSTONE (Lib) 1868 – 1874
BENJAMIN DISRAELI (Con) 1874 – 1880
WILLIAM EWART GLADSTONE (Lib) 1880 – 1885
MARQUESS OF SALISBURY (Con) 1885 – 1886
WILLIAM EWART GLADSTONE (Lib) 1886 – 1886
MARQUESS OF SALISBURY (Con) 1886 – 1892
WILLIAM EWART GLADSTONE (Lib) 1892 – 1894
EARL OF ROSEBERY (Lib) 1894 – 1895
MARQUESS OF SALISBURY (Con) 1895 – 1902
ARTHUR JAMES BALFOUR (Con) 1902 – 1905
HENRY CAMPBELL BANNERMAN (Lib) 1905 – 1908
HERBERT HENRY ASQUITH (Lib) 1908 – 1916
DAVID LLOYD GEORGE (Lib) 1916 – 1922
ANDREW BONAR LAW (Con) 1922 – 1923
STANLEY BALDWIN (Con) 1923 – 1924
JAMES RAMSAY MacDONALD (Lab) 1924 – 1924
STANLEY BALDWIN (Con) 1924 – 1929
JAMES RAMSAY MacDONALD (Lab) 1929 – 1935
STANLEY BALDWIN (Con) 1935 – 1937
NEVILLE CHAMBERLAIN (Con) 1937 – 1940
WINSTON CHURCHILL (Con) 1940 – 1945
CLEMENT ATTLEE (Lab) 1945 – 1951

INDEX

1869 – 1945